KU-038-330

For my mother and father,
my sisters and brother,
my wife and my son

Contents

Preface

If the misery of our poor be caused not by the laws of nature, but by our institutions, great is our sin.

Charles Darwin, *Voyage of the Beagle* (1839/1936:781)

This book is about suffering, healing, and evolved human nature. It is about the mundane suffering that is wrought by our very nature, and why knowledge of this nature is our best hope for healing the suffering that it so often brings. The shape of my argument is this: (1) what our nature is, (2) why it is this way, and (3) why knowledge of why it is this way has therapeutic implications. I believe that my overall argument follows logically from my most basic assumption, which is that human beings have a nature. There are two reason why I am happy with this assumption. First, I believe that we are part of nature, part of life. Therefore, because evolutionary theory is our only scientific theory of life, for me, literally everything about life is ultimately explainable in terms of evolutionary theory or terms compatible therewith. Second, not only do I believe that human nature is a fact of nature, I also believe that value exists as a fact of nature and that knowledge of the value that is in life, including ourselves, would constitute an extremely valuable set of facts. Indeed, since the continuation of our species (our descendants) may depend on knowing and accepting our nature, I cannot imagine any more valuable set of facts. This book is about using evolutionary theory to understand human nature in order thereby to heal and preserve human life and life in general. It is therefore an essay in evolutionary medicine. It is an essay on the use of evolutionary theory as a rational basis for human problem-solving. It is therefore also an exercise in what Julian Huxley (1964) called "evolutionary humanism."

Human nature is that which we have in common despite our differences. It is that which transforms us from local partisans with cramped loyalties into *kosmou politēs*, "citizens of the universe," with allegiances to what we undeniably share: the qualities of life. In the coming pages I will paint a picture of human nature that is emerging from recent thinking at the interface of evolutionary theory and human development about the evolved nature and contingent development of human reproductive strategies. I will describe this thinking and what we know about reproductive strategies in considerable detail in succeeding chapters. For now, however, it is enough to define a reproductive strategy loosely as the sum of all the adaptations – anatomical, physiological, psychological, and developmental – that enabled all of the (direct) ancestors of all organisms that ever lived to solve the problems that had to be solved in order for them to have left descendants. These adaptations are the qualities of life.

To set the stage for what follows I must emphasize at the outset that, while evolutionary biologists believe that organisms actually do possess – indeed *are* – such adaptations (and their by-products), and that many can be convincingly demonstrated, the concept of reproductive strategy is fundamentally an *assumption,* which means that it is a working hypothesis, a mental model, an image or a way of seeing, rather than an empirically established entity. An assumption is the *if* that comes before a *then.* In the act of determining whether some *then* that we predict actually exists, we have assumed that the *if* that precedes it is true. Or, as Pierre Ryckmans put it recently, "The saying 'to see is to believe' must be reversed: to believe [to assume] is to see" (1996:13). Darwin was getting at the same idea when he wrote to Alfred Russel Wallace in 1857, "I am a firm believer that without speculation there is no good and original observation" (Burkhardt 1996:183).

In evolutionary theory this has proved to be an extraordinarily powerful and productive problem-solving gambit. To assume that human nature is fundamentally, essentially about reproduction is to adopt what Dennett (1987, 1995; see also Fodor 1994) calls the "intentional stance," which is to assume that the qualities of life – adaptations – are *for* something, that they were *intended* by some imaginary agent (say, a blind watchmaker [Dawkins 1986]) to solve some problem. We do not *really* believe this, of course, any more than we believe that each and every biological trait actually is an adaptation (more on this later). However, the fundamental logic of the process of adaptation by natural selection that is embodied in the intentional stance allows us to make predictions about the nature of the problems that organisms in particular ecological or political–economic circumstances will face, which, in turn, often gives hints about the kinds of solutions (adaptations) that we might look for. This is what evolutionary ecology is all about. This why I believe that the concept of reproductive strategy can contribute substantially to new perspectives on human nature: because it helps us to understand the adaptive problems that each and every one of our (direct) ancestors logically had to have solved before each and every one of us could exist. Knowing what these problems are, I believe, will help us understand how their solutions are represented phenotypically – that is, how solutions to adaptive problems (the problems of life) are materially instantiated, literally embodied in flesh, blood, bone, neural networks, and other physicochemical structures and processes. Knowing what these problems are, in other words, may help us understand how the *ifs* of human reproduction give rise to their various *thens*. Knowing these *ifs* and *thens* would constitute a supremely valuable set of facts.

From these basic assumptions, I work toward the conclusion that it is not only possible, but indeed valuable to view human nature as a manifestation of our reproductive strategies and thus as a natural, biological phenomenon. I maintain, however, that this can be only cold comfort to outdated "greedy" reductionists who believe in some fixed, universal human nature. This is because an essential part of human nature is the way that it evolved to be reliably, adaptively affected during development by certain kinds of information about young human beings' local socioecology. From my combined evolutionary/developmental perspective, in fact, human nature comes to be seen as essentially, biologically, adaptively local, contingent, and emergent.[1] Not only does the view of human nature as a manifestation of our reproductive strategies increase our understanding of human nature, such a view also provides a rational, scientific basis for a theory of value and an ethical stance that combines reason and compassion, that says it is rational to be compassionate, and that can help us *ameliorate* our all-too-human condition. From assumptions about the essential reproductive function of human nature – that human nature is ultimately *for* reproduction – I develop a rational, evolutionary theoretical foundation for an ethical stance that aims to be therapeutic by increasing our practical reason. Indeed, in some ways this book amounts to one long argument against G. E. Moore's (1903) naturalistic fallacy – the idea that it is wrong to argue from facts to values. The structure of my therapeutic argument is the proposition that if human nature is a manifestation of our reproductive strategies, and if our reproductive strategies evolved to be reliably affected by certain features of the environments in which we develop, then the essence of human nature,

---

[1] Emergent in the literal sense of *coming into view*, not necessarily in the technical sense of *arising unpredictably* from what comes before (Dennett 1995:415).

the part we care about most, our minds and moral sentiments, must be at least partly contingent on these same environmental features.

And what environmental features are these? What are our minds and moral sentiments *for*? What particular problems did they evolve to solve? As I will show in the coming chapters, evolutionary theory and human development are (for different reasons) coming to conceive of these problems in terms of environmental risk and uncertainty, which is how evolutionary ecologists refer abstractly to threats to an organism's survival or its potential for leaving descendants. I believe that when human nature is viewed from a conjoined evolutionary/developmental perspective, our minds and moral sentiments emerge as essentially adaptations for predicting the future. Predicting the future reduces environmental risk and uncertainty, thereby reducing the chance of death, nurturing growth and development, and providing hope for future generations. For evolutionists, future generations are what reproductive strategies – sex – are meant to achieve. In short, predicting the future maximizes the chance of *reaching* the future. This, I shall argue, is the origin of value itself. And, because inequality is a major source of risk and uncertainty, it is also a reason for valuing equality and human rights.

Acknowledgments

This book has many beginnings. One was in Gregory Bateson's famous seminar at the University of Hawai'i. This was a heady affair, for I was just a first year graduate student, and doubly lucky to be enrolled while he was writing *Steps to an Ecology of Mind* (1972). His mark on my thinking about mind and nature has been enduring. I am also plainly indebted to him for my subtitle, which I have appropriated as a way of honoring his vision of the importance of ecology for understanding the mind.

Parts of the book began as papers presented at conferences. Portions of chapters 2, 3 and 5 were presented in November, 1991, in Teresópolis, Brazil, at the Wenner-Gren Foundation for Anthropological Research International Symposium, "The Politics of Reproduction," organized by Rayna Rapp and Faye Ginsburg (this paper is now Chisholm 1993). In December 1992, I presented another version of these ideas in the symposium, "The Anthropology of Romantic Passion," that Bill Jankowiak organized for the annual meeting of the American Anthropological Association in San Francisco (now Chisholm 1995a). In 1994, I made two preliminary attempts to sketch the whole argument. One was "Steps to an evolutionary ecology of mind," which I presented in April at the conference "Biocultural Approaches to the Mind and Human Development," which was organized by the Cognitive Studies Group of the Institute for Behavioral Research at the University of Georgia (now published in *Beyond Nature–Nurture: Biocultural Approaches to the Emotions*, edited by Alex Hinton and D. Harper-Jones [Cambridge University Press 1999]). The other was in December, in the symposium "Ethnicity and Health," organized by Linc Schmitt and Len Freedman for the annual meeting of the Australasian Society for Human Biology in Perth (now Chisholm 1995b). Portions of chapter 2 were presented in the symposium, "Nature, Culture, and the Question, 'Why?'" organized by Lutz Eckensberger and Michael Lamb for the biennial meeting of the International Society for the Study of Behavioral Development in Quebec City in August, 1996. Portions of chapter 3 were presented in the symposium, "Childhood in Life History Perspective," organized by Gilda Morelli and Paula Ivey for the annual meeting of Society for Cross-Cultural Research in Santa Fe in February, 1994 (now Chisholm 1996a). Finally, portions of chapter 4 were presented at the symposium, "The Evolution of the Ontogeny of Enculturation," organized by Keith McNeal and John Bing for the Annual Meeting of the American Anthropological Association in San Francisco in November 1996.

Much of this book began in the minds of teachers, students, colleagues, and friends who over the years have shared their ideas with me and encouraged me by their example to forage for ideas and insights across traditional disciplinary boundaries. Many of them also read and commented on various early sections and versions of the book. I want to acknowledge in particular the inspiration and advice of Jay Belsky, Nick Blurton Jones, Berry Brazelton, Ric Charnov, David Coall, Ellen Dissanayake, Pat Draper, Robin Fox, Len Freedman, Sara Harkness, Henry Harpending, Murray Head, Sarah Hrdy, Mel Konner, Michael Lamb, Jane Lancaster, Jim McKenna, Neil Pelkey, Scott Rushforth, Barb Smuts, Charlie Super, Ross Thompson, Lionel Tiger, Noel Wescombe, and Carol Worthman. I am fortunate to have had such a collection of mentors.

The book also began with support from the Australian Research Council and the University of Western Australia. A grant from the ARC relieved me of my other academic reponsibilities for a term, resulting in the blissful but altogether necessary luxury of writing full time. UWA, through its Deputy Vice-Chancellor, Professor Alan Robson, provided an additional term of leave. This second consecutive semester of leave more than doubled the value of the first, and I am grateful to Alan for his support and vision.

As might be expected of a developmentalist, I also discern beginnings for this book in my past. My father was an engineer and my mother a poet, so for me Snow's two cultures were so familiar and warm as to become one. My brother Doug became an engineer as well, and from him and my father I learned long ago that things can be "reverse engineered." From my sister Jean I learned more about engineering (managing) social relations. I am especially grateful to her for her concept, and practice, of the "ideology of concern."

Finally, this book had a number of important beginnings all in one person, my wife, Victoria Katherine Burbank. I am enormously grateful for her inspiration, guidance, grace, and insight. She was the one who showed me that, although inequality is a social fact, it has critical biological implications and might therefore serve as another basis for a unified biosocial science.

1   Evolution and explanation

Empty is that philosopher's argument by which no human suffering is therapeutically treated. For just as there is no use in a medical art that does not cast out the sicknesses of bodies, so too there is no use in philosophy, unless it casts out the suffering of the soul.

Epicurus (341–271 BCE)

Explanation is not achieved by description of the patterns of regularity, no matter how meticulous and adequate, nor by replacing this description by other abstractions congruent with it, but by exhibiting what *makes* the pattern, i.e., certain processes.

Fredrik Barth (1966:2)

All organisms are all of the time problem-solving.

Karl Popper (1994:55)

Clarity about what it means to be human constitutes not only the highest political and therapeutic vision, but also the height of practical reason. This is because it is from conceptions of human nature that access to all social resources flows. Aristotle argued that humans become aware of their political ideals only through their understanding of shared human nature. Taking his lead, Epicurus and the Hellenistic philosophers developed the idea that both philosophy (knowledge) and politics were medicine (i.e., healing, therapy) carried on by other means (Nussbaum 1994). At some point, everything human has philosophical and political implications, but, as Western philosophers have known at least since Aristotle, in order even to see these implications it is necessary first to have knowledge of human nature – otherwise, what would the implications be *for*? For Aristotle and the Hellenistic philosophers, knowledge of human nature could only lead to *eudaimonia* – i.e., "human flourishing." They believed that it was only through knowledge of shared human nature that we become aware of where we want to go, the ideals at which we should aim. As Aristotle put it in the *Nichomachean Ethics*, illustrating the practical value of therapeutic arguments, "Won't knowledge of it [i.e., the good; the conditions for *eudaimonia*] make a great shift in the balance where life is concerned, and won't we, like archers with a target before us, be more likely to hit on what is appropriate?" (quoted in Nussbaum 1994:60). Knowledge of shared human nature would establish what is appropriate for achieving human flourishing – the target which ought to guide our aim whenever we decide how best to make our way in the world.

Human nature and practical reason

Knowing how to make our way in the world is practical reason. I am grateful for Charles Taylor's (1993) conception of practical reason for it shows that rational and moral arguments share common features. (It also fits nicely with the evolutionary epistemological approach to knowledge that I shall examine shortly.) If we accept human flourishing as our target, Taylor writes,

> . . . then the activity of explaining why things are as they are (what we think of as science) is intrinsically linked to the activity of determining what the good is, and in particular how human beings should live . . . The notion that explanation can be distinct from practical reason, that the attempt to grasp what the world is like can be made independent of the determination of how we should stand in it, that the goal of understanding the cosmos can be uncoupled from our attunement to it, made no sense to the pre-modern understanding. (1993:217)

Note that explaining "why things are as they are" entails the use of facts to describe the processes that cause "things" to come into being. These facts are then used to determine "what the good is" and "how human beings should live." Practical reason thus uses facts to approach values.

For Taylor, practical reason is when "we understand an environment [and] can make our way about in it, get things done in it, effect our purposes in it" (1993:218). The environment that we need to understand is the one comprised of our individual and collective human natures, and their products and residues, so to speak, in the rest of nature, over time. For now, Aristotle's *eudaimonia* is as good a way as any to conceive of the ultimate purpose that we try to effect when we make our way and get things done in this environment. Later, however, I will develop the idea that this purpose is a deeply moral purpose and that the reason we experience it as such (i.e., as a feeling – a moral sentiment) is because these feelings were the best way that natural selection could devise to reflect or represent a value that exists in nature – the nature of evolutionary biology as it is instantiated in each of us.

To effect our purposes – to approach *eudaimonia* – it is necessary to have a concept of human nature. Without such a concept no target can be better than any other. And if all targets are equally good, how do we know where to aim? If there is no human nature, no target, then anything goes, and we can aim anywhere we please – or where our aim pleases someone else. If there is no pre-existing, a priori human nature that we can look to for guidance, then anyone with sufficient wealth, power or prestige can have us aim wherever *they* please, at the targets *they* construct. If there is no human nature, then Michel Foucault and Jacques Derrida are right: might makes epistemological right and there is no truth outside of power. But such a stance is not just wrong, it is irresponsible, a counsel of despair, and dangerous, for it opens the door to bullies and despots. As Robin Fox put it:

> If there is no human nature, then any social system is as
> good as any other, since there is no base line of human
> needs by which to judge them. If, indeed, everything is
> learned, then surely men can be taught to live in any kind
> of society. Man is at the mercy of all the tyrants – be they
> fascists or liberals – who think they know what is best for
> him. And how can he plead that they are being inhuman if
> he does not know what being human is in the first place?
> (Fox 1975:13)

Likewise, Noam Chomsky observed that

> . . . one can easily see why reformers and revolutionaries should
> become radical environmentalists, and there is no doubt that
> concepts of immutable human nature can be and have been
> employed to erect barriers against social change and to defend
> established privilege. But a deeper look will show that the
> concept of the "empty organism," plastic and unstructured,
> apart from being false, also serves naturally as the support for
> the most reactionary social doctrines. If people are, in fact,
> malleable and plastic beings with no essential psychological
> nature, then why should they not be controlled and coerced by

those who claim authority, special knowledge, and a unique
insight into what is best for those less enlightened? . . . The
principle that human nature, in its psychological aspects, is
nothing more than a product of history and given social
relations removes all barriers to coercion and manipulation by
the powerful. This too, I think, may be a reason for its appeal to
intellectual ideologists, of whatever political persuasion.
(Chomsky 1975:132)

And Charles Taylor argued that without a theory of value (i.e., without a
rational basis for moral action) only power remains:

In a neutral universe, what agreement there is between
attitudes seems merely a brute fact, irrelevant to morals, and
disagreement seems utterly inarbitrable by reason, bridgeable
only by propaganda, arm-twisting, or emotional manipulation.
(Taylor 1993:213)

In a similar vein, Karl Popper labelled "intellectually evil" the belief that
all rational arguments inevitably rest on a framework of assumptions
that are beyond examination:

What I call "the myth of the framework" is a very widely held
and often even unconsciously accepted view, that all rational
argument must always proceed within a framework of
assumptions – so that the framework itself is always beyond
rational argument. One could also call this view "relativism",
for it implies that every assertion is to be taken as relative to a
framework of assumptions . . . A fairly common form of the
myth of the framework also holds that all discussions or
confrontations between people who have adopted different
frameworks are vain and pointless, since every rational
discussion can operate only within some given framework of
assumptions . . . I regard the prevalence of this myth as one of
the great intellectual evils of our time. It undermines the unity
of mankind, since it dramatically asserts that there can, in
general, be no rational or critical discussion except between
men who hold identical views. And it sees all men, so far as
they try to be rational, as caught in a prison of beliefs which
are irrational, because they are, in principle, not subject to
critical discussion. There can be few myths which are more

destructive. For the alternative to critical discussion is violence and war. (Popper 1994:137)[1]

Finally, consider Nancy Scheper-Hughes' recent deductions concerning our moral nature:

> To speak of the "primacy of the ethical" is to suggest certain transcendent, transparent, and essential, if not "precultural," first principles ... The extreme relativist position assumes that thought, emotion, and reflexivity come into existence with words and words come into being with culture. But the generative prestructure of language presupposes, as Sartre (1958) has written, a given relationship with another subject, one that exists prior to words in the silent, preverbal "taking stock" of each other's existence. Though I veer dangerously toward what some might construe as a latent sociobiology, I cannot escape the following observation: that we are thrown into existence at all presupposes a given, implicit moral relationship to an original (m)other and she to me. (Scheper-Hughes 1995:419; see also 1992:22–3)

If some conception of human nature is a prerequisite for the pursuit of human flourishing, as well as the *sine qua non* of practical reason and ethical action, then why are so many set against it?[2] I think the answer can only be that the naysayers are made anxious by the very concept of human nature because of their unexamined belief that not only does such a thing really exist, but that it is *essentially, irredeemably evil*. They believe, as William Blake wrote in *The Marriage of Heaven and Hell*:

1   That man has two real existing principles: viz: a body & a soul.
2   That energy, called evil, is alone from the body: & that reason, called good, is alone from the soul.
3   That God will torment man in eternity for following his energies.

In his sweeping social history, *In Search of Human Nature: The Decline and Revival of Darwinism in American Social Thought*, Carl Degler (1991) made the same point: that resistance to Darwinian thought (read Blake's "energy")

---

[1] Although not published until 1994, Popper wrote these words for a series of lectures at Emory University in 1969.
[2] Clifford Geertz, for example, once argued notoriously that the facts of human nature (if any existed) would amount to a "portrait of man" that was no more than a "cartoon" (1973:40).

rested on an "ideology or a philosophical belief that the world could be a freer and more just place" if only "the immutable forces of biology played no role in accounting for the behavior of social groups" (1991:viii). In short, just as Scheper-Hughes fears that the very "precultural" foundation for her ethical stance causes her to "veer dangerously toward what some might construe as latent sociobiology," so, too, do many others fear that the essence of biology – evolutionary theory – is inherently, essentially, deterministic and insensitive to historical contingencies, especially those affecting inequalities associated with race, ethnicity, class, and gender. As Brad Shore put it, "Until the issue of cultural diversity could be unhooked from its evolutionary (and racial) moorings, modern anthropologists were not free to contemplate the implications of cultural differences for an understanding of mind" (1996:17–18).

Despite the obvious misuse to which evolutionary theory has been put (and by some still is) I believe that this is wrong and that we have nothing to fear from evolutionary biology. On the contrary, I believe that viewing human nature as a manifestation of our evolutionary biology is the height of practical reason and our best hope for making our world "a freer and more just place." In this I again follow Robin Fox, who argues that

> . . . to look hard at, and accept the limitations of, human nature as a basis for political action, may turn out to be the least reactionary and most strenuously radical act of the twentieth century. But it will, in the nonpejorative sense of the word, be also a truly conservative act. (1989:51)

In the same vein, and fully in the spirit of Huxley's evolutionary humanism, Jerry Fodor observes that "Naturalism might turn out to be more of a humanism than, until quite recently, anyone had dared to hope" (1994:103).

Science and wisdom

If some conception of human nature is a prerequisite for rational, moral political action, this raises the question: who gets to define human nature? If human rights derive ultimately from concepts of human nature, then this is a question of some weight, for, threatened as we are by our deteriorating social and physical environments and expanding population, we cannot afford to define ourselves wrongly much longer. It goes without saying, therefore, that I immediately reject science's traditional antagonists, magic and received religion, for they depend for their existence not on rational argument but on the power, prestige, and wealth of their practitioners (Taylor's "propaganda, arm-twisting, [and] emotional manipulation"). This leaves science – but what kind of science? To put the question another way: if I am going to do justice to my central argument that viewing human nature as a manifestation of our reproductive strategies provides a rational basis for a theory of value and a rationally compassionate ethical philosophy, then I should explain why I think the foundation for my argument is sound.

My argument rests on a foundation of two interlocking parts: (1) evolutionary epistemology and (2) an emerging approach to science that is based on what Nicholas Maxwell (1984) called the "philosophy of wisdom" (some call it postpositivism or postempiricism). After a brief look at the anti-science sentiment that has lately become so pervasive, I will begin with the philosophy of wisdom, for, of the two elements in my foundation, it confronts most directly this growing antipathy toward science.

Anti-science
In recent years, the opponents of science have included not just the usual suspects, magic and received religion, but also some adherents of a branch of humanism that has come to be known as postmodernism. All scientists and most philosophers view reality as an "out there" (or "in here" – i.e., the very real [to us] quality of our sensations and feelings) that really exists. Some extreme postmodern interpretivists and deconstructionists, on the other hand, view reality not as something "out there," but as something that is inherently "constructed" by the inevitable interaction between data and observer. Knowledge, or truth, for them, is thus always "negotiated" and ultimately cannot exist except in its interpreters. While this is true in the sense that it certainly takes a knower for something to be known, it strikes me as a narrow view of knowledge because it comes down unfairly on the side of unknowability; it emphasizes our imperfection as observers and interpreters at the potentially catastrophic expense of failing to understand adequately the reality that really exists (either "out there" or "in here").[3]

This postmodern emphasis on our ultimate incapacity for perfect

---

[3] One almost suspects that postmodernism itself developed as a psychological defense against the painful realization that we cannot have perfect knowledge. It is as if someone who wished to be god was so upset on learning that he could not have god's perfect, pure knowledge that he blamed reality instead: If reality does not exist, then it is not my fault that I cannot know it!

knowledge may be another manifestation of the ancient antipathy between reason and desire, or cognition and emotion, that Blake captured in his opposition between "reason" and "energy." I wonder if postmodernism gives pride of place to the internal, subjective side of the relationship between reality and its internal, subjective representations because of its unargued belief that the essence of human nature – that which all people share – is actually their *individuality*: their separateness, their particular subjective experiences, their unique histories. Paradoxically, then, in postmodernism, human nature – that which all of us share – may be precisely that which makes us *different* from each other. If this is so, then viewing people as individuals rather than as a whole, as a species, makes sense as a way of preserving their essential humanity; as Geertz put it, "Becoming human is becoming individual" (1973:52). To do otherwise, to submerge individuals in their species, is abhorrent because it seems to reduce human nature to . . . well, to nature, for, if we are stripped of our individual experience, our acts of observation and interpretation (i.e., our "reason," which is "called good"), all that will remain (they fear) is some impersonal, universal, species "energy" ("called evil"), which merely manufactures our capacity for individual experience.

After the Enlightenment, as science, technology, and commerce fuelled the quickening pace of political and economic change everywhere, and so threatened the family, kinship, and religion as the organizing principles of society, Romantic anti-science sentiments have never been hard to find. Lately, however, with looming environmental and population catastrophes, world-wide economic downturns and increasing inequalities in the distribution of wealth, greater emphasis in business and politics on short-term results and payoffs, and everywhere the rise of fundamentalism, anti-science sentiments have become fervent and epidemic. In such a climate, the "hard" sciences, medicine, and engineering have fared better than the "soft" social, behavioral, and historical sciences. Indeed, for many, scientist and non-scientist alike, the hard sciences have become the very model for *all* of science. One reason for this is that the reality studied by hard sciences like physics and engineering seems more obviously to be "out there" than the reality studied by soft sciences like anthropology, sociology, or psychology (which seems to range rather more freely between "out there" and "in here" than the reality of the hard sciences).

Another reason, however, is that the hard sciences, including medicine, are often seen as value-free or neutral and therefore nonthreatening, safe and familiar, because they are morally neutral, rational tools for solving relatively narrow, short-term, practical problems. But, when by extension all of science then comes to be seen as value-free, then science in general is seen to have failed us, and people come to distrust or abhor it, because it seems bound to treat them as providers or products and to deprive them of their humanity and what they value most – their personal, subjective experience, which is the very basis by which they value anything at all. Myth and magic then abound, and science loses (e.g., Gross and Levitt 1994; Holton 1993). Vaclav Havel, President of the Czech Republic, expressed clearly this anger and dismay in his acceptance speech after receiving the Philadelphia Liberty Medal on July 4, 1994:

> The dizzying development of science, with its unconditional faith in objective reality and complete dependency on generally and rationally knowable laws, led to the birth of modern technological civilization. It is the first civilization that spans the entire globe and binds together all societies, submitting them to a common global destiny . . . At the same time, the relationship to the world that modern science fostered and shaped appears to have exhausted its potential. The relationship is missing something. It fails to connect with the most intrinsic nature of reality and with natural human experience. It produces a state of schizophrenia: man as an observer is becoming completely alienated from himself as a being . . . Experts can explain anything in the objective world to us, yet we understand our own lives less and less. (*New York Times*, Friday, July 8, 1994. p. A17)

Both playwright and politician, Havel has the gift of speaking for many; disaffection for science is indeed widespread. It is also clear to many, however, that Havel's problem – and postmodernism's – is not with science, but with *scientism*, which, in Paul Roscoe's words (he quotes from other definitions), is a version of science that "aims to construct a 'perfectly impersonal or objective,' 'value-free,' cognitive representation (or 'mental map') of reality as a whole" (1995:493). It is scientism's impersonal, value-less vision of reality that Havel, postmodernists, and humanists of all sorts (including me) abhor. But there is more to science than scientism, and epistemologists, philosophers of science, and scientists of all sorts are well along in the intellectual task of constructing a humanistic science – as are humanists (Crook 1991; Roscoe 1995; Turner 1995).

The philosophy of wisdom

For example, consider the work of the philosopher Nicholas Maxwell (1984). It was to criticize scientism and to provide a rational basis for a humanistic science that he set out to describe what a philosophy of wisdom might look like. In Maxwell's terms, scientism is standard empiricism, i.e., inquiry that is based on the traditional Western philosophy of knowledge, as developed primarily by Bacon, Newton, and Descartes. Standard empiricism holds that because human beings do not possess a priori knowledge of the world, everything that passes for knowledge, truth, or fact must be assessed empirically, impartially, through our own sensory experience. For standard empiricists, of course, sensory experience does not include emotional experience, for they do not consider emotions to be senses. (In fact, as I argue later, just as vision is a priori evidence that light exists, emotions are a priori evidence that value exists.) Therefore, standard empiricism of the traditional philosophy of knowledge sort holds that:

> Only by dissociating itself decisively from the goals, values and beliefs of common social life, so that claims to objective knowledge can be subjected to scrupulously *rational* assessment, can inquiry accumulate genuine knowledge, thus ultimately being of benefit to humanity. Rational inquiry must, as it were, ignore human need in order to help fulfil such need. (Maxwell 1984:10)

On this view, and given standard empiricism's huge successes, it is no wonder that so many, scientist and nonscientist alike, accept uncritically the view that:

> Feelings, desires, human social interests and aspirations, political objectives, values, economic forces, public opinion, religious views, ideological views, moral considerations, must not be allowed, in any way, to influence scientific or academic thought. (1984:16)

As a consequence, we are now in the curious position that, if we sense that something is *not* value-neutral – then we fear it cannot also be true! And, if something is not true, how can it be worth our consideration? This is the position that Havel so decries, and is the reason why distrust of science is so high: when science excludes from discussion any mention of human values, wisdom, and moral sentiments on the grounds that they are beyond rational argument, then people begin to devalue rationality itself – because they *know* that these things matter. This is what happens when, like Moore, you separate facts from values. For Maxwell, this is the "major intellectual disaster at the heart of western . . . thought" (1984:7). As an antidote, he outlines a philosophy, not of knowledge, but of wisdom, in which fact and value are not separated, but joined to make inquiry *even more rational*. He argues that there is no rational, but only a historical, basis for excluding values from rational consideration, and, indeed, that to include them in the realm of rationality makes possible a new scientific inquiry with a radically different aim, viz.,

> . . . to enhance personal and social wisdom. This new kind of inquiry gives intellectual priority to the personal and social problems we encounter in our lives as we strive to realize what is desirable and of value, problems of knowledge and technology being intellectually subordinate and secondary. For this new kind of inquiry, it is what we do and what we are that ultimately matters; our knowledge is but an aspect of our life and being. (1984:v)

Maxwell's philosophy of wisdom is a key part of the foundation for my central argument that an evolutionary view of human nature provides a basis for a scientific theory of value and a rational concern for human rights. The primary role of the new rational inquiry, Maxwell argues, is to give us not just truth, but *valuable* truth; it is to help us "discover, and perform . . . those actions which enable us to realize what is of value" (1984:66). That which is of value in a person's life comes to be judged as such only through his or her personal, subjective experience. Nor can any rational argument about value be effective unless it touches a person's personal, subjective experience (e.g., Nussbaum 1993, 1994; Taylor 1993). But this does not mean that what we experience as value bears no relationship whatsoever to anything that exists in reality. Nor does it mean that value is not a fact of nature, or that rational inquiry cannot help us learn what is of value. Indeed, a critical part of the argument of this book is that value exists in nature, that we experience this value subjectively, and that rationality evolved *for* value – i.e., to achieve value. Learning what is of value is the height of practical reason, for "valuable truth" helps us to make our way in the world, to make good choices, so as to better effect our purpose – which is to realize the greatest good, human flourishing. If, as Taylor put it, science is "intrinsically linked to determining what the good is" – and thus indispensable for realizing *eudaimonia* – then our best hope, Maxwell argues, is a science of value:

> What ought to have been realized long ago is that the Rationalist espousal of the philosophy of knowledge is actually irrational precisely because it excludes Romantic intellectual ideals of motivational and emotional honesty, truth to personal experience, imagination employed in the exploration of possibilities of value. The philosophy of wisdom is intellectually more rigorous than the philosophy of knowledge precisely because it incorporates such vital Romantic intellectual ideals. Aim-oriented rationalism [rationalism aimed at *eudaimonia*] heals the traditional split between Rationalism and Romanticism – the split between Snow's two cultures. It puts the two together, very much improving each as a result, the two uniting to form a coherent intellectual–cultural movement . . . capable of devoting itself far more effectively to the cooperative realization of value in life. (1984:118)

But where do we start? Where should we look for a science of value? The most obvious place is with our best science. But how are we to judge science? What is good science?

Good scientific theories are like old-fashioned American football players: They play well on both defense and offense. A theory may be said to play well on defense when unremitting efforts to disprove it have failed; it is a good theory because it has not yet been scored upon (Popper 1959). A theory may be said to play well on offense when it fosters its own growth – i.e., when it is generative, when it stimulates new research and new insights, and when it "makes contact with what scientists of different sorts are thinking and demonstrating" (Plotkin 1994:x). It is a good theory because people find it useful; it is useful because it allows people "to interact successfully with and toward other scientists" (Roscoe 1995:497). What matters in science, as Roscoe notes in his spirited critique of the postmodern antipathy toward science (i.e., scientism), is precisely that which matters in postmodern interpretation – which is *not* pure, disinterested truth, but the *success* of one's ideas – with success being defined as acceptance by other scientists (Chalmers 1978; Dunbar 1995; Hull 1988; Plotkin 1994). Postmodern critics of science, Roscoe argues, have aimed at the wrong target. Scientists and philosophers have been working on the knowledge problem for a long time and are agreed (as we will see in more detail shortly): truth – pure, neutral knowledge – is a fantasy; it is simply not ours to have. Martha Nussbaum puts it this way:

> . . . the error of the sceptical opponent of practical reason consists in remaining too much in the grip of the very picture of rational argument that is allegedly being criticized. While objecting to the hegemony of the natural sciences, and while seeking to restore to the human sciences their own rich humanistic character, the opponent has, presumably without full awareness, imparted into her analysis one very central part of the natural science model, namely, its understanding of what constitutes a rational argument. For she seems to assume that rational argument requires neutrality, and deduction from premises that are external to all historical perspectives. (1993:235)

By the twin criteria of (1) not yet disproved and (2) productivity or generativity, evolutionary theory is a good theory. Despite the best efforts of scientists and nonscientists alike, for well over 100 years, evolutionary theory has not been seriously challenged, let alone disproved. Quite the contrary, it has dramatically fostered its own growth, because it helps scientists of all sorts make their way in the social world of other scientists (despite the latter's concerted attempts at disproof). Indeed, so great has been evolutionary theory's generativity that scientists, philosophers, and other thinkers accept not only *that* "nothing in biology [*bios* = "life"] makes sense except in the light of evolution" (as Theodosius Dobzhansky [1973] said a quarter-century ago), but they are beginning to understand as well *how and why* everything comes to make sense. Therefore, unless humans are somehow apart from life, any good (rational) theory of human nature must at least be compatible with evolutionary theory if not actually an extension of it. On the face of it, then, evolutionary theory is well equipped to be our science of value.

But is evolutionary theory well equipped to include humanism's specific concerns with "ideals of motivational and emotional honesty" and "truth to personal experience"? What would it mean for a science to be "well equipped" to study human values? If we accept *eudaimonia* as our criterion, then a science is well equipped in this humanistic regard when it can conceive of values in a way that increases practical reason – that is, in a way that helps us make our way in the world and effect our purposes in it. This is why I believe that evolutionary theory is the only candidate for a science of value, because, in *explaining* human nature – how and why our ancestors made their way in their worlds – it simultaneously helps us realize what is *good* in ours.

Evolutionary epistemology

Evolutionary epistemology (Campbell 1974) is the branch of evolutionary theory that is concerned with the origin and nature of knowledge. Its fundamental *raison d'être* is the proposition that, if knowledge is part of life, then it must be capable of explanation in evolutionary terms. I will begin this section with a brief account of evolutionary epistemology and its key principles and arguments. I will then explain why I believe that evolutionary epistemology adds a number of big rocks to the foundation of my central argument – the idea that viewing human nature as a man-ifestation of our reproductive strategies provides a rational basis for a theory of value.

Knowledge as adaptation

Evolutionary epistemologists are scientific realists. Martha Nussbaum refers to scientific realism as "metaphysical realism," by which she means

> . . . the view (commonly held in both Western and non-Western philosophical traditions) that there is some determinate way the world is, apart from the interpretive workings of the cognitive faculties of living beings. Far from requiring technical metaphysics for its articulation, this is a very natural way to view things, and is in fact a very common daily-life view, in both Western and non-Western traditions. We did not make the stars, the earth, the trees: they are what they are there outside of us, waiting to be known. And our activities of knowing do not change what they are . . . On such a view, the way the human being essentially and universally is will be part of the independent furniture of the universe, something that can in principle be seen and studied independently of any experience of human life and human history. (1995:68)

Scientific realists believe three things. First, they believe that the real-ity described by evolutionary theory corresponds to a reality that exists independently of their own thoughts and theoretical commitments.

They are thus foundationalists, which means they believe that "common realities underlie the different experiences of persons, species, and forms of matter" (Turner 1995:28), and that the principles of evolutionary theory are not dependent for their justification on other beliefs. Indeed, they believe that evolutionary processes are the *ultimate* foundation for all of our other beliefs (after a long series of intermediate ontogenetic and historical steps). Second, they believe that the history of science is generally one of progressively greater correspondence between our constructions of reality and reality itself. Third, they also believe that knowledge itself is an adaptation. Viewing knowledge as an adaptation has an important consequence: if knowledge itself is an adaptation – but if no adaptations can ever be perfect (which they cannot; more on this later) – then neither can knowledge ever be perfect. Evolutionary epistemologists thus hold out no hope for complete or infallible knowledge. It could not evolve and therefore cannot exist in principle.

In denying that perfect knowledge can exist, evolutionary epistemologists are in superficial agreement with postmodern critics of science who deny the same thing. What makes all the difference, of course, are the reasons why each side denies that perfect knowledge is possible. Evolutionary scientists believe that reality exists but that the costs of knowing it, even just passably, are great – but also that knowing it passably has been good enough for enough organisms to effect their purposes such that the living world is the way it is today. Postmodernists, on the other hand, believe that knowledge is inherently imperfect because it is inevitably socially constructed. This is a difference that makes a difference, for if knowledge of reality is completely socially constructed then reality is completely determined by power, prestige, and wealth. But if, as Kitcher (1993) points out, knowledge of reality is socially constructed by those who have sufficiently similar experiences of an underlying reality that really exists, then there is hope for rational argument.

Postmodernism's error was to tie knowledge too closely to language (e.g., "thought, emotion, and reflexivity come into existence with words" [Scheper-Hughes 1995:419]). If knowledge exists only in and through language, and if language is inescapably social and thereby open to our hidden and not so hidden agendas of power, then knowledge is always, inevitably socially constructed. Postmodernists thus ask the (for them) rhetorical question: "Is there a knowledge that we can have that is independent of any social construction whatsoever? Can one imagine knowledge, for example, that exists without language?" (Wark 1996:28).

One can. While it is certainly not possible to have knowledge without a *knower*, it *is* possible to have knowledge that is absolutely independent of any social construction whatsoever. The issue, of course, is how to define knowledge. If knowledge is defined as that which is known through language, then the answer, by definition, is obviously no, knowledge cannot exist without language. But where is it written that we (or any form of life) can know things only through language? Language makes it possible to *talk* about knowledge (Pinker 1994), and perhaps even to *think* about knowledge (e.g., Fodor's [1975, 1983, 1994] "mentalese"), but knowledge itself should not be confused with our capacity to talk or think about it. There are many forms of life that have no language, but I would hesitate to say that because of their silence they also have no knowledge.

In fact, all forms of life have knowledge. Indeed, there is a real sense in which organisms *are* knowledge, for, as the evolutionary epistemologists Hahlweg and Hooker (1989:23) put it (following Konrad Lorenz 1941/1982), "life itself is to be characterized as a cognitive process." The knowledge that all organisms possess is information about their ancestors' environments that has become represented materially, phenotypically, in their bodies. This knowledge is universal in living forms and totally independent of all social constructions. This knowledge is the a priori knowledge of its ancestors' environments that each organism acquires via the DNA it inherits from these ancestors (i.e., its genotype: its endowment of genetic possibilities). This view of knowledge allows at least one form of knowledge (the original) to exist in the utter absence of social construction (but, again, *not* without a knower to do the knowing – that is, a living thing to *embody* the knowledge).

Evolutionary epistemology conceives of knowledge in representational terms, i.e., as the representation of aspects of an organism's environment (reality) in that organism's body (its phenotype: the particular set of its genetic possibilities that were actualized during development in a specific environment). The laws of aerodynamics, for example, are represented in the shape of birds' wings, while the laws of optics are represented in their eyes. Thus Plotkin (1994:ix) calls gaining knowledge the "incorporation of the world" into living organisms, much as Piaget (1970) describes learning as that which happens when the thing learned has been "assimilated" into existing cognitive structures. To incorporate something is to take it "into the body," which makes the thing taken in an "embodiment" in flesh and blood of some aspect of the world. Plotkin proposes that: "To know something is to incorporate the thing known into ourselves. Not literally, of course, but the knower is changed by knowledge, and that change represents, even if very indirectly, the thing known" (1994:ix). For Plotkin then, "knowledge is the relationship between the organization of *any* part of a living creature's body and particular aspects of order in the world outside of that creature" (1994:21) (and *inside*, he might have added; see below). Paul Volkmann had the same insight, almost 100 years earlier, in 1910:

> Under the constant influences of the external necessity . . . an internal necessity of thinking evolved, which is nothing else but a copy of the external necessity . . . If one accepts this view as at least partially true, he would admit the fundamental importance of natural science for any logic and theory of knowledge. Natural science, indeed, would be the Archimedian point for all questions of human knowledge. (Quoted in Danailov and Tögel 1991:20)

More recently, Fodor has also emphasized the internal–external relational quality of mental representations:

> . . . the essence of mental representations [is] that they face two ways at once: They connect with the world by representing it, by and large veridicially; and they connect with behavior by being its typical proximal cause. Because they do both of these things at once, they're custom-made to be what mediates the world's behavioral effects. (Fodor 1994:83)

Knowledge is thus an adaptation. As Plotkin (1994:xv) put it, "Adaptations are biological knowledge, and knowledge as we commonly understand the word is a special case of biological knowledge." He argues further that all adaptations have two qualities: (1) they are "for" something and (2) they are "relational." Literally, they are "fit" or "suited" (*aptus*) "to" (*ad*) some purpose or function in nature. Adaptations are "for" solving problems posed by nature. Thus wings are *for* flight. Adaptations are "relational" in that they are material representations of some aspect of an organism's environment (or that of its ancestors). By virtue of this representation there is thus a relationship between the organism's phenotype – its material, physical being – and its environment. Wings are thus the *relation* between the physical being of birds' bodies (molecules, cells, tissues, organs, etc.) and that part of the bird's environment described by

the laws of aerodynamics. An organism's environment is its total surround – including, of course, its social surround (i.e., its conspecifics). But
organisms are also surrounded, so to speak, by their sensations and
perceptions, which reflect their *internal* environment (conventionally
divided into affective, cognitive, and sensory realms) as well as their
external environment.

Nature in mind

Evolutionary epistemology is thus about nature in mind: Nature really
exists, and our minds evolved to represent it (or rather, parts of it, imperfectly). Evolutionary epistemologists would thus argue (paraphrasing
Geertz [1973:5]) that "man is an animal suspended in webs of significance
that he *evolved to spin*." Our minds, of course, do not represent all of
nature. The question thus becomes, of all of nature's aspects, which did
our minds evolve to represent, and why?

One way to approach this question is to ask what problems would
organisms living in a certain environment have to solve in order to leave
descendants (Dennett 1995; Parker and Maynard Smith 1990; Tooby and
Cosmides 1989, 1990; Tooby and DeVore 1987). For example, consider
why minds evolved at all. Plotkin (1994) suggests that the first minds
evolved to represent space in order to co-ordinate movement. When the
resources that are necessary for life are sufficiently constant over space
and time, the primary problem posed by nature is less about *obtaining*
resources (for they do not move very much) than about their efficient *processing*. Thus plants – which harvest relatively constant and predictable
resources from soil, sun, and water – are immobile. Animals, on the other
hand, move. Some animals make their way by eating plants, which,
although they do not move, are patchily distributed in space and time;
having consumed one plant, an animal has not the time to wait for
another to grow in its place. And some animals make their way by eating
other animals, which are not in one place for very long. The primary
adaptive problems for animals were to obtain resources and avoid becoming another animal's resource. Selection thus favored anatomical and
physiological mechanisms (i.e., adaptations) which made it possible for
animals in general to make their way more or less efficiently in space.
Making one's way in space is movement. Minds first evolved to represent
space in order to solve the problem of controlling movement – which is
behavior: where should I be next? What should I do next? But we are not
animals in general. We are an extraordinarily intelligent and intensely

social animal. What particular environmental problem did *our* minds evolve to represent and solve?

The perennial adaptive problem for any species, but especially our slowly developing, long-lived, highly intelligent, and intensely social species, is that of environmental uncertainty. This is the problem of obtaining sufficient information to make our way through complex social space in the face of virtually continuous sociocultural change. No environment is free of uncertainty, but such uncertainty has been a chronic, defining problem for our species because of an ultimate sort of environmental uncertainty that Plotkin (1994) called the "uncertain futures problem."

The uncertain futures problem arises from the biological fact of "generational deadtime."[4] This is the time-lag between an organism's conception, when it receives its complement of genetic "instructions" for making its way in the world, and the time that it reproduces – parenthood being the state that these "instructions" were supposed to have brought it. The ultimate function of genes, after all, is to leave copies of themselves in subsequent generations. This, however, takes time. Until it can reproduce, the organism's primary adaptive problem is to survive. But it also has to grow and develop. Then it has to find a mate, reproduce, and rear its young so that they can start the process all over again. The problem is that during this "deadtime," before it reproduces, the environment may have changed, so that the genetic "instructions" that manifestly worked well enough for one's parents might not work so well for one's own survival, growth, development, mating, or parenting. The essence of the uncertain futures problem is how to produce an adaptive match between organism and environment when the organism takes time to "build" but the "instructions" for building it are received all at once and the organism's environment is changing the whole time.

If reproductive success depends on some degree of match between organism and environment, but the organism's environment is changeable and uncertain, then selection may be expected to favor mechanisms which enabled developing organisms to track their environments – to aim at a moving target, as it were. And, indeed, the broad solution to the uncertain futures problem has been to equip organisms to track their environments, so that their adult, fully reproductive phenotypes are co-constructed by "instructions" from their environments as well as their

---

[4] Plotkin attributes the phrase to Konrad Lorenz (Plotkin 1994:137).

genes (e.g. Oyama 1985; Slobodkin and Rapoport 1974; Stearns 1982). There are many examples of adaptations that allow developing organisms to track their environments (some to come in later chapters), but, because our concern just here is with representations of nature in our own minds, we must be concerned with *representations* of risk and uncertainty that enable us to reduce *actual* risk and uncertainty.

The adaptation that allows us to represent and reduce environmental uncertainty is our intelligence – in which I specifically and emphatically include the intelligence of emotion (i.e., the "reasons that reason does not know at all" [Pascal 1670]). As Plotkin put it, "Intelligence is an adaptation that allows animals, including ourselves, to track and accommodate to change that occurs at a certain frequency" (1994:150). All adaptations are *for* something and are *relational*; intelligence is a mechanism *for* gaining knowledge in order to reduce uncertainty, and it is the *relationship* between the material being of our neuroendocrine systems and the real risk and uncertainty that really exists in nature. For evolutionary epistemologists, the way that intelligence reduces uncertainty is clear. Kim Sterelny put it this way:

> . . . to the considerable extent that our behaviour is adaptively flexible and informationally sensitive, to that extent it must be directed by representations. There can be no informational sensitivity without representation. There can be no flexible and adaptive response to the world without representation. To learn about the world, and to use what we learn to act in new ways, we must be able to represent the world, our goals, and options. Furthermore, we must make appropriate inferences from these representations. (Sterelny 1990:21)

and Popper this way:

> [Intelligence] allows us to *dissociate ourselves* from our own hypotheses, and to look upon them critically. While an uncritical animal may be eliminated together with its dogmatically held hypotheses, we may *formulate* our hypotheses, and criticize them. Let our conjectures, our theories die in our stead! We may learn to kill our theories instead of killing each other. (Popper 1978:354)

On this view, our minds evolved to represent reality (however imperfectly) and to perform mental operations (however imperfectly) on these representations with the intermediate goal of reducing environmental risk and uncertainty (the ultimate goal being reproduction). This amounts to learning about the world (embodying it) and forming conjectures or hypotheses about the nature of the world in order to make better decisions about what we should do – that is, in order better to make our way in the world and effect our purposes in it. This is science in the service of practical reason. To learn about the world is to collect data about it; to form a hypothesis about the world on the basis of these data and then to criticize it is to perform an experiment. An experiment is "a device that's designed to cause the state of your mind to correspond to the state of the world . . . 'Know thyself' Socrates said; 'or no science' he might have added" (Fodor 1994:95). Science is something that comes naturally to all normal human infants (Harris 1991, 1994; Johnson-Laird 1983; Piaget 1970, 1971) (as well as postmodern critical theorists [Roscoe 1995]) because it helps us make our way in the world.

But how do we decide that one way is *better* than another? How do we *experience* the decision-making process? How do we *evaluate* the results of our experiments? The answer to these questions is the reason why I believe that evolutionary theory is well equipped to include humanism's specific concerns with "ideals of motivational and emotional honesty" and "truth to personal experience" – the reason, in other words, why I believe that evolutionary theory is well equipped to be our science of value and the foundation for a humane ethical philosophy. And the answer to these questions (the very subject of this book) is that our minds evolved to represent (imperfectly, as always) not just the *facts* of nature, but the *value* that these facts hold for each us. If it were otherwise, how could we evaluate our experiments and (ever) make *good* decisions?

Value in mind: evolutionary ethics and the naturalistic fallacy

This brings us to the naturalistic fallacy. Since I am going to argue that we can base a theory of value and a rational ethical philosophy on the fact that our minds evolved to represent not only certain facts of nature but also the value that these facts hold for us, it clearly behoves me to address G. E. Moore's (1903) claim (via David Hume 1740) that it is illegitimate to argue from the facts of nature to human values. Like others of late I believe that this is wrong, and to show why I will outline recent critiques of the naturalistic fallacy in philosophy and evolutionary ethics.

The fundamental assumption of evolutionary ethics is akin to that of evolutionary epistemology: just as knowledge is part of life and must therefore ultimately be capable of explanation in evolutionary terms, so, too, is ethics part of life and must ultimately be explainable in evolutionary terms as well. Perhaps because it has served so honorably in the war against Social Darwinism, however, the naturalistic fallacy is still received wisdom among many philosophers and evolutionary biologists (Richards 1987, 1993). Even so, there is a growing consensus that it has outlived its usefulness. Mark Johnson, for example, says that

> By claiming that empirical evidence about who we are and how we function is simply irrelevant to the fundamental questions of moral philosophy, Moore initiated a serious decline in ethics (and in value theory) in this century, from which we are only beginning to recover. (1993:140)

The problem with the naturalistic fallacy is not in arguing from facts to values, but doing so unwisely. Two things matter: what we take to be the facts of nature (where we look for our facts and how we recognize them) and how we make the passage from these facts to particular values.

First the facts. The major stumbling-block for Moore's assertion that we cannot argue from facts to values is simply that values have to come from somewhere. While showing that any particular value flows logically from any particular fact may be problematical, the fact remains that values themselves exist as facts of nature and must be capable of rational explanation in terms of nature. As Daniel Dennett said, "If 'ought' cannot be derived from 'is,' just what *can* 'ought' be derived from? Is ethics an *entirely* 'autonomous' field of inquiry? Does it float, untethered to facts from any other discipline or tradition?" (1995:467). His answer is that ethics must be based on "an appreciation of human nature – on a sense of what a human being is or might be, and on what a human being might want to have or want to be" (1995:468). Robin Fox makes the same point, arguing that any political order which fails to consider human nature is an "unnatural order; that is, an order made according to rational decision, not an order evolved from the needs of human nature" (1989:41). Likewise, Robert Richards holds that:

> The first principles of an ethical system can be justified only by appeal to another kind of discourse, an appeal in which *factual evidence about sentiments and beliefs* is adduced . . . So moral principles ultimately can be justified only by facts. The rebuttal, then, to the charge that at some level evolutionary

ethics must attempt to derive its norms from facts is simply
that every ethical system must. (1993:127; emphasis added)

The other discourse on which the first principles of an ethical system
must be justified is the discourse of motive – that is, of emotion. It is our
emotions that allow us to pass from is to ought. As Martha Nussbaum put
it: "the great moral virtues all require some high evaluation of uncon-
trolled external things" (1994:470). The *ought,* the moral imperative, is
that of promoting human flourishing, i.e., *eudaimonia.* The *is* from which
this *ought* flows has two faces: the emotional truth – that is, the fact of our
own and other people's personal emotional (value) experience, which is
the driving force behind all moral action – and the facts of evolution and
development that explain where these emotional truths come from, why
they exist, and why, ultimately, such feelings have a rational basis. (I will
return to this point in the final chapter.)

The fallacy within the naturalistic fallacy is its Cartesian separation of
reason and emotion and blindness to the fact that without emotion there
is no value. As Mark Johnson put it in his *Moral Imagination: Implications of
Cognitive Science for Ethics,* "The source of the problem is the mistaken
assumption that desire is always nonrational, arbitrary, and subjective"
(1993:132). J. Q. Wilson agrees: "morality does not rest on *mere* sentiment,
because there is nothing 'mere' about certain sentiments . . . the teach-
ings of the heart deserve to be taken as seriously as the lessons of the
mind" (1993:238). And, as we shall see in more detail in chapter 3,
Andrzej Elzanowski (1993) suggests that the neurophysiological source of
human value is what he calls "value experience," which is the positive or
negative emotional valence that is universally, innately linked to sensations such as hunger, pain, body contact, social responsiveness, etc. To be
understood, he argues, "value experience has first to be accepted as a natural phenomenon, as an objective source of subjectivity" (1993:272–3).
Johnson also grounds his theory of value in bodily experience:

> There are universal human experiences of pain, pleasure,
> suffering, joy, and fulfilment. There are universal human
> needs, such as shelter, food, love, and protection from harm.
> There are widely, if not universally, shared moral prototypes
> (e.g., *the bully, fair distribution, undeserved kindness*). All of these
> universals, if they are universals, place general constraints on
> what moralities must be like. Furthermore, the facts of human
> psychology – how we conceptualize, what motivates us, how

our identity is formed, and how we develop – place restrictions on the form of any humanly realistic morality. (1993:259)

The philosopher Grant Gillett sums it up this way: "there may be a large number of truths to be derived from the needs (and therefore the good) of human beings" (1993:320).

There is a growing sense, in other words, that moral claims not only can, *but can only* rest on the facts of human nature. But not just any fact will do. Charles Taylor (1993) makes the critical point that commitment (value) is not enough for morality. He denies that something is a moral goal simply in virtue of the fact that we are committed to it. He argues instead that we need to feel that this goal *demands* our commitment. Such demanding commitment, he says, comes from the "strong evaluation" of some goal: "A strongly evaluated goal is one that, were we to cease desiring it, we would be shown up as insensitive or brutish or morally perverse" (p. 210). For example, were most people to cease desiring health, well-being, and justice for all they would feel insensitive or morally perverse. A weakly evaluated goal, by contrast, is one that we could imagine giving up without feeling that we had let ourselves down in any important way. For example, people who have broken their addictions to heroin do not ordinarily feel that they have let themselves down. Taylor holds that the naturalistic fallacy holds for weak evaluations but not strong evaluations. He agrees with Moore: the fact that someone values heroin does not make heroin inherently valuable and does not mean that she should take heroin. However, the fact that most of us would feel "insensitive or brutish or morally perverse" if we gave up caring about the sick, the weak, the poor, and the down-trodden suggests that such caring is inherently valuable and that we should continue to care. Taylor's claim is that if we can show as a fact that our feeling of worth or self-value would be lessened by giving up some value, then that value has been shown to be good, and it is legitimate to say that we ought to pursue it. In other words, moral claims must be based on what human beings need – that is, on *facts* about what they *value,* which is what they feel *strongly* about, and which is how people everywhere judge an act as moral: "our basic moral concepts are never pure abstractions, but are always permeated with the passion and emotion that moves us to action" (Johnson 1993:191).

But what do humans passionately need, and value, such that their resulting action is judged empathic, moral, and in some sense rational? The short answer is *the future.* "Once one is up against [the] sheer fact of species survival, then the nature of the basic needs is obvious; and assuming that survival is accepted as a goal, the question of what to do about it is not difficult" (Fox 1989:45). The long answer will occupy me for the remainder of the book as I set out the evolutionary biological and developmental psychological reasons why it is both accurate and useful (valuable) to think of the future (i.e., relative risk and uncertainty) as a contingent fact of nature, the personal implications of which (i.e., the value of which) our minds evolved to represent – as subjective value experience, as personal emotional truth. To conclude this introductory chapter, however, I will provide one final foreshadowing of this long answer.

Humans must always have been enthralled by the possibility that there might be a way of living which is objectively better than others. Following philosophers since Aristotle, Grant Gillett suggests that a "general understanding of human function" will lead to such objective moral knowledge:

> The objectivity of moral claims would be secured if the "internal good" constituted by moral action were essentially connected to some general understanding of human function ... and therefore to some determinate reading of human well-being. For instance, it is possible to determine what makes for excellence in a hawk or in a surgeon because we know what functions they serve. Thus, if we had a conception of excellence of activity in accordance with reason, we would have some positive or contentful conception of good or well-being for a human being. (1993:288)

In one of the best recent critiques of the naturalistic fallacy, Lewis Petrinovich (1995) points out that in fact we already have an excellent "general understanding of human function" and a corresponding conception of "excellence of activity in accordance with reason." Evolutionary theory provides the general understanding – according to which "excellence relates to those actions that increase the likelihood of reproductive success" (Petrinovich 1995:31). In accordance with evolution's reason, then, the ultimate value in life (*bios*) is having descendants. Without ancestors we could not exist; without reproduction life itself could not exist, nor could value. To effect our purpose in life is to foster reproduction, which is the continuation of life.

In the following pages I will propose that our minds evolved in part to represent not only certain facts about our environments that are relevant to our capacity for reproductive success (i.e., for leaving descendants – what evolutionary biologists call reproductive value [Fisher 1930]), but that the way we experience these facts is emotionally, as value experience. On this view, as eyes sense light and ears sense sound, emotions sense value. I will also suggest that when we experience our environments as low in risk and uncertainty we are, for very good evolutionary biological reasons, more likely to place a high value on our futures, and that we experience this value, in part, as the moral imperative to promote human flourishing. In a nutshell, I am going to argue that our moral sentiments are (1) contingent, facultative adaptations *for* achieving a future (even if we cannot live to see it) that is valuable for our ultimate reproductive success (or would have been in our evolutionary past), and (2) that these moral sentiments represent the *relationship* between current and recent indicators (socioecological and cultural) of the evolutionary value of our futures and the state of our nervous system, which we tend to experience as a variety of love – the personal moral command to promote human flourishing.

If value cannot exist without life, and life cannot exist without reproduction, then, according to our only scientific theory of life, the ultimate value in life is having descendants. But what does this mean for humans? How do we achieve this ultimate value? How are moral sentiments (which "require high evaluation") linked to reproductive value? How is value represented phenotypically? How does morality come to be embodied? Why does not everyone have the same morality? These are the questions that I will begin to address in the following chapter. I must be cautious, however, for, as Dennett (1995) notes, these are also the questions on which earlier evolutionary theories of morality stubbed their toes. Wilson (1978), Ruse and Wilson (1985), and Alexander (1987) have all advanced versions of the argument that morality "is an illusion fobbed off on us by our genes to get us to cooperate" (Ruse and Wilson 1985:51) and that "genes hold culture on a leash. The leash is very long, but inevitably values will be constrained in accordance with their effects on the human gene pool" (Wilson 1978:167). Dennett points out, however, that people in fact *do* have wrong ethical beliefs (in case you need examples see Brown 1991 and J. Q. Wilson 1993). The mistake, says Dennett, is in assuming "that our genes are powerful enough, and insightful enough, to keep us from making policies quite antithetical to their interests" (1995:471), and he calls "massively misleading" (p. 473) the essential argument of Wilson, Ruse, and Alexander that because the *ultimate* explanation of everyone's ethical stance has to do with reproductive success, therefore considerations of reproductive success explain *each and every step* on the complicated causal pathway that leads each of us from the genes we inherit from our ancestors to the particular moral sentiments that we come to hold as we mature.

As Dennett says, this is not so much wrong as misleading. The reason it is misleading is that yes, of course, considerations of reproductive success are involved in each and every step of these causal pathways, but this is simply a truism, exactly analogous to the truism that nature and nurture, genes and environments, are involved in the production of every aspect of all organisms. What matters is *how* nature and nurture, genes and environments interact; what matters is precisely *what* these considerations of reproductive success are (and how they are measured) and *how* they are involved in the causal pathways which lead from our ancestors, through the developmental history of our interactions with our environments, and on to our own personal moral sentiments. Furthermore, it is only knowledge of these causal pathways that could contribute to our practical reason and help us to make our way in the world. Knowing *that* considerations of reproductive success are involved in moral development is not valuable truth; knowing *how and why* they are involved is what could have valuable therapeutic implications.

What has been missing from previous evolutionary perspectives on morality, in other words, is a thorough appreciation of development: the processes of gene × environment interaction whereby information about our ancestors' environments – especially the predictable contingencies of reproductive value – becomes literally embodied as adaptations in us, their descendants, during ontogeny. My task now, therefore, is to show how evolution and development can be usefully joined.

2   Evolution and development

No living being can be happy or even exist unless his needs are
sufficiently proportioned to his means.   Emile Durkheim (1951:246)

The main issue in evolution is how populations deal with unknown
futures.   C. H. Waddington (1969:122)

Individual adaptability is, in fact, distinctly a factor of evolutionary
poise. It is not only of the greatest significance as a factor of evolution
in damping the effects of selection . . . but is itself perhaps the chief
object of selection.   Sewall Wright (1931:147)

The preceding chapter broached the idea that viewing human nature as
a manifestation of our reproductive strategies provides the basis for a
science of value and a liberal ethical philosophy. My aims in this chapter
are, first, to explain how modern evolutionary theory justifies the assumption that the ultimate value in life is reproduction (the continuation of
life), and second, to point out some of the implications that flow from
this assumption. But to do this it is necessary first to show why evolutionary theory is incomplete without a thoroughly integrated theory of
development (and vice versa), and why it is only when evolutionary and
developmental perspectives are combined that questions about the phenotypic representations of reproductive value, including our subjective
experiences of it, can begin to be answered. A large part of this chapter is
devoted to the argument that life history theory is the best candidate for
integrating evolutionary and developmental perspectives.

The missing phenotype
In just three decades, inclusive fitness theory (Hamilton 1964; Trivers
1971, 1972, 1974) has massively transformed the study of behavior in
both the biological and social sciences, but has had considerably less
impact in the historical sciences (e.g., Gould 1989), especially developmental biology and psychology (e.g., Goodwin 1994; Hall 1992; Oyama
1985). The reason for inclusive fitness theory's huge success is the com-

pelling logic at its heart. On the other hand, the reason for its lesser standing in the developmental sciences is that this logic is silent about the relationship between genotype and phenotype (e.g., Bateson 1982; Gould and Lewontin 1979; Oyama 1985). Since selection operates on phenotypes, not genotypes, and, since the relationship of the genotype to the phenotype can only be a developmental one, it follows that any evolutionary approach to behavior has to include a major developmental component.

As is well known, Darwin had no knowledge of genetics, and his theory of adaptation by natural selection needed Gregor Mendel, J. B. S. Haldane, Ronald Fisher, and Sewall Wright, and, more recently, George Williams, William Hamilton, Robert Trivers, and John Maynard Smith, before it could achieve the explanatory and predictive power that it has today. The reason that evolutionary biology has tended to disregard the phenotype is precisely because of this power. Equipped with population genetics, demography, inclusive fitness theory, and game theory, evolutionary biologists now routinely generate elegant and powerfully predictive formal models of how gene pools behave and what genes selection should favor. A model is a metaphor, image, or schema of how some aspect of the world is believed to work. A formal model is an image of these workings that has been represented in mathematical terms. Using such models, evolutionary biologists have gained an immense amount of empirical support for their hypotheses (models, schemas, etc.). But, in their focus on genes as the product of natural selection, evolutionary biologists have sometimes been inclined to neglect the phenotype, and thus to neglect as well the fact that selection operates on phenotypes, not genotypes; that it is the success of the phenotype that determines which genes get copied into subsequent generations; and that phenotypes, to do their adaptive work, must first develop – they must first be *produced*. Steven Stearns described the problem this way:

> Population genetics was the first attempt at a predictive quantitative theory of evolution. Its founders made a series of simplifying assumptions that had the effect of reducing the objects of study to changes in gene frequencies: the organism disappeared from view, and with it went the phenotype, the ecological interactions of the phenotype with the environment that determine fitness, and the developmental interactions with the environment that produce the phenotype. (1982:238)

The situation that Stearns describes is a manifestation of the dichotomy in biology between *adaptationist* and *mechanist* thinking. In his words, adaptationists ask the question, "What should selection favor?" while mechanists ask the question, "How does the organism work?" (1982:238).[1] Evolutionary theory is nothing if not adaptationist. Nor is there any necessary or fundamental opposition between the two perspectives. And it is important not to exaggerate their differences. Nonetheless, differences exist, and, while they stem from straightforward differences in perspective, the two approaches have developed along divergent pathways with different implications for theory and method.

The adaptationist perspective
The adaptationist school, with roots in quantitative genetics, works, implicitly or explicitly, with abstract mathematical models of natural selection and its products, i.e., the traits selection is supposed to favor. For example, the compelling logic at the heart of inclusive fitness theory is the equation

$$k > 1/r$$

(Hamilton 1964).[2] Exploring adaptation as they do through the logical manipulation of such symbols, adaptationists have to trade off a certain amount of biological realism to achieve analytic precision and generality. Consequently, they occasionally run the risk of conflating real phenotypic traits with the hypothetical genes "for" such traits by treating the organism as if it *were* their representation of it – i.e., a genotype (Kitcher 1985; Oyama 1985; Plotkin and Odling-Smee 1981).

Possibly to rationalize their subtle inattention to the phenotype, some evolutionary biologists make use of the *phenotypic gambit*, which is the simplifying assumption that the relationship of the genotype to the phenotype is not especially important for understanding adaptation. As Stearns put it, "optimality models assume simple, unrealistic genetics, but that assumption does not appear to make a crucial difference to the

---

[1] This is essentially the distinction that Tinbergen (1963) made between phylogenetic/ultimate questions (what selection should favor) and ontogenetic/proximate questions (how the organism works).

[2] Hamilton demonstrated that selection should favor altruistic behavior when k (the benefit to the recipient of some altruistic behavior, compared to the cost of that behavior to the altruist) is greater than 1 divided by r, the coefficient of genetic relatedness between the altruist and the recipient.

design of the phenotype" (1992:131; see also Grafen 1984; Smith and Winterhalder 1992). But for many purposes it *is* important, for without an understanding of how phenotypes emerge developmentally from gene × environment interactions we can have no clear picture of the trait that is supposed to be the adaptation. To understand what selection *should* favor it is necessary to test predictions from our abstract formal models against the phenotypes of real organisms. This is the phenotypic gambit: if our models of the genotype successfully predict the phenotypes that we actually observe in nature, then the relationship of the genotype to the phenotype is deemed not very important. However, to understand what selection *does* favor we must understand how organisms work, which includes understanding the developmental mechanisms whereby genes and environments mutually construct phenotypes. Without a description of the processes that actually *make* the phenotypic patterns that our abstract models predict, we have not really explained them, but have merely replaced our abstraction with a description that is congruent with it. Congruence, like correlation, is not explanation. Or, in the words of the zoologist Joseph Bernardo:

> The most significant difficulty with current [life history] models is the assumption that the analysis of patterns of phenotypic variation can identify the underlying biological mechanisms responsible for generating or maintaining the variation . . . [W]hile optimal control and other phenotypic optimization models may implicate potential sources of phenotypic variation, they cannot predict whether organisms are capable of producing such phenotypes, or how that variation is generated. (1993:172)

The potential pitfalls of the phenotypic gambit are nicely illustrated by the uncommonly perceptive work of Dmitry Belyaev and his colleagues (1985) at the Institute of Cytology and Genetics of the former USSR Academy of Sciences. In an effort to improve production and save fingers, he and his team studied hundreds of litters of silver foxes, an obstreperous little animal widely farmed for its fur. Investigating the physiological changes that underlie animal domestication, they observed the development of two strains of silver fox pups. One strain had been selected for 25 years for outstanding aggressiveness (the "wild" strain), while the other had been subject to 25 years of selection for outstanding ease of handling (the "tame" strain). In all mammals, friendly, affiliative, or positive approach behaviors emerge developmentally before fearful (and thus also aggressive) behaviors. Human infants, for example, typically first evidence clearly positive, affiliative behavior at around 6 or 8 weeks when the social smile appears; they first show clear signs of social fear at around 8 months when fear of strangers ordinarily appears. This period of time between the onset of positive, affiliative behavior and negative, fearful behavior is sometimes referred to as the "period of primary socialization." Belyaev and his team observed that, compared to wild pups, those from the tame strain had significantly longer periods of primary socialization; compared to wild pups, the tame ones were significantly developmentally delayed in the appearance of social fear. Belyaev's team concluded that selection for tameness resulted in lower levels of aggression because those animals who showed a longer sensitive period of primary socialization *had more time* to explore their social environments, and thereby more time to develop the habit of positive, friendly, affiliative social interactions before their innate fearful (and thus also aggressive) responses developed. Simply with more time *to experience* positive, affiliative behaviors, the neural pathways involved in their expression would receive more functional validation, and thus be less likely to atrophy or be extinguished from insufficient use when fearful behaviors began to emerge.[3]

The relevance of Belyaev's research to the phenotypic gambit is this: If I make the simplifying assumption that the relationship of the genotype to the phenotype is not very important for understanding the lower aggressiveness of tame silver fox pups, then I am more likely to conclude that, having selected for lower aggressiveness, and actually achieved it, I must therefore have selected the genes "for" lower aggressiveness. In fact, what seems to have been selected was genes "for" a longer period of primary socialization. Now for some purposes it does not matter whether it was genes "for" aggressiveness or "for" an altered pattern of behavioral development that actually made the difference. But, if I am trying to understand individual differences in aggressiveness in silver foxes, it makes all the difference in the world. First, Belyaev's results suggest that the genetic basis "for" silver fox aggression should more properly be conceived as the genetic basis "for" a pattern of development that affects young foxes' *opportunity* for a certain kind of experience with their

---

[3] This is an example of what Changeux (1985) called "epigenesis by selective stabilization" (see below p. 64).

environments. (Which is nature here, and which is nurture?) Second, when many people think of genes "for" a trait like aggression they do not think of the genes involved in the correct technical sense of the genes that *make a difference* in the expression of aggression (e.g., Dawkins 1976, 1982), but in the all-too-common sense that the genes "for" aggression *determine* aggression, so they then believe, too, that aggression is somehow "programmed," or, even worse, "natural." Such a view is wrong, of course, as the work of Belyaev's team shows, for what matters as much as the potential (genotypic) *opportunity* for experience is the actual, historical (phenotypic) *experience* of nonaggression itself.[4] Again, for some purposes the precise nature of the relationship of the genotype to the phenotype might not matter very much, but for others it matters a lot. If the species in question were humans rather than foxes, for instance, and the purpose was therapeutic, then knowing that the early experience of nonaggression could make a developmental difference might make a very big difference indeed.

There will be more on the adaptationist perspective shortly, when I examine its supreme strength to explain why evolutionary biologists are justified in making the *optimality assumption*, which is an adaptationist concept through and through. However, to set the stage for a more involved account coming later in this chapter and in the next, I must first provide a brief account of the mechanist approach in biology.

The mechanist perspective
The mechanist school, with roots in anatomy, physiology, embryology, and whole organism natural history and classical ethology focuses more on individual organisms and the mechanisms that produce phenotypes (and thus adaptations) and how organisms and their environments interact throughout life to affect fitness. Adaptationists and mechanists are in perfect agreement that the ultimate cause of evolutionary change is the differential reproduction of inherited variation, and they also agree that ultimately genes underlie everything an organism is or ever can be. Mechanists, however, may be less apt to conflate phenotypic traits with the genetic basis "for" such traits because mechanist thinking emphasizes that the environment also underlies everything an organism is or ever can be, and that the phenotype is not resident in or isomorphic

---

[4] For an account of the "*unnaturalness*" of aggression, see *Aggression: The Myth of the Beast Within*, by a group of behavioral and developmental scientists known as J. Klama (1988).

with the genotype, but emergent – developmentally (i.e., historically) contingent on the dialectic between organism and environment from conception to death. As Stearns put it, "More is known about what evolution ought to produce . . . than about what developmental systems can produce" (1982:237).

Developmentalists are thus uncomfortable with models of evolution formulated only in terms of the genotype and the phenotypic gambit. Life history theory offers an attractive alternative because its subject-matter is the evolutionary study of life cycles, which are inherently developmental phenomena. Again, Steven Stearns:

> Life history theory emerged . . . as a reaction to the lack of empirical content forced upon population genetics by its simplifying assumptions. Along with other optimization approaches in evolutionary ecology, it constitutes the second attempt at a predictive quantitative theory of evolution [and] motivates a new look at development because developmental mechanisms could connect population genetics with life history theory to form a predictive theory of evolution more powerful than either of the first two attempted. (1982:238–9)

As we will see, life history theory offers the best hope for combining adaptationist and mechanist perspectives. The adaptationist heart of this book is a series of arguments from life history theory as to why selection should favor the capacity of all human beings to experience moral sentiments – but also why we would not expect all humans to have the same moral sentiments. A critical part of the adaptationist heart of my argument, in short, is the rationale in life history theory for expecting adaptive individual differences in human value experience.

Adaptationism is not enough, however. Even if you should find compelling the coming arguments about why selection should favor the capacity for individual differences in value experience, this would not be enough, as the silver foxes helped us see. The question would then become, how are these adaptive individual differences in value experience *produced*? How are they actually embodied? How does value experience come to be represented materially, phenotypically, in each of us? Since my ultimate goal is therapeutic – to increase practical reason – then I have to describe the developmental mechanisms involved. The mechanist heart of this book, then, is an exercise in reverse engineering (Dennett 1995), in which I try to uncover the developmental mechanisms (themselves produced by natural selection) that produce the individual differences that may be adaptive in particular social and physical environments.

Life history theory: developmental evolutionary ecology

Life history theory is the evolutionary study of life cycles and life history traits in an ecological context. Examples of mammalian life history traits are gestation length, size at birth, age at first reproduction, number of offspring, lactation period, reproductive rate, and length of life.[5] The initial impetus for life history theory was the realization that, just as anatomy, physiology, and behavior are exposed to selection and evolve, so, too, are life cycles exposed to selection and evolve. (Or, better, the developmental mechanisms that *produce* life cycles are exposed to selection and evolve.) Arising 30 years ago from developmental biology, evolutionary ecology, demography, and quantitative genetics (e.g., Bonner 1965; Bradshaw 1965; Williams 1957, 1966), life history theory today is one of the most vital areas in all of evolutionary biology. I think that there are two reasons for life history theory's dramatic growth. The first is its critical (adaptationist) insight that life cycles themselves are usefully conceived as evolved reproductive strategies. The second is its (mechanist) concern with the developmental systems that actually produce life cycles.

The principle of allocation
Why does life history theory conceive of life cycles as evolved reproductive strategies? To nonbiologists this may seem (at best) a curious narrowing of reference, but it makes sense to evolutionists because of life history theory's principle of allocation (Levins 1968; see also Darwin 1871; Fisher 1930; Lack 1947).

The principle of allocation originates at the intersection of biology, our science of life, and physics, our science of matter and energy. According to the laws of evolution, to be alive is to have ancestors who were themselves once alive.[6] To have left descendants (i.e., to have achieved a degree

---

[5] Because mammals provide the most appropriate comparative context for understanding human life history traits I limit my discussion to members of this class. Menopause is the only human life history trait that is not found in other primates or mammals – except, apparently, in some whale species (Peccei 1995; for additional life history perspectives on menopause see Hill 1993; Hill and Hurtado 1991; Pavelka and Fedigan 1991).

[6] How did life itself arise? How could life have come from nonlife? For a splendid rational account of what might have happened see Dennett (1995), especially chapter 7.

of reproductive success or fitness) each of our direct ancestors had to have survived long enough to reproduce. This takes work, for, according to the Second Law of Thermodynamics, entropy (disorganization, dissipation, death, decay) tends to increase. In nature, as in culture, there is no such thing as a free lunch. Therefore, in order for life to arise at all, to become more complex over time, and for each of our ancestors to fend off their own decay long enough to reproduce, work had to be done.

This was the work of acquiring the resources required to survive and reproduce. At a minimum, such resources include energy, nutrients, safety or security, information, and time. Energy and nutrients are required to maintain organismic structure and function. Security is the statistical or actuarial resource required to avoid accidental death (technically, extrinsic mortality) or failure to reproduce. If you live in a dangerous environment, with no way to ward off the dangers arrayed against you, you have less chance of surviving and reproducing than someone living in a secure environment. And the more you persist in risky activities (e.g., hang-gliding, gang violence, childbirth) the greater the chance that your number will come up. Information is a resource in the sense that it can be used to obtain energy and nutrients and to ward off danger. Finally, time is a resource, for it is in the nature of work that it takes time to complete.

What makes things interesting is that all of these resources are limited. While occasionally some individuals (particularly of our species, and in our time) have access to more energy and nutrients than they can possibly use, the vast majority do not, and we have known since Malthus that population growth is ultimately curbed by starvation. In any event, safety is always limited in the sense that no environment is perfectly secure, absolutely without risk. Information is always limited in the sense that no environment is absolutely predictable; no organism ever has perfect, complete knowledge of every aspect of its environment. And time is always limited, in two senses. First, time is limited in the sense that there are always occasions when it is impossible to do two things at the same time (opportunity costs). If one is searching for food to stay alive, for example, it may not be possible at the same time also to search for a mate. Second, and of special relevance for my central argument, time is limited in the sense that all sexually reproducing animals have a genetically determined maximum life potential. Ultimately, the price of sex is death. Even if we were to possess all of the other resources in perfect abundance we would still die. This is because selection has favored genes that help us to reproduce, not survive. If these genes have deleterious effects that show up *after* we have finished reproducing, well, that is too bad (Medawar 1952; Rose 1991; Williams 1957).[7]

All of our direct ancestors, in an unbroken chain back to the beginning of life, with no exceptions, possessed sufficient energy, nutrients, security, information, and time to do the work required to produce us, their descendants. All of our ancestors achieved a degree of fitness, which is defined in terms of reproductive success, or the number of copies of genes passed into subsequent generations (more later on the critical questions of *how many* copies and *how many* generations). But, because there is more to fitness than simply producing offspring, we are connected to the beginning of life by more than an unbroken chain of copulations. Sex, while necessary for fitness, is not sufficient; in order for newly produced offspring to reproduce, they must first survive. But neither are sex and mere survival sufficient to achieve fitness, for, by definition, only adults reproduce, and newly produced offspring must not only survive, but at the same time grow, develop, mature, and learn before they have a chance of attracting a mate and successfully rearing their own offspring. Thus, while fitness is ultimately *measured* in terms of number of descendants, it *consists* of separate components, which may be thought of as "work that needs to be done to leave descendants." Such work includes, at a minimum, (1) survival; (2) growth and development, maturation, learning and other preparations for reproduction; and (3) reproduction itself. The work of survival and growth and development is called *somatic effort*, while the work of reproduction is referred to as *reproductive effort*. Reproductive effort, in turn, is conventionally subdivided into (3a) the actual *production* of offspring (sometimes referred to as *mating effort*), which increases the *quantity* of offspring, and (3b) the *rearing* of offspring (sometimes referred to as *parenting effort*), which increases offspring *quality* or reproductive value (see Table 2.1) (Alexander and Borgia 1979; Hirschfield and Tinkle 1975; Low 1978).

The fact that resources are always limited would not be so interesting if selection didn't always favor greater fitness too. What matters in evolution is not leaving *many* copies of your genes in subsequent generations,

---

[7] Actually, it is years of *reproductive* life that matters, not simply lifespan *per se*. Thus, although women tend to live longer than men (at least in the West), because of menopause they have considerably fewer years in which they can produce offspring.

Table 2.1 The components of fitness.

Somatic effort	(1) Survival, maintenance
	(2) Preparations for reproduction (e.g., growth, development, learning, maturation, etc.)
Reproductive effort	(3) Reproduction
	(3a) Production of offspring (increases offspring *quantity*)
	(3b) Rearing of offspring (increases offspring *quality*)

but leaving *more* copies than other individuals in your population who carry different genes. Selection does not favor traits associated with reproductive success *per se*, but with *greater* reproductive success; fitness is intrinsically a relative concept. There is thus no a priori way to say what high or low fitness might be. In this sense, while the resources that organisms hold are always limited, they simultaneously face unlimited (i.e., unending) pressure to leave *more* descendants.

The inherent conflict between means (limited resources) and ends (unremitting selection for greater fitness) is where biology (the work of life) meets physics (the origin and nature of work) and where life history theory's principle of allocation originates. "If you wanna live, you gotta eat" is how Dennett (1995:128) put it. But if you wanna live and wanna grow and develop and wanna have babies (and your babies to have babies) you gotta eat more. What if there is no more? Then you gotta decide what to do: continue living, continue growing, or have babies. Can you do all three? If you cannot, what gives? If *any* of your ancestors gave up on having babies you would not be here. What is the best way to use your time and energy and risk your security? Because there can never be sufficient resources to meet selection's never-ending demand for greater fitness (i.e., longer survival; faster, slower, or better growth and development; and ultimately more offspring of higher quality), something has to give. Because the Second Law of Thermodynamics takes precedence over the laws of evolution, the only thing that can give is one or more of the components of fitness.

All of this necessitates the existence of *trade-offs* among the components of fitness. A trade-off occurs when an increase in one thing entails a decrease in another: "Trade-offs represent the costs paid in the currency of fitness when a beneficial change in one trait is linked to a detrimental change in another" (Stearns 1989:259). Resources allocated to the work of survival, for example, cannot be allocated as well to the work of growth and development. Thus, if resources are insufficient both to maintain life and support growth, there exists a trade-off between survival and growth, and something has to give. If survival is what gives, then the organism leaves fewer or no descendants. End of story. If growth is what gives, however, the story (like a good hypothesis) continues. By trading off growth to stay alive, the organism may survive to grow again later, and then to pass on to its descendants the genetic basis for allocating limited resources to ("making decisions" about) survival instead of growth under severe conditions.[8] Trade-offs may be either *intraindividual* (e.g., own survival vs. own growth) or *intergenerational* (e.g., own survival vs. survival or growth of offspring) (Stearns 1989).[9]

Similarly, if resources are insufficient to produce a large quantity of offspring who are also of high quality (reproductive value), something has to give – either quantity or quality (or both). Consider two mothers, A and B, each with the same amount of limited resources (time, money, capacity to go without sleep, etc.). Mother A puts hers into rearing, say, four offspring, while mother B puts hers into rearing just two. Having to divide her parental investment into only two portions, Mother B can give half of what she has to each offspring, who grows strong and healthy as a result. Mother A's offspring, however, receiving only one-quarter each, are somewhat smaller, weaker, or less secure as adults. Mother A is thus said to have "traded" some of her offsprings' quality in order to increase their quantity. But why would a mother ever make such a trade, even if unconsciously? Is not quality always a good thing? Not when it does not make a difference. I'll have more to say about the nature and cost of quality later, but in the meantime, imagine that the environment in which these mothers live is highly dangerous, but *randomly* so, so that survival to adulthood is largely a matter of luck, that what parents can do for their children makes little difference for their children's reproductive value, and that on average, of every four offspring produced, only one

---

[8] This may be the ultimate explanation for "hospitalism" (Spitz 1945) or nonorganic failure to thrive, a serious pediatric condition in which highly stressed but otherwise adequately nourished infants cease to grow (Drotar 1991; Monckberg 1992). Shunting the energy and nutrients they take in away from growth and into survival may be an adaptive response to stress, allowing infants to "buy time" on the chance that conditions will improve.

[9] Trade-offs may also be *interindividual* (or *intragenerational*, which amounts to the same thing). For example, if I have sufficient power, prestige, or wealth I may be able to induce you to trade off some component of your fitness in order thereby to increase my own.

survives and reproduces. In this extreme scenario, both of mother B's high-quality offspring would likely have perished, while one of mother A's low-quality offspring would have carried her genes into the next generation. The point is that quality (reproductive value) is not an absolute, but is always contingent on the nature of the environment. It follows that, when environments change, so can the nature of the trade-off between quantity and quality or any of the other components of fitness.

Some of the more commonly studied trade-offs are survival vs. growth, survival vs. reproduction, growth vs. reproduction, and quantity vs. quality of offspring. For an example of the trade-off between survival and reproduction consider the now-classic work of Tim Clutton-Brock and his colleagues (1982). They showed that among red deer, lactating females suffered significantly higher mortality during the winter than non-nursing mothers. From a mechanist perspective, the reason was that the lactating females had smaller fat reserves, and were thus more vulnerable during the harsh winter months. The reason they had smaller fat reserves was because they had to allocate energy from the food they took in both to fat reserves (which stores energy and is thus an adaptation for winter survival) and to milk production (which benefits offspring survival and growth and is thus an adaptation for reproduction, i.e., parenting). Many lactating females did not take in enough energy to support both survival and lactation. From an adaptationist perspective, the reason they died was because of the trade-off between survival and reproduction. Those who died were apparently less able to strike the appropriate balance (achieve the optimal trade-off) between survival and reproduction (and so did not pass on copies of whatever genetic material might have a made a difference in their capacity to do so).

For an example of the trade-off between quantity and quality of offspring consider the research of Montserrat Gomendio (1991). To reproduce at all, female mammals are obligated by their anatomy and physiology to expend a great deal of reproductive effort in the form of ovulation, menstruation, gestation, parturition, and lactation – i.e., parenting effort. Allocating more of their limited resources to rearing offspring (which increases their quality), they have less to put into producing offspring (which increases their quantity) (Trivers 1972). Since a minimum amount of both quality and quantity are required to leave descendants, we expect selection to have favored mechanisms which enable female mammals to find the optimal balance between number and quality (reproductive value) of offspring. Studying this trade-off in a colony of rhesus macaques,

Gomendio observed mother–infant interactions associated with nursing in two groups of mothers: those who conceived in their first estrus after the birth of the current offspring, and those who did not conceive. There was no difference between the groups in the frequency of infants' attempts to nurse. However, mothers who did conceive were more rejecting of their infants (especially during the breeding season) than those who did not. The lower rejection rate of the mothers who did not conceive resulted in a higher nursing frequency by their infants, which probably helped prevent conception (Lee 1987). Everything else being equal, the less-rejecting mothers would have fewer offspring – i.e., lower quantity. At the same time, because they nursed more frequently, the infants of the less-rejecting mothers would be expected to show greater weight gain and higher survivorship – i.e., higher quality.

Finally, for an example of both intergenerational and intraindividual trade-offs between survival and reproduction in humans, consider why humans usually have singleton births. Using old census records (1769–1850) from rural Finland, Haukioja, Lemmetyinen, and Pikkola (1989) studied a total of 316 children from singleton births and 168 children from twin births. Women giving birth to twins ended up with significantly greater lifetime fertility – but at great (intergenerational) cost to their children's health. While 71% of the singleton children survived to age 15, only 34% of the children from twin births lived that long (a difference significant at $p < 0.0001$). Likewise, the mothers of twins paid a significant (intraindividual) cost themselves. While 95.6% of the mothers of twins survived the first year after delivery, fully 99.1% of the mothers of singletons survived, also a significant difference. In this population, the optimal number of children per pregnancy was one. The trade-off for increasing offspring production (maximizing offspring quantity) by one additional offspring per pregnancy significantly reduced survival for both the women themselves and their children (offspring quality).

The existence of trade-offs among the components of fitness implies the existence of phenotypic mechanisms for actually making trade-offs. That is, we expect natural selection to favor mechanisms or algorithms for *selecting between* or *making decisions about* alternative ways to allocate resources. More than this, it implies the existence of mechanisms or algorithms for making the best possible (optimal) decisions, for we expect natural selection to favor those mechanisms whose operation on average resulted in more descendants – i.e., the continuation of life. This is the rationale for the principle of allocation: life history theory assumes that natural selection will tend to favor phenotypic mechanisms that achieve the optimal allocation of limited resources among the components of fitness: survival, growth and development and other preparations for reproduction, and reproduction itself.

Which returns us to the question at the beginning of this section: how does the principle of allocation justify life history theory's view of life cycles as evolved reproductive strategies? What is the rationale for this apparent narrowing of reference? The answer is that evolution is not driven by differential survival or differential growth and development, but by differential reproduction. Survival and growth and development are necessary for leaving descendants, but not sufficient.[10] Adaptations for survival and growth and development are thus evolutionarily significant only in so far as they contribute to ultimate fitness – which requires reproduction: the production and rearing of offspring. Life cycles themselves evolved because they enabled organisms to make trade-offs among more components of fitness, which is what life cycles *are* – the components of fitness ("work that needs to be done to leave descendants"): cycles of conception (new life), continuing survival, growth and development, reproduction, and then death (one of the costs of reproduction). For example, John Bonner, the eminent developmental biologist, argued that "development is the inevitable result of sex and size. The single-cell stage is required for sexual reproduction, and the larger size is the result of selection for reproductive success in new niches" (1993:35). Increased size conferred fitness benefits because competition for resources put an adaptive premium on larger, more complex and competitive bodies. The only way to get from the single-cell stage to larger, more complex, competitive bodies, however, was through the evolution of processes of growth and development. This was the origin of the life cycles of multicellular organisms (Buss 1987). Growth and development take time, which is another reason why time itself is a resource. Development is what produces life cycles; life cycles *are* development. But development, the result of sex and size, is *for* reproduction. Therefore, from the perspective of life history theory, life cycles themselves may be conceived as evolved reproductive strategies. Reproductive strategies, in turn, are thought of as suites or constellations of

---

[10] Until reproduction is physically possible, however, survival and growth and development and all preparations for reproduction are always the most important adaptive problems. This is because continued survival and growth and development are the immature organism's *only* pathway to reproduction (Chisholm 1996a).

functionally integrated[11] anatomical, physiological, psychological, and developmental mechanisms for optimizing the trade-offs among the components of fitness in the way that maximizes number of descendants, throughout the life cycle.[12]

The assumption of optimality
But what does it mean to "optimize" the trade-offs among the components of fitness? What does it mean to *assume* that this optimization occurs? Why do evolutionists make this assumption, and what are its implications? Having raised the contentious topic of optimality, I must pause to explain what the all the fuss is about and why there need not be any.

The assumption of optimality, as it is known, is the fundamental and thoroughly adaptationist assumption at the core of life history theory, indeed of all evolutionary theory. When misunderstood, however, it is probably the one concept that most hinders the acceptance of evolutionary thinking in other disciplines. My goal here is to review the optimality assumption in the hope of persuading skeptics that not only is it valid, but it can also make an important contribution to practical reason.

Most objections to the optimality assumption revolve around the mistaken assumption that those who use this approach believe that organisms actually are optimally (i.e., "perfectly") adapted or are trying to prove that they are (Parker and Maynard Smith 1990; Seger and Stubblefield 1996). From this first false step a number of others can follow, the worst being when the critics project their own fears of biological determinism ("energy, called evil, is alone from the body") onto the misunderstood optimality assumption, which tempts them to conclude that if evolutionary biologists believe that a trait is optimal, then they must also believe that its very optimality means that it is inevitable, if not morally or politically justified as well (e.g., Segerstråle 1992).

---

[11] Some of an organism's traits are functionally integrated, in the sense that they work together to carry out some metabolic, endocrine, or developmental process which is or was favored by selection. Such traits are integrated in a network of adaptive causation; they cause something to happen (e.g., a developmental process that produces an anatomical feature or behavioral predisposition) that may be adaptive. Other traits have no function and do not cause anything adaptive to happen. Instead, they are "by-products" (see below), merely correlated with each other or with other integrated traits (e.g., Stamps 1991; Stearns 1992). The distinction is not always easy to make in practice.

[12] The best statements of life history theory include Boyce (1988); Charnov (1993); Charnov and Berrigan (1993); DeRousseau (1990); Hill (1993); McNamara and Houston (1996); Pereira and Fairbanks (1993); Roff (1992); Stearns (1992).

In fact, the assumption of optimality does not imply any a priori definition of an optimal trait, life cycle, or reproductive strategy, for optimality is local and contingent; what is optimal in one environment is likely to be suboptimal in another. The key to understanding the assumption of optimality is knowing that "optimal" means "best available given existing circumstances" and not "best imaginable." However much we might wish otherwise, there is no perfection in life, nor can there be. An optimal design is not a perfect design, only the best that can be produced with the available genes, the available resources, and in the available time. Because resources are always limited, organisms are always bundles of compromises or trade-offs between and among their various traits. Selection cannot produce perfection – the best imaginable – when there is no genetic or developmental basis for achieving it, nor when constrained by a changing environment or inadequate resources. The best selection can do is to maximize the probability that the optimal phenotype – the best *available* design – will become manifest (Mangel and Clark 1988; Mayr 1983; Parker and Maynard Smith 1990; Seger and Stubblefield 1996; Williams 1966).

We expect selection to maximize the probability that the best available phenotype will be produced because really we have no choice. We *have* to expect or assume that when Mother Nature (evolution and development) produces a trait, she has her reasons, she has some *intention* in mind. There are two justifications for this superficially audacious claim. The first is a straightforward methodological justification: The assumption of optimality is simply a logical tool that helps us to ask better questions. The second justification is from deep within evolutionary theory, best appreciated, in my opinion, through the twin concepts of the intentional stance and reverse engineering. As mentioned, the intentional stance is the assumption that Mother Nature has a purpose – that at least some traits are *for* something. This is the adaptationist approach. Reverse engineering is "artifact hermeneutics" (Dennett 1995:212), which is the interpretation of phenotypic "artifacts" (traits) on the basis of this assumption in order to determine how such traits come to serve Mother Nature's purpose – i.e., how they work to continue life. This is the mechanist approach. I will review this latter justification first.

We know that work is a precondition of life. For life to exist, organisms must do the work of life: survival, growth and development, and reproduction. The work of life is done only by phenotypes (information in genotypes helps to *control* work but does not actually *do* work). Therefore, selection must have designed phenotypic traits (more precisely, adaptations) so that they were good at (i.e., *for*) keeping organisms alive while they grew and developed, so that ultimately they could reproduce (and do it all on limited resources, too). This is the intentional stance. When the intentional stance is used to understand phenotypes, the result is the reverse engineering of evolutionary and developmental processes, which is viewing the phenotypic trait in question "as a product of a process of *reasoned* design development, a series of *choices* among alternatives, in which the *decisions* reached were those *deemed best* by the designers" (Dennett 1995:230; original emphases). Design, as Darwin deduced, does not imply a designer (Dawkins 1976, 1986, 1996; Dennett 1995). All that it takes is a large number of choices (i.e., decisions, selections) – not of the perfect phenotype (for it does not exist), but simply of the best available at the time, which is all that optimal means: best available. "Selection favors existing variants with higher fitness, not necessarily the best possible or imaginable variant; it trades in relative rather than maximum advantage" (Smith and Winterhalder 1992:52).

The assumption of optimality does not mean that everything is an adaptation; it does not mean that each and every phenotypic trait either (1) gives (or once gave) a fitness advantage or (2) is (or once was) "for" something and "relational" (as in Plotkin's notion of adaptations as knowledge). It means simply that everything is (or was) either a product or a by-product (epiphenomenon) of natural selection. By-products of selection, in turn, may be useful (adaptive) or not useful. Products of selection must be produced – literally embodied during ontogeny – before they can actually be adaptations or do adaptive work. The developmental processes that carry out this material instantiation of adaptations not only leave the adaptations themselves, but also typically traces of their construction work. Some such traces may be thought of metaphorically as scaffolding that supported part of the phenotype or its builders while it was being erected. This scaffolding itself would qualify as an adaptation – i.e., an adaptation for building, for growth and development. Other traces of construction may be thought of metaphorically as useful by-products of functional architectural features – for example, the space that comes into being underneath a staircase as the treads are laid. The staircase itself would constitute an adaptation, but if the space underneath the stairs were to be used (for storage, say), then it would constitute an *exaptation*. Exaptations are "features that now enhance fitness, but were not built by natural selection for their current role" (Gould and

CHESTER COLLEGE LIBRARY

Vrba 1982:4). Still other traces of the construction process include the equivalent of building rubble scattered about a job site: the cut-off ends of joists and rafters, unused boards and bricks, the plastic wraps from new plumbing fixtures. Such rubble does not serve a purpose and is neither adaptation nor exaptation, but is none the less *necessary* to the construction process in that it is an inescapable *cost of construction*. It is, therefore, a useless by-product or epiphenomenon of evolved developmental processes. It is possible that the human chin – the projecting wad of bone at the tip of our lower jaw – is the equivalent of such building rubble. Although controversial, one interpretation is that the chin is not "for" anything, but arose as a by-product of natural selection for slower rates or shorter periods of growth in the tooth-bearing parts of the jaw, which left the (unselected) chin jutting out below like so many unused bricks cluttering up a building site (Gould 1977). While in any given case our lack of knowledge may thwart us, in principle at least we can use our understanding of how evolution and development mutually construct phenotypes to carry out reverse engineering on any trait to determine (1) whether it is (or was) an adaptation, exaptation, or epiphenomenon (Gould and Lewontin's [1979] "spandrel"), and (2) how constraints analogous to bricks with too much straw, rain delays, or the carpenters coming down with the flu may prevent some trait from reaching its theoretical optimum.

The second justification for the apparently audacious claim that "optimality must be the default assumption" (Dennett 1995:213) is a straightforward methodological one: if we do not assume that there is a good reason for every phenotypic trait, adaptive or not, to be the way it is, then we cannot begin to analyze the trait at all. After all, we have to start somewhere. If we assume instead that there *is not* a good reason for a trait to be the way it is, then there must be no reason at all – or worse, even a bad reason, in which case we will have to try to make our way in the world using magic and received religion ("propaganda, armtwisting, [and] emotional manipulation"). To assume that selection optimizes the trade-offs among the components of fitness means only that *if* natural selection works the way we think it does, *then* it should favor traits (and accompanying by-products) which function to allocate limited resources among competing uses in the way that results in relatively more descendants (the vital issue of *when* to count descendants is coming soon). Again, this is not a statement that everything that exists in life is an adaptation, and certainly not perfect or the best imaginable. Nor is it a statement that everything that exists in life *actually is* optimal (the best available). In the end, the assumption of optimality is just that – an assumption, a model, a working hypothesis: *If* the living world works the way we think it does, *then* we should find such-and-such. It is simply a methodological strategy (informed by theory) for generating hypotheses about the nature and origin of adaptations. When these hypotheses have been rigorously tested and not disproved we may feel that we have a tentative explanation, *but the optimality assumption itself is not the explanation.* The explanation is the *description* of the evolutionary and developmental *processes* that produce the trait. On the other hand, when our hypotheses have not been supported by evidence, we suspect that there is a flaw in our description (model, image, metaphor) of nature and we can then alter that model in an attempt to come up with a better model from which better hypotheses may emerge. Changing models when they are not supported by data is not a sin; it is not *ad hoc*, evolutionary just-so-storyism. When their models are not supported by data, all scientists (and humanists) sooner or later change them (or should) so that they can gain the acceptance of other scientists (and humanists) whose models are better supported by data. The assumption of optimality is simply a logical gambit that allows evolutionists to speed up the process of generating new hypotheses (Emlen 1985; Mangel and Clark 1988; Orzack and Sober 1994; Parker and Maynard Smith 1990). Nor has this assumption been proved wrong. As Dennett said, "if there weren't design in the biosphere, how come the intentional stance *works*?" (1995:237). In sum, to paraphrase Fodor, the optimality assumption is a device that is designed to cause the state of our minds to correspond to the way that natural selection works.

However, while the assumption of optimality has indeed proved itself extraordinarily good at generating new hypotheses and has not been seriously challenged, to me it has another, equally conspicuous virtue, one that I believe has implications for the development of a humanistic biosocial science: contrary to much popular wisdom, the assumption of optimality implies that perfection cannot exist and that it is wrong to think of human nature in terms of fixed essences. Essentialist thinking seems to be part of human nature, a natural assumption about the nature of things that may take special training and conscious effort to overcome. Prototype theory, for example, suggests that to think at all is to use categories, which are organized in terms of prototypes, which are themselves a kind of logical essence (Jackendoff 1993; Johnson 1987,

1993; Lakoff 1987). Children seem to assume naturally, by default, that things are structured in terms of essences, perhaps especially in the realm of biology (Keil 1992). And Mayr (1988) points out that the assumption that biological kinds have fixed essences long predates evolutionary theory, and indeed that essentialist thinking originally worked *against* the Darwinian notion that species are not fixed entities, but change over time and evolve.

The assumption of optimality thus works *against* our nature, as an antidote to our propensity to essentialize. It implies that it is misleading at best to think of human nature (as we seem naturally to do) in terms of certain prototypical, fixed, or essential qualities of humans in general (say, altruistic, selfish, evil, rational, noble), males and females in particular (respectively aggressive, competitive, and sexually voracious vs. coy, passive, promiscuous, and nurturant), or myriad other racial or ethnic groups (fill in your favorite stereotype). Because of the inevitable tradeoffs that exist among the components of fitness, neither a "perfect" nor an "essential" phenotype (whatever they might be) can exist. When the laws of life (evolution) meet the Second Law of Thermodynamics, sooner or later life always loses to disorganization, dissipation, and decay. Thus, in the long run, in the face of limited resources and limited time, natural selection will always favor whatever traits are associated with reproductive success. This means that people, like all other organisms, are not evolved to maximize health, wealth, happiness or any other trait – but to have descendants, which is the continuation of life. Since there can be no perfect health, wealth, happiness or any other trait, then, in Rick Shweder's words, "in some ultimate sense we must all live in error, ignorance, and confusion (or in 'mystery,' if you prefer that word)" (1996:5). But accepting this, as Robin Fox said, may turn out to be "a truly conservative act." I will return to this point in the final chapter.

Even more, the assumption of optimality compels us always to go beyond what is "normal" (in the sense of merely common or statistically average) and to contemplate instead the adaptive significance of the *full range* of variability in any phenotypic trait. It demands an analytical focus on the potential adaptive function of *individual differences* in their local socioecological and political–economic contexts. If we assume that selection tends to favor mechanisms that produce the best available phenotype, and if the genes and environments that construct phenotypes differ, then we have to entertain the possibility that each phenotype we observe represents the best available in its *particular* conditions, under its *particular* constraints (or would have in the EEA[13]). Thus, what is optimal for the individual is not always what is normal (average) for a group, and what looks like pathology might sometimes represent instead the best available (i.e., the optimal) option under unique or extreme conditions (or what would have been so in the EEA). It is no longer possible to assume that what is average or species-typical implies normality or indicates the target of selection (e.g., Caro and Bateson 1986; Nesse and Williams 1995; Tauber 1994; Wiley 1992).

By the same token, critics of evolutionary perspectives on human behavior can no longer assume that evolutionary theory entails an essentialist view of human nature. There is some irony here, because it is the much-maligned assumption of optimality itself that has most contributed to evolutionary theory's move away from its earlier, sometimes essentializing focus on species-specific behavior and average or "normal" behavior. We must never lose sight of the importance of "population thinking" in biology (Mayr 1982), but the pendulum is swinging, and thinking about the nature and origin of individual phenotypes as well as populations will improve our thinking in general (e.g., Emlen 1995; McNamara and Houston 1996; West-Eberhard 1989, 1992). And as Stephen Emlen put it in his recent evolutionary theory of the family, the kinds of phenotypic variation in which we ought now to be interested are those involved in decision-making:

> The condition-dependent expression of many social behaviors in no way precludes them from genetic influence. The work of researchers such as Maynard Smith [1982] and Parker [1989] has clarified the relationship between conditionality and the evolution of behavior. Indeed, the last decade has seen a marked shift toward viewing organisms as "decision makers," selected to accurately assess the consequences of different behavioral options available to them and to express those behavioral variants that maximize their fitnesses. (1995:8092)

Theory and data suggest that selection tends to favor the capacity for making "decisions" (they need not be conscious) when socioecological

---

[13] "EEA" is the acronym for John Bowlby's (1969:50) "environment of evolutionary adaptedness," which is simply the material and socioecological contexts in which natural selection favored the genotypic basis for the way we are today.

conditions vary so as to present individuals with a succession of novel environments – i.e., when the environment is predictably unpredictable. This puts an adaptive premium on the organism's capacity to respond flexibly to changing conditions. To respond flexibly to changing conditions is to make a decision about how to respond to the environment such that what ends up being done is *contingent* on the particular (historical) environmental conditions encountered (e.g., Fagen 1982; Johnston 1982; Mayr 1974; Plotkin 1994; Slobodkin and Rapoport 1974). There is no point in making decisions, however, unless they are (relatively) good ones. Like every other aspect of the phenotype, decisions are evaluated naturally in the currency of fitness. Ultimately, a good decision is one that fosters continued survival, better growth and development, and ultimately, more descendants, or *any* descendants after more generations (e.g., Cooper 1987).

Nothing is more predictably unpredictable than the interactions of highly intelligent, highly social decision makers like ourselves as we go about adjusting our behavior according to what we believe others will do. Selection for behavioral flexibility and decision-making was an important cause (and effect) of increased individual differences, and surely the reason why the variety of ways in which humans can be different from each other is greater than in any other species (consider our cultural differences alone). The manifest evolution of our capacity to make decisions (consciously or not) about behavioral alternatives thus forces our attention (both adaptationist and mechanist) to the origin and nature of these individual differences. This suggests a point of contact between current scientific, evolutionary approaches to human behavior and humanistic views that emphasize our essential humanity in terms of "truth to personal experience." This includes the Geertzian view that "Becoming human is becoming individual." The evolution of behavioral flexibility and Machiavellian decision-making suggests that to view ourselves as a species in a way *is* to view ourselves as uniquely individualized.

In sum, the optimality assumption is not only scientifically, logically, and methodologically valid, it may also help us bridge the troubled waters between scientific and humanistic views of human nature. Because virtually all aspects of our behavioral phenotypes seem to be at least "fine tuned" by (i.e., contingent on) local developmental trade-offs and constraints, the assumption of optimality implies that (1) perfection cannot exist, (2) the concept of a fixed or "essential" human nature is not useful, (3) the concept of "normal" is ambiguous, and (4) to understand human nature we would do well to adopt a processual approach, focusing on the evolutionary and developmental contingencies (selections, decisions, choices) that produce the phenotype.

The General Life History Problem

Having planted the idea that it is logically legitimate and scientifically and humanistically valuable to assume that natural selection tends to favor traits that optimize the trade-offs among the components of fitness, I will now focus on one trade-off in particular. Of all the trade-offs that have been identified (at least 45 [Stearns 1992]), there is now a consensus that the most important or inclusive trade-off is that between current and future reproduction (e.g., Charnov 1993; Stearns 1992). The General Life History Problem, as the current–future (C–F) trade-off is also known (Schaffer 1983), is a model that predicts the optimal allocation of resources to reproduction at a given age based on the assumption that there is a trade-off between current and future reproduction (Stearns 1992). The trade-off between current and future reproduction may be intraindividual or intergenerational. For some purposes, current refers to reproductive opportunities that are more-or-less at hand, in the current mating season or the immediate or near future, while future refers to reproductive opportunities that may arise later, sometime during the remainder of the individual's lifetime – i.e., within a generation. At issue in the intraindividual trade-off is whether it would be better for the individual's lifetime reproductive success to reproduce now or to wait for another opportunity later. In other contexts, however, current refers to the individual's lifetime reproductive success, while future refers to the number of descendants (grandchildren, great-grandchildren, etc.) that he or she might be expected to have after some arbitrary number of generations. At issue here is whether it would be better for one's genetic representation in arbitrarily distant future generations to have more offspring in this generation.

This brings us finally to the great question of *when* to measure fitness. We saw earlier that fitness is never high or low, only higher or lower. But, just as fitness is inherently a relative measure, the *time* at which it is measured is always somewhat arbitrary. How can we measure today something that our theory says cannot properly be measured until some uncertain point in the future? How can we know today how many descendants an individual will have in the future? Sure, we have to count offspring, because they are always the *sine qua non* of both short-term and long-term fitness (not counting descendants through collateral kin). They are also relatively easy to count. But what assurance do we have that any offspring produced will also reproduce? And, if our children give us grand-children, what assurance do we have that they too will reproduce? What matters in evolution is *staying in the game* (Gould 1989; Slobodkin and Rapoport 1974). We are here because *none* of our direct ancestors failed to reproduce. So to see how successful our reproductive strategies *really* are, counting only children, and even grandchildren, is not enough. We must count as well great-grandchildren, great-great-grandchildren, great-great-great-grandchildren and go on counting every generation into the mists of the future. Whenever we stopped counting would be arbitrary. The significance of this point will emerge as we continue to explore the C–F trade-off.

Let us begin with the intraindividual C–F trade-off. Consider a nursing mother (the example is from Bateson 1994). To assume that there is a trade-off between current and future reproduction means that if selection works the way we think it does, then for this mother to *increase* her current reproductive effort (in this case nursing, i.e., parenting effort) beyond a certain amount, or to extend current levels for a longer period, there should be a corresponding *decrease* in the number of offspring she would have in her lifetime (future reproduction). There are two reasons for expecting this trade-off. The first is that increased current reproduc-tion (i.e., reproductive effort – more frequent or prolonged nursing) means that she has to increase or prolong her consumption of current resources. Logically, this means that there has to be a point of diminishing fitness returns for her, such that some of the resources she consumed to support her increased current reproductive effort would have had greater fitness returns if they had been used instead to support future reproduction. Even if the mother is in good condition and her baby grows rapidly, the longer she nurses the worse her condition will become. If she persists in nursing there will even come a point at which her condition becomes bad enough to jeopardize her chances of conceiving or rearing another child. But, while the cost to the mother is increasing, the benefit to her baby from prolonged nursing is decreasing as the baby gains weight. In other words, at some point the lifetime fitness benefits accruing to the mother from allocating her resources to *current* reproductive effort (her existing child) will be less than those she would receive if she ceased investment in her current child and allocated her resources instead to *future* repro-duction – i.e., a new baby.

The second reason that increased short-term reproductive effort is expected to decrease lifetime reproductive success is that, under some conditions, continued reproductive effort decreases parents' chances of surviving to bear or rear additional children. For example, imagine another nursing mother, but this time one who, along with her baby, is in poor condition with few resources (again Bateson 1994). For the mother to continue nursing (prolonging parenting effort) would only detract from her already poor condition and from her capacity to nourish her baby. At the same time, as the baby's condition also worsens, its chances of survival decrease, thus decreasing the probability of any fitness returns to its mother. Especially if the mother is young, then, and has some probability of recovering and having another child in the future, everything else being equal, her optimal strategy would be to cease all current investment. In other words, the lifetime fitness benefits accruing to the mother from allocating her resources to future reproduction (ceasing to nurse her existing child) will be greater than those she would receive if she put them into current reproduction by continuing to nurse the current child and to delay getting pregnant.[14]

To summarize, increasing current reproductive effort (mating or parenting) is expected eventually (1) to consume resources that would have had greater fitness returns if allocated in the future, and/or (2) to reduce parents' probability of surviving long enough to bear and rear additional children in the future. For these reasons we no longer expect natural selection always to favor traits that simply maximize number of offspring in each generation (current reproduction), as early sociobiological models often did. Instead, we now expect, in principle, not one, but a *variety* of optimal reproductive strategies that are contingent on local conditions, with a major dimension of differences along an axis defined by the C–F trade-off.

Let us now explore the intergenerational C–F trade-off and the question of whether it would be better for one's genetic representation in arbitrarily distant future generations (i.e., for staying in the evolutionary game) to have more offspring in this generation. Perhaps the easiest way to grasp this trade-off is to understand why age-specific extrinsic mortal-

---

[14] This disturbing scenario is all too common in societies where mothers and children fail to receive adequate nutrition and health care. Nancy Scheper-Hughes' *Death Without Weeping: The Violence of Everyday Life in Brazil* (1992) is a forceful account of how generations of mothers have adapted to such realities.

ity rates are among the most important determinants of the optimal between-generation C–F trade-off, both within and between species.[15] To paraphrase Stearns, the key problem in life history theory is not that of understanding how habitats affect life histories, but how habitats affect *mortality regimes* – and then how mortality regimes affect life histories (Stearns 1992:208).[16] Extrinsic mortality refers to death from predation, disease, accidents, homicide, and other environmental hazards that are not affected by changes in the allocation of reproductive effort. Intrinsic mortality, on the other hand, refers to death from the costs or trade-offs of reproductive effort. As we will see in chapter 6, for example, physiological costs (trade-offs) of early menarche (first menstruation) in women (which facilitates current reproduction) may include increased risk later in life for unhealthy weight gain (Wellens et al. 1992), breast cancer (Apter et al. 1989), or giving birth to low birthweight infants (Scholl et al. 1989).

In risky or uncertain environments, where extrinsic mortality rates are high or unpredictable, the short-term reproductive strategy of maximizing the *production* of offspring in the current generation may be the optimal strategy, because, by maximizing the probability of having at least *some* offspring who manage to survive and reproduce, it thereby minimizes the probability of lineage extinction – that is, of having one's own genes vanish from the gene pool (Ellison 1994; Keyfitz 1977). On the other hand, in environments that are safe and predictable the long-term strategy of maximizing the *rearing* of offspring – that is, of consistently producing fewer offspring over many generations and investing more in

---

[15] For fuller discussions see Charnov (1993); Charnov and Berrigan (1993); Gadgil and Bossert (1970); Harpending, Draper, and Pennington (1990); Pagel and Harvey (1993); Promislow and Harvey (1990, 1991); Purvis and Harvey (1995); Roff (1992); Seger and Brockmann (1987); Stearns (1992).

[16] Until recently, life history theory was dominated by the concepts of *r*- and *K*-selection. Natural selection works in its *r*-selection mode when environments are highly unpredictable and large numbers of organisms die or fail to reproduce not so much because they are unfit but because they are unlucky. *r*-selection thus tends to favor individuals who reproduce most rapidly and/or in the greatest number. Natural selection works in its *K*-selection mode when environments are predictable, mortality rates are low, and more organisms die or fail to reproduce because they are unfit than because they are unlucky. *K*-selection thus tends to favor individuals who produce "fewer and better" offspring. There were always problems with *r/K* theory, especially the way it tried to map habitats *directly* on to life histories (Stearns 1992:206–8). Consequently, when bet-hedging theory (e.g., Seger and Brockmann 1987) and models of the effect of age- and size-specific fecundity and mortality on life histories began to appear in the late 1980s, *r/K* theory quickly lost its allure.

each – may be optimal because, *ceteris paribus*, over a period of generations, *consistently* having a small number of high-quality offspring who
survive and reproduce results ultimately in more descendants (future
reproduction) than would having *more* relatively low-quality offspring
whose chances of survival are low or unpredictable (Gillespie 1977;
McNamara and Houston 1996; Rubenstein 1982; Seger and Brockmann
1987; Stearns 1992). What this means, in Hillard Kaplan's words, is that
"it may be necessary to measure fitness in terms of third generation (or
longer) effects. Models including these effects are likely to predict lower
optimum rates of fertility than the one-generation model that maximizes
number of surviving offspring" (1994:770-771).

At one end of the between-generation C–F axis, then, are what might
be called current, or short-term reproductive strategies, whose fitness
motto might be "minimize chances of lineage extinction by maximizing
current reproduction." At the other end of this axis are the future, or
long-term reproductive strategies, whose fitness motto might be "maximize number of descendants in arbitrarily distant future generations by
minimizing intergenerational variance in number of offspring." While
not exactly catchy, these slogans have the virtue of capturing the adaptationist rationale that underlies this C–F trade-off. To see how, consider
Figure 2.1.

Figure 2.1 is a schematic representation of the reproductive success of
each member of two hypothetical lineages, A and B. Lineage A occupies
a risky, unpredictable, high-mortality environment, while Lineage B
occupies a safe, predictable, low-mortality environment. For ease of illustration only I have assumed asexual reproduction. Sexual reproduction
would obviously be a more realistic assumption, but would also be harder
to illustrate and would not materially affect the C–F trade-off that I want
to depict.

The key thing to notice in Figure 2.1 is that, while members of Lineage
A enjoy greater short-term or current reproductive success than those of
Lineage B (a maximum of 3 vs. 2 offspring per parent, each generation),
members of Lineage B none the less enjoy greater long-term or future
reproductive success (16 vs. 9 descendants after four generations). This is
because on average two-thirds of the offspring in every other generation
of Lineage A fail to reproduce (note that to save space only those offspring
who survive to reproduce have been shown). Thus, while both lineages
average 2 offspring per generation who survive and reproduce, the
between-generation variance in the number of offspring doing so is

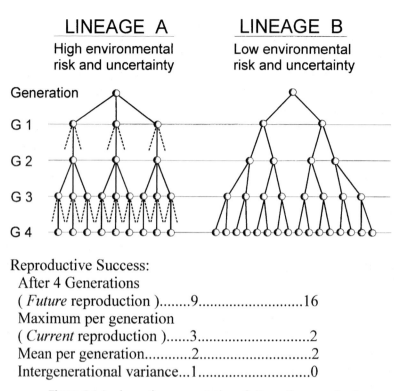

LINEAGE A
High environmental
risk and uncertainty

LINEAGE B
Low environmental
risk and uncertainty

Generation

G 1

G 2

G 3

G 4

Reproductive Success:
After 4 Generations
(*Future* reproduction)........9...........................16
Maximum per generation
(*Current* reproduction)......3.............................2
Mean per generation............2.............................2
Intergenerational variance...1.............................0

Figure 2.1 A schematic representation of alternative reproductive strategies that illustrates the trade-off between current and future reproduction.

higher in Lineage A than in Lineage B (1 vs. 0) because of Lineage A's more dangerous and uncertain environment. In effect, Lineage A has "traded" diminished long-term or future reproduction for greater short-term or current reproduction while Lineage B has done the opposite, "trading" current reproduction (which increases the risk of lineage extinction should conditions change) for a greater number of descendants in the future.

When mortality rates are high or unpredictable, in other words, the most pressing adaptive problem is likely to be the immediate one of avoiding extinction, and (everything else being equal) Lineage A's short-term, high-fertility reproductive strategy is the optimal strategy. When mortality rates are low and predictable, on the other hand, there are fewer, or at least less urgent adaptive problems, and Lineage B's long-term, low-fertility, "less is more" reproductive strategy is optimal. It is important to note, however, that each strategy works best *in its own environment.* If Lineage A were moved to the low-risk environment it is unlikely that its long-term fitness would be as high as Lineage B's unless it adopted B's strategy. Likewise, if Lineage B were moved to the high-risk environment it is unlikely that its short-term fitness would be as high as Lineage A's unless it adopted A's strategy. Therefore, everything else being equal, of these two strategies, that of Lineage A is the optimal strategy in high-risk, high-mortality environments, while that of Lineage B is the optimal strategy in low-risk, low-mortality environments.

Life, however, is complex and things are rarely equal. Because reproductive success depends on more than mere survival, mortality rates are not the only determinant of the optimal between-generation C–F trade-off. Instead, parents' capacity to invest in their children – to increase their children's reproductive value by fostering their preparation for reproduction – is also expected to influence the optimal C–F trade-off. Thus, from the perspective of life history theory (and contrary to a great deal of "common sense") when parents' resources are limited it is *not* necessarily adaptive or rational for them to have fewer offspring so as to be able to invest more in each one. In other words, even when mortality rates are not high the optimal strategy for parents who lack the material or social resources (e.g., power, prestige) to *make a difference* in their children's reproductive value (e.g., health, education, employment or marriage prospects, competence as parents – i.e., children's capacity to produce *grand*children with good reproductive value) may well be to *increase* fertility (to maximize current reproduction) while reducing investment in each child (which tends to decrease future reproduction). Even for mammalian females, who by virtue of numerous anatomical and physiological adaptations (notably for conception, gestation, parturition, and lactation) are often thought of as the "nurturant" sex, it is not always true that reproductive success depends exclusively on the resources a mother is able to accrue for her offspring. Sometimes it depends instead on her producing *more* offspring, or producing them earlier (e.g., Hrdy 1997). The "nonintuitive message" here (as Monique Borgerhoff Mulder [1992:350] described this apparent paradox) is that when the flow of resources is chronically low or unpredictable – which is when we might otherwise expect parents to be most solicitous of their offspring – it may in fact be (or have been) evolutionarily adaptive for parents' to "hedge their bets" against lineage extinction by *reducing* parental investment and allocating their limited resources not to parenting effort (or even, beyond some

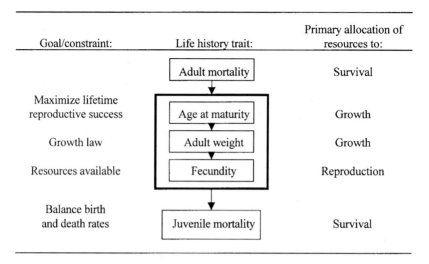

Goal/constraint:	Life history trait:	Primary allocation of resources to:
	Adult mortality	Survival
Maximize lifetime reproductive success	Age at maturity	Growth
Growth law	Adult weight	Growth
Resources available	Fecundity	Reproduction
Balance birth and death rates	Juvenile mortality	Survival

Figure 2.2 A summary of Charnov's model of mammal life history evolution (after Harvey and Nee 1991 and Worthman 1996).

threshold, to their *own* health or longevity), but to *offspring production* instead (Borgerhoff Mulder 1992; Harpending et al. 1990; Kaplan 1994; Pennington and Harpending 1988; Rogers 1990, 1994; Weinrich 1977).

For these reasons, then, we expect that both mortality rates and the resources available to parents for conversion into parenting effort should influence reproductive strategies. Combining optimality theory and comparative life history data, Eric Charnov (1990, 1991, 1993; Charnov and Berrigan 1990, 1993) developed a model of mammal life history evolution that explains in principle how these environmental contingencies interact to drive the C–F trade-off. Figure 2.2 is a schematic representation of his model.

Charnov's model is intended to explain what selective forces molded mammal life history traits and thus what predicts them today.[17] For simplicity he assumes that populations are stationary (i.e., not growing

---

[17] Although developed initially to account for differences between species, such models are regarded as appropriate for understanding individual differences within species as well. As Charnov put it, "life history evolution theory aims to account for both within and between-group variation" (1993:15). McNamara and Houston (1996) and Stearns (1992) make the same point: there is no reason in principle why models of between-species differences in life history patterns cannot also be used to understand within-species differences.

or shrinking) so that birth and death rates are balanced, and that reproductive value is a function of body size (i.e., bigger animals are stronger
and healthier and produce and/or rear more offspring than smaller
animals). He also assumes that the environment determines a constant
rate of extrinsic mortality among adults, which in turn establishes the
average lifespan. Mortality rates among juveniles, in contrast, are assumed
to be density-dependent, so that when there are few juveniles in the
population, fewer of them die; when their numbers rise, more of them
die.

Given these assumptions, Charnov proposes that the optimal age at
first reproduction, optimal body size, and optimal reproductive rate
(fecundity) of mammals can be predicted from (1) the extrinsic mortality
rate of adults, (2) a growth law (the inherent metabolic determinants of
the maximum rate at which body size can increase), which determines
the minimum age and size at maturity, and (3) the resources available to
parents (which determines how much they can allocate to parenting
effort) and to weaned juveniles (which determines their rate of growth up
to that set by the growth law). Natural selection acts on age at maturity to
optimize the trade-off between body size and risk of death. Late-maturing
animals have more time to grow, and so (when resources are available)
they grow bigger. At maturity the utility or value (e.g., energy or security)
that has accrued from these resources is reallocated from growth to
reproduction, which enables (well-nourished, nonstressed) late-maturing
individuals to produce/rear more offspring. At the same time, however,
late-maturing individuals (especially if they are malnourished or unduly
stressed) are less likely to survive to reproductive age because they are
exposed for longer to all sources of mortality. In turn, age and size at
maturity and rates of resource flow to adults determine their optimal
reproductive effort. The capacity of parents to increase offspring reproductive value (which depends on their size and their available resources)
is used to determine the particular trade-off between quantity and quality (body size) of offspring that maximizes parents' fitness. Because rates
of birth and death are equal, juvenile mortality rates are determined by
the differences between the quantity of offspring produced and adult
mortality rates. When the juvenile population is high, resources become
limited, parents are less able to increase their offsprings' reproductive
value, and the juvenile mortality rate begins to increase (Charnov 1993;
Charnov and Berrigan 1993; Harvey and Nee 1991; Hill 1993; Purvis and
Harvey 1995).

In sum, the rate at which adults die from extrinsic causes, the inherent rate at which children grow, and the capacity of parents to affect their children's reproductive value can, in principle, be used to predict two of the most critical biobehavioral components of mammalian reproductive strategies – age at first reproduction and reproductive rate. While a model as sweeping as Charnov's deserves especially close scrutiny, it has already passed one early test with flying colors. In a rigorous examination of his model, Purvis and Harvey state that their "analysis of life-table data from 64 species, ranging across nine orders, supports all of Charnov's assumptions and most of his predictions" (1995:259). In any event, it is certainly not premature immediately to draw one implication in particular from his model: What Charnov's model (and life history theory generally) makes very clear is that, in principle, there can be no a priori, noncontingent, "best" reproductive strategy. It all depends; contingency rules. And what the optimal strategy seems to depend on most are the contingencies (i.e., risk and uncertainty) that affect the flow of (1) security, which sets the probability of death (extrinsic mortality), and (2) energy and nutrients, which set the capacity of parents to invest in offspring.

But, if the optimality assumption and comparative life history data are pointing us in the right direction – so that reproductive strategies are indeed adaptations – then, as such, reproductive strategies must (1) function to affect ("make decisions about," i.e., be for) the allocation of resources among survival, growth and development, and reproduction over the lifespan, and (2) represent the *relation* between environmental risk and uncertainty and the organism, the phenotype. How is this done? How is the environmental information on which the optimal strategy is supposed to depend represented phenotypically? How is information about mortality rates and resource flows embodied, processed, and evaluated such that the best available alternative strategy is likely to be chosen? These are among the most pressing questions in current life history research, for, as we have seen, without some understanding of the mechanisms that actually produce adaptations we cannot adequately test life history models nor fully understand the process of adaptation. Without some understanding of the processes of gene × environment interactions that produce adaptive phenotypes we have merely replaced our model of life history evolution with a description that is congruent with it. What is more, since my goal is ultimately therapeutic, I must have a *point of entry* into the mechanisms that produce the phenotypes that I hope to treat. Taking the phenotypic gambit would absolutely defeat this purpose. For these reasons I now switch my focus from life history theory's adaptationist concern with the reproductive function of life cycles to its mechanist concern with the developmental systems that actually produce life cycles. In the remainder of this chapter I will outline a model of gene × environment interaction that I believe can help us understand, in principle, how environmental risk and uncertainty come to be represented phenotypically. In the two following chapters, I will fill in this model with theory and data from empirical studies of human development in the hope that we may understand better in practice.

Developmental systems: adaptations for reducing uncertainty

As we saw earlier, development is *for* reproduction; in Bonner's (1993:35) words, "development is the inevitable result of sex and size." What this means is that life cycles (development) evolved to carry multicelled organisms "from sex to size" – i.e., from their one-celled beginnings as zygotes to their many-celled adulthoods. Sexual reproduction occurs when egg and sperm (two haploid cells) join to create a zygote (a single diploid cell), which is the beginning of a new individual. However, while sexual reproduction requires this single-cell stage, a single cell is not sufficient for reproduction. Ultimately, this is because small (single-celled) organisms are less reproductively competitive than large (multi-celled) organisms. In any event, zygotes are not capable of reproduction. The adaptive function of growth and development (the reason they evolved) is to convey new single-celled individuals to the state of multi-cellularity – which is required for sexual reproduction (Buss 1987). Thus, development is *for* reproduction.

As is adaptation's wont, however, the solution to one problem is often the cause of another. In resolving the sex–size problem, the evolution of development caused a new kind of uncertainty. In chapter 1 (pp. 19–20) we saw that a critical source of uncertainty is Plotkin's (1994) uncertain futures problem: how to produce an adaptive match between organism and environment when the mature organism takes time to "build" but the "instructions" for building it are received all at once while the organism's environment is constantly changing. The uncertain futures problem arises from the biological fact of generational deadtime: the period of time between an organism's conception (as a single-celled zygote) and the time it reproduces (as a multicelled adult). The evolution of development essentially created the trade-off between current and future reproduction. On the one hand, reproducing immediately, as soon as possible after coming into existence as a single cell (current reproduction), reduces the probability of dying before reproduction can occur. On the other hand, reproducing later, after one has reached a larger, more competitive, multicellular state (future reproduction), makes it possible for parents to allocate more resources to parenting effort, thereby increasing offspring reproductive value. Development provides a way to resolve the sex–size problem, but the downside of development is generational deadtime, which greatly exacerbates the uncertain futures problem. With the evolution of development, then, came the adaptive problem of reducing the very uncertainty that it entails. Phenotypic plasticity provided a way to solve this new problem.

The evolution of phenotypic plasticity

Information reduces uncertainty – and good, up-to-date information reduces it even more. Phenotypic plasticity is the capacity of a single genotype to produce a wide range of phenotypes that are contingent on environmental information. The range of phenotypes permitted by a single genotype (its reaction norm) may be wide, but the adaptive significance of phenotypic plasticity comes not from the width, *per se*, of this range, but from the phenotype's capacity to *track* its developmental environment – to be affected by changes in this environment in ways that promote fitness.

Adaptations are environmental information that has become represented in phenotypes. The information that is embodied to produce phenotypes can be of only two kinds: (1) old information about an organism's ancestors' environments that it acquired via copies of their DNA, and (2) more up-to-date information about its own environment that it acquired via experience with this environment. When environments change too quickly, old information is not good enough. Phenotypic plasticity provides an adaptive advantage when an organism's fitness depends on information that is more up to date than that contained in its genotype. Selection then favors phenotypic mechanisms for acquiring more up-to-date information. Everything else being equal, the more – and more current – sources of information that an organism has, the less uncertain will be its future. This is the adaptive function of phenotypic plasticity: learning about one's environment, being affected by it, in order to track it, to go with its flow (Fagen 1982; Gottlieb 1992; Johnston 1982; Plotkin 1994; Slobodkin and Rapoport 1974).

Phenotypic plasticity is at the heart of what Lawrence Slobodkin and Anatol Rapoport (1974) called the "optimal strategy of evolution." In their very big-picture view of evolution, organisms are seen as having evolved a hierarchy of mechanisms or processes for responding to (tracking) environmental changes. Intelligence, especially social intelligence, is at one end of this hierarchy; it is the zenith of environmental tracking mechanisms. Then come a series of anatomical, physiological, endocrine, and developmental mechanisms for responding to somewhat slower, more pervasive change. At the nadir is the latent, potential, and ultimately least flexible way to respond to still slower and more pervasive environmental changes: that of genetic change. The capacity for intelligent (appropriate, contingent) responses to environmental changes was selected, Slobodkin and Rapoport suggest, because intelligent behavior was quick and highly flexible. To the extent that intelligent responses were successful, they tended also to protect or conserve the slower, deeper, and less flexible adaptive capacities farther down the response hierarchy.

The principle behind Slobodkin and Rapoport's model of the evolution of highly sophisticated phenotypic plasticity is nicely illustrated in their game theory analog of the optimal strategy of evolution. The game, a form of poker called Gambler's Ruin, has four rules, each more bizarre than the last: (1) all players have a fixed number of chips (analogous to limited resources); (2) all promise to play indefinitely – no one can drop out (just as organisms ordinarily strive to avoid death; species, of course, cannot opt either in or out); (3) all promise to wager something, no matter how little (there is no such thing as a free lunch; there is always the work of life to be done), on each hand (each environmental perturbation); and (4) whenever a player loses all his chips he is dead (when the Laws of Life meet the Second Law of Thermodynamics, sooner or later life always loses). It is immediately obvious that there is only one rational strategy for playing this ultimately losing game: players should always minimize their bets in order to maximize their chances of simply staying in the game. The evolution of phenotypic plasticity enabled flexible organisms to minimize their bets. The capacity to respond to environmental changes quickly, appropriately, flexibly, and contingently reduces the need for organisms with plastic phenotypes to draw on their ultimate stakes: their genetic capital. You know you are in trouble when you have to start betting your genetic chips; when you are out of genetic chips, you are out of the game (the "existential game of life"). This was Sewall Wright's point in the epigraph cited at the head of this chapter: "Individual adapt-

ability [phenotypic plasticity] . . . is not only of the greatest significance as
a factor of evolution in damping the effects of selection . . . *but is itself
perhaps the chief object of selection."*

In keeping with my dual adaptationist/mechanist perspective, it is
worth pausing briefly to describe an important mechanism for acquiring up-to-date information about the developmental environment. This
is Jean-Pierre Changeux's (1985) "epigenesis by selective stabilization"
(Edelman's [1987] "neural selection"). Changeux argues that, while the
core architecture and number of neurons in adult vertebrates seem quite
narrowly genetically determined and are established before birth, "phenotypic variability" (as he calls phenotypic plasticity) is nevertheless inherent
in the processes of neural development. On his view, neural development
proceeds by the laying down of redundant and variable synaptic connections which provide the raw material for epigenesis by selective
stabilization to preserve or stabilize (i.e., choose, select) those synapses
that have functional significance in a particular local context. To have
functional significance means that a neural pathway laid down during
the development of the brain is actually *used*, it serves a real function as
the organism interacts with its particular environment. In a different
environment, this same pathway might not be used, and in virtue of not
being used, not serving a function, it would atrophy and then disappear
from lack of use. On the basis of comparative neurological developmental data, Changeux also notes that there is a progressive decrease in the
effect of the genotype on the neural phenotype from invertebrates to
vertebrates, from lower vertebrates to higher, and from nonhuman
primates to humans because of the indeterminacy[18] that is inherent in
neural developmental processes:

> This phenotypic variability is intrinsic. It is the result of the
> precise "history" of cell division and migration, of the
> wandering of the growth cone and its fission, or regressive
> processes and selective stabilization, which cannot be exactly
> the same from one individual to another even if they are
> genetically identical. (1985:247)

Epigenesis by selective stabilization may explain why the brains

---

[18] C. H. Waddington, who pioneered the integration of evolutionary and developmental
biology, used to argue that the relationship of the genotype to the phenotype was a developmental one of "adaptive indeterminacy" (1968:364).

of rats reared in enriched environments (with plenty of playmates, intricate mazes, numerous objects, etc.) show more dendritic branching and an increased density of synapses over those of controls reared in impoverished environments (e.g., Rosenzweig, Bennet, and Diamond 1972).

Whatever knowledge-gaining mechanisms are involved, however, they are bound to involve individual differences in motivation (emotion). This is because in order for phenotypic plasticity to work, to be adaptive, not just any phenotype will do. To reduce uncertainty, the information acquired during development must be *about* the future – in the sense that it enables the developing organism somehow to predict, anticipate, or prepare for that future. The organism is unlikely, therefore, to be a mere passive receptacle for environmental information, but is expected instead *to seek out* – to be *motivated to have* – the kinds of experiences that would tend to have fitness-promoting developmental consequences in the particular environment that engendered its taste for this certain kind of experience in the first place. In other words, do not be misled by the concept of phenotypic *plasticity*. Plasticity does not imply *randomness*; it does not mean that there is a chancy, haphazard, or indiscriminate relationship between phenotypes and the environments in which they develop. On the contrary, it implies the contingent development of various kinds of learning biases or predispositions – which are evaluative or motivational phenomena (Boyd and Richersen 1985; Johnston 1982).

The contingent predisposition of young animals to play provides a good example of the adaptive potential of phenotypic plasticity. Robert Fagen's (1977, 1982, 1993) comparative life history analyses of animal play, for example, show how an animal's motivation to play may be affected by information about its current environment in such a way that the developmental *consequences* of play (the effects of this early experience) constitute a kind of *preparation for the future* – and thereby function to reduce environmental uncertainty. Fagen argues that animal play has few current benefits for fitness because resources allocated to play must on average reduce those available to support survival and growth. On the other hand, he suggests, play may have considerable future benefits for fitness, which accrue from the enhanced behavioral flexibility made possible through the power of play to increase functionally significant neural interconnectivity – in the way that rats reared in enriched environments show more dendritic branching and an increased density of synapses. By altering the relationship of the young animal to its developmental environment, play (creativity) effectively makes that environment an "enriched" one (it "recreates" it in an enriched form). And, because of the long-term neural effects of development in an enriched environment, animals that play as juveniles tend to show more adaptability as adults, through having a greater motivation or capacity to explore their environments, to switch rapidly between different behavior patterns, and to reverse previous learning and engage in new learning (e.g., Fagen 1977; 1982; Johnston 1982).

Anticipating bet-hedging theory and more recent models of the effect of age- and size-specific fecundity and mortality on life histories, Fagen concludes that higher-order taxonomic differences in animal play are due primarily to differences in survivorship – i.e., mortality rates. In small, energetically inefficient species, where high mortality rates place an adaptive premium on rapid attainment of adult body size, the costs of diverting resources from growth to play are believed to select against any powerful or obligate motivation to play regardless of local circumstances. On the other hand, among larger, more energetically efficient animals, who typically also have lower metabolic rates and higher survivorship, the costs of diverting resources from growth to play are generally lower. And, with higher survivorship, especially among juveniles, and longer lives overall, larger and more energetically efficient animals are more likely to live long enough to reap the delayed, future benefits of play.

Fagen finds that lower-order (e.g., within-species) differences in play are usually due, however, to differences in the availability of resources (including security) and the animal's capacity to use them efficiently. Thus, the motivation to play seems to be facultatively (i.e., contingently) suppressed in animals otherwise expected to show it when their chances of living long enough to reap the delayed benefits of play are compromised – for example, by disease, hunger, predation, and the other components of risky and uncertain environments. Horn and Rubenstein (1984) make the same point when they argue that "behavioral decisions about life history" (i.e., phenotypic plasticity in behavior) should occur most frequently in large animals with low reproductive output (i.e., high levels of parental investment) who are in good condition with large amounts of stored energy and nutrients. This is because simply being in good condition and having large amounts of stored resources tend to be reasonable indicators of (i.e., correlated with) continued survival – and thus the capacity to benefit in the future from the delayed effects of play.[19]

However, while being in good condition and having many resources are associated with a greater motivation to play, the association is not perfect. In kittens, for example, it appears that a particular kind of resource *shortage* – early weaning – is associated with a *greater* motivation to engage in play (of certain kinds). It is worth pausing a moment to examine this (partial) exception, for it proves a wider and more important rule about phenotypic plasticity.

It has long been known among cats that, when nursing mothers are placed on restricted diets, they wean their offspring early. The question for Bateson, Mendl, and Feaver (1990) was why food-stressed mothers weaned their kittens early rather than late, for, in principle, *prolonging* nursing – to make up for the lesser nourishment received in each nursing bout – might be as good a strategy. To learn why, Bateson and his colleagues studied the effects of early weaning on kittens' behavioral development. They found that compared to normal controls, early-weaned kittens engaged in significantly more *object* play but not more social play; early weaning did not have a general effect on play, but a *specific* effect on *object* play. The reason, they propose, is that object play is more important for the development of cats' hunting skills than is social play. Put differently, the benefits of object play (the developmental effects of object play) are more valuable than those of social play because they are both more immediate and functionally significant in an environment where food shortages mean (or meant, in the EEA of cats) that young cats could not long depend on their mothers but would soon have to become independent and begin foraging (hunting) for themselves. Similar effects have also been reported for rats (Smith 1991). Bateson, Mendl, and Feaver conclude that "it seems likely that, by responding to cues from the

---

[19] Note that in addition to their variety of types, resources may also be stored in a variety of ways. Some may be stored in an individual's body, say in the form of fat. Others may be stored in the physical environment, in the form of an individual's control over some territory. Note too, however, that resources may also be stored in the social environment, in the form of nepotism from kin and reciprocal obligations from nonkin. Finally, for humans at least, resources may be stored in the cultural environment, in the form, say, of banks, or more generally, in the form of traditions and laws of ownership, access (including education), and privilege. See Kaplan's (1994) theory of "embodied human capital" for an analysis of the ways that these latter stores can affect fertility.

mother, the individual animal is able to move along a developmental route that is appropriate to the conditions it will encounter in later life" (1990:524).

And this is the wider and more important rule about phenotypic plasticity that is proved by these hungry but playful kittens. The issue is not the narrow one of whether it is an abundance or a shortage of early resources that affect play. Rather, the important issue is the wider one of how certain early experiences move the developing organism "along a developmental route that is *appropriate to the conditions it will encounter in later life*." Young mammals are not passive recipients of just any information about their developmental environments. Instead, when we look at young mammals (especially humans) from a dual evolutionary/developmental perspective (i.e., as individual reproductive strategies/life cycles emerging in particular socioecological niches) then I think that we should expect that they will be especially attracted to certain kinds of environmental information, to the point of actively seeking out the kinds of early experience that tend to have fitness-promoting developmental consequences in the environments that engendered their taste for this certain kind of experience in the first place (or did in their EEAs). The environmental information that is embodied in phenotypes to constitute an adaptation comes either from an organism's ancestral environments (its own DNA) or its own environment. However, as we will soon see, it is also true that the (ancestral) environmental information that comes to an organism via its DNA can be used to make the organism sensitive to, even prefer, the *kind* of current environmental information that would be adaptive for it to have. Thus, when young mammals of some species are in good condition, with large amounts of stored resources, it has generally been adaptive for them to be motivated to engage frequently in play, because being in good condition and having plenty of resources were long correlated (in their EEAs) with relatively long life – and therefore their relatively high capacity to benefit *in the future* from the delayed effects of play. Equally, however, when the young of other species (say, kittens or rat pups) are in *poor* condition, with *few* stored resources, it has generally been adaptive for them also to engage frequently (or earlier) in object play. This is because being in poor condition and having few resources were long correlated (in their different EEAs) with a relatively risky or uncertain future – and therefore their greater capacity to benefit from the short-term pay-offs of object play. Through their presumed greater/earlier motivation to engage in object play, kittens whose mothers were food stressed are able to "squeeze in" enough object play to acquire its relatively immediate adaptive developmental effects before they have to put their lives on the line when they are thrust into early independence. This illustrates how *accelerating* development as a response to early stress can be an adaptive strategy – because it makes it more likely that individuals will gain the developmental effects of some early experience that increases fitness under the conditions that cause early stress.

As mentioned, natural selection is expected to favor the genotypic basis for phenotypic plasticity when socioecological conditions vary so as to present a succession of novel environments – i.e., when the environment is "predictably unpredictable" (Fagen 1982; Johnston 1982; Mayr 1974; Plotkin 1994; Slobodkin and Rapoport 1974). And no environment is more predictably unpredictable than the social environment created by long-lived, highly intelligent, intensely social animals like ourselves as we try to effect our individual purposes in the midst of everyone else doing the same thing. In so doing we constantly create novel social environments.

However, even in the midst of all this flux, the work of life has to continue. Phenotypically plastic as our ancestors came to be, open as they became to learning and change, decoupled as their phenotypes came to be from their genotypes, they could not avoid the laws of evolution. Even as each and every one of our phenotypically plastic (direct) ancestors responded adaptively to socioecological factors that were changing more and more over periods of time that were shorter than their lifespans, they still managed to do what had to be done in order for each and every one of us to exist: they survived, grew and developed, and reproduced. This implies that, just as there are benefits to be had from phenotypic plasticity (the capacity to learn, the capacity to be affected by one's environment), so too are there costs. No organism is perfectly plastic; plasticity is constrained by the demands of the work that needs to be done to leave descendants. Knowing these constraints could only help us make our way in the world.

Perhaps the major risk associated with an increased capacity for learning is the increased chance of learning gone wrong or failing to occur. The very flexibility of behavior that is the benefit of learning, in other words, implies an increased possibility of *mistakes* in learning. This, in turn, implies the existence of mechanisms that protect against failing to learn or learning gone wrong (Boyd and Richerson 1985; Johnston 1982). Since evolution is driven not by differential survival or differential growth and development, but by differential reproduction, then if there is any aspect of human activity where we might expect selection to have buffered us against wrong learning, it is in the realm of reproduction – either the production of offspring, their rearing, or, more likely, both. As Stephen Jay Gould expressed this idea, "adaptive explanations" of human behavior are most useful for analyzing "explicitly biological traits shared with other related species lacking our cultural richness – e.g., . . . behaviors of sexual and parent–child bonding" (1991:60).[20]

For this reason, the most important question about human phenotypic plasticity is how certain early experiences move us along a developmental route that is appropriate to the *reproductive* conditions we will encounter in later life. What early learning matters for our reproductive futures? To reduce the most important uncertainty the information that we acquire via early learning must be *about* our reproductive futures; it must somehow enable us to predict, anticipate, or prepare for these futures. In the remainder of this chapter I will describe a model of gene × environment interaction that shows, in principle, how we predict these futures.

Nature, nurture, and the future: organism as hypothesis
The essence of developmental systems theory is the idea that nature and nurture are inherently inseparable because what organisms inherit in reproduction is not only copies of their parents' genes but their parents' environment as well (Lickliter and Berry 1990; Oyama 1985, 1994). It is therefore impossible, in principle, to explain phenotypic traits in terms of separate genetic and environmental causes or sources. Donald Hebb (1953) used to make this point by arguing that all behavior is both 100 percent innate and 100 percent acquired. Plotkin expressed it less enigmatically:

> The instinct–intelligence and genes–experience dichotomies,
> or any other of the dichotomies that characterize the
> nature–nurture distinction, are false dichotomies. This is

[20] Dennett (1995) argues that Gould's subtle form of adaptationism gives unnecessary aid and comfort to creation "scientists" and their ilk and invites them to misunderstand evolution. There may be some truth in this, but in my opinion the fault lies more with the creationists than with Gould, for, as this quote suggests, Gould is not the anti-adaptationist some make him out to be. More to the point, I believe that Gould's subtle adaptationism has helped to make the world safe for evolutionary theory by serving as a corrective to the vulgar adaptationism and "scientific" racism that are still the theory's worst enemies.

> because all genes require an environment in which to develop.
> Since development requires both genes and experience, and
> since every trait is constructed by a developmental process,
> every trait requires both nature and nurture. (Plotkin 1994:164)

On this view, all aspects of all phenotypes are always constructed by
processes of gene × environment interaction. This is true enough, but
unfortunately it is not valuable truth, for it furthers our understanding
of development not one whit. It is analytically, conceptually vapid, for it
fails utterly to address the question of how genes and environments
interact. While everyone agrees that some form of interactionism is the
only way to resolve the perennial nature–nurture dichotomy, what does
it mean for genes and environments to "interact"? Because the nature of
this interaction is illusive, to say the least, despite high hopes and good
intentions this pernicious dichotomy is still very much with us (e.g.,
Oyama 1985).

Change is in the wind, however. In addition to the many thoughtful
"horizontal" models of gene × environment interaction that we have
painstakingly accumulated,[21] we now have Plotkin's "vertical" model.
Plotkin's view of life as a knowledge-gaining process, and of adaptations
as environmental knowledge that has become embodied, have given him
a novel way to think about gene × environment interaction.

As we have seen, the essence of Plotkin's uncertain futures problem is
how to arrive at an adaptive relationship between organism and environment when the organism takes time to "build" but the "instructions"
for building it are received just once, at conception, and the environment
that the organism has to live in may change considerably before it is completely "built." In broad terms, the answer is that selection favored mechanisms that enabled developing organisms to track their environments,
to aim at a "moving target," such that their adult, fully reproductive
phenotypes were constructed by "instructions" from their environments
as well as from their genes. By opening the developing organism to more
information ("instructions") from its environment, selection reduced
the uncertain futures problem. Plotkin's model of gene × environment
interaction is one in which postconception "instructions" for "building"

---

[21] Some of the best discussions and models of gene × environment interaction are Bateson
(1976, 1982); Featherman and Lerner (1985); Gottlieb (1992); Hinde (1987); Oyama (1985,
1994); Plomin (1986); Plomin and Bergeman (1991); Sameroff (1975); Scarr and McCartney
(1983); and Worthman (1993, 1994, 1996).

an organism are constructed for the organism by mechanisms which juxtapose two kinds of information: old information about the organism's ancestors' environments that it acquired via copies of their DNA, and new information about its own environment that it acquired via interaction with this environment. *Neither the old nor the new information constitutes the new "instruction" for building the organism.* Instead, the new "instruction" emerges from, or is constructed by, the interaction of both old and new information; it is the *output* of the mechanism for juxtaposing old and new information.

Plotkin sees adaptation by natural selection as a "knowledge-gaining procedure," in which information about the environments experienced by an organisms' ancestors becomes represented during epigenesis in the organism's body via the DNA it inherited from them (interacting, as always, with the environment it also inherited from them). For Plotkin, the essence of this "knowledge-gaining procedure" is the GTR heuristic – for *generate, test,* and *replicate.* A heuristic is a procedure or algorithm for gaining knowledge or information. Whenever the GTR heuristic is "run" or "implemented," information is gained – i.e., information about the environment becomes represented or embodied in the organism of which the GTR heuristic is part. The G component of the GTR heuristic generates variability; it generates variant forms of that which is adapting. In adaptation by natural selection, G consists of processes like mutation and recombination that generate variant forms of (i.e., individual differences between members of) a single species. The T component of the GTR heuristic is natural selection – some element of the organism's environment that tests each variant against some selective filter or criterion; it selects or chooses those variants (if any) that in virtue of being selected may continue to be part of the adapting (evolving) system. In adaptation by natural selection, of course, T is a problem posed by some aspect of an organism's environment that it did or did not have the means to solve. Lastly, the R component of the GTR heuristic is the mechanism whereby the selected variants (or some aspect thereof) are carried into the future; it is the processes for copying or reproducing the variants who passed their particular T, even if only by luck. In adaptation by natural selection, all R mechanisms reduce to the capacity of the DNA molecule to copy itself.

For evolutionary epistemologists like Plotkin, however, adaptation by natural selection is not the only knowledge-gaining procedure. Learning, intelligence, and cultural learning, he argues, are knowledge-gaining procedures as well, for they increase the exposure of the developing organism to "instructions" from its current environment, and so increase the organism's knowledge of its own environment. Plotkin refers to the first knowledge-gaining procedure (adaptation by natural selection) as the *primary heuristic*. He refers to learning and intelligence (adaptation by acquiring new information) as the *secondary heuristic*. Cultural learning (adaptation through learning what *others* have learned) he calls the *tertiary heuristic*. I will have more to say about the GTR heuristic and its various manifestations in the next chapter. Right now I want to focus on Plotkin's primary and secondary heuristics.

The key difference between the primary and secondary heuristics is that they are sensitive to different frequencies and degrees of environmental change and uncertainty. Plotkin envisions the relation between the two heuristics as a "nested hierarchy," with the secondary heuristic, adaptation by learning and intelligence, "always tucked under the wing," as he put it, of the primary heuristic, adaptation by natural selection. (Figure 2.3 is a schematic representation of Plotkin's model.) As in Slobodkin and Rapoport's optimal strategy of evolution, Plotkin's nested heuristics constitute a hierarchy of mechanisms or processes for responding to, or tracking, environmental change: the secondary heuristic (adaptation by learning and intelligence) is for controlling responses to uncertainty brought about by relatively rapid, frequent environmental change, while the primary heuristic controls responses to much slower change.

It is with his notion of a "nested hierarchy" of adaptations that, in my opinion, Plotkin makes an important contribution to thinking about gene × environment interaction. He is critical of standard interactionism

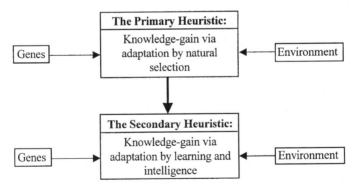

Figure 2.3 Plotkin's nested hierarchy of knowledge-gaining procedures.

on the grounds that it sees interaction occurring only *horizontally*, so to speak, with genes on one side, environments on the other, and epigenesis or interactionism in between, "purporting," he says, "to get rid of the separateness of the two components" (1994:164). He suggests instead that to understand gene × environment interaction we may need an *additional* dimension of interaction – a *vertical* dimension, as it were, in which genes and environments interact both *within* and *between* the two knowledge-gaining procedures, the primary and secondary heuristics. But whether behavior is caused by internal (genetic) or external (environmental) factors is not the issue for Plotkin, for they always interact, at both levels (which interaction still needs to be described, of course). The issue instead is what integrates the response hierarchy vertically and how the two heuristics interact.

Both heuristics are *for* gaining knowledge, Plotkin argues, and so what integrates the hierarchy that they establish is their common function of producing adaptive responses to environmental change. They differ only in the frequency or periodicity of change to which they respond. It is the precise manner in which he sees the two heuristics interacting, however, that I believe gives us a new way of thinking about gene × environment interaction, for it is in their interaction that these two adaptive mechanisms combine to perform a *single, joint* function – that of predicting the future – thus providing a new rationale for the inseparability of nature and nurture.

To see how the primary and secondary heuristics working together constitute a single adaptation for predicting the future, think of the kind of knowledge that each brings to the organism. The primary heuristic, adaptation by natural selection, brings to the organism old information about its ancestors' environments. When this information becomes embodied, materially instantiated in the organism's phenotype, through processes of gene × environment interaction, then it becomes *accessible* to the organism, *available* for the organism to use or process further. The secondary heuristic, adaptation by learning or intelligence, brings to the organism, via sensory data of its world (including its internal world of sensations and feelings), information about the environment in which it has been and currently is living. But the data coming in is data that the organism's genes determined was adaptively relevant or important in the first place, because this kind of data enabled the organism's ancestors to solve the problems that had to be solved in order for them to have left descendants. Therefore, even information about the organism's current environment arriving via the secondary heuristic is *constructed* by inevitable processes of gene × environment interaction. The secondary heuristic, in other words, provides data that the primary heuristic *predicted* would be important. In Plotkin's words, "These innate determiners [of knowledge], themselves *a priori* forms of knowledge, are *a priori* to us as individuals, but they have been gained *a posteriori* by the long evolutionary history of our species" (1994:241).

Like all adaptations, the interaction of the two heuristics is *for* something and it is *relational*: it is for predicting the future and it is the relation between information about the past and the present – information about the past environments experienced by an organism's ancestors (as it comes to be embodied in the organism) and about its own present environment. The interaction of old and new (current) information guides behavior by enabling the organism, metaphorically speaking, to project a line from its evolutionary past through its socioecological present and then on into its future. On this view, learning and intelligence are adaptations for actively extracting information from the environment in order to juxtapose the present to the past and thereby reduce environmental uncertainty by predicting the future. For evolutionary epistemologists, the way that learning and intelligence reduce environmental uncertainty is clear: as Popper said, "While an uncritical animal may be eliminated along with its dogmatically held hypotheses, we may formulate our hypotheses, and critcize them. Let our conjectures, our theories die in our stead!"

To predict the future is to form a hypothesis about it. Organisms are a kind of hypothesis advanced by their ancestors (natural selection) about future environments. Individual organisms are good hypotheses, however, to the extent that their past and present environments are not too different. To predict the future when it is likely to be different from the past requires more and better information about both the past and the present. From the perspective of life history theory and evolutionary epistemology, then, at least part of the reason for the extensive and intensive interaction of nature and nurture in the causation of human behavior is that it is their very interaction that enables us to track our developmental environments – so that we can form hypotheses about our futures, "on the run," as it were, updating them quickly as we go. We seldom think of prediction as something that organisms in general can do, yet even a bacterium, for example, when it follows a chemical gradient, implicitly predicts that food lies in that direction (Holland 1992). It moves in that direction, in effect, by comparing incoming sensory information about its current environment with old, a priori information about the chemical environments of its ancestors that it received via copies of their genes. For humans, of course, many of these predictions are much more explicit. Or, as Plotkin put it, adaptation by natural selection gives us the "ability to generate [our] own causes for [our] behavior" (1994:175) – these causes being our mental representations of the past and the present that allow us to look ahead to the future consequences of current action, without actually carrying out any particular action. In the following chapter, we will begin to look more closely at these mental representations – these mental models of past, present, and future – what they are, where they come from, and the dimensions of their differences.

3 The nature of value

Rationality recognizes truth; the recognition of some ethical truths is impossible without emotion; indeed, certain emotions centrally involve such recognitions. Martha Nussbaum (1994:96)

There is but one passion . . . Hope and fear, sorrow and joy are the motions or properties of love. Jean François Senault, *The Use of Passions* (1649), as quoted in Ainslie (1992:34)

As we saw in the previous chapter, all adaptations are for something. The argument in this chapter is that the process of infant–mother attachment is an adaptation for a special kind of learning. I begin by explaining why I approach human development from the perspective of attachment theory. This I do by using the assumption of optimality to identify the jobs that need to be done during development. I then outline attachment theory and research to show that the attachment process does these jobs. Attachment, I shall argue, is for learning about (gaining knowledge about, representing) one's past and one's present in order to predict one's future – and thereby to "evaluate" one's alternatives and "choose" (i.e., not necessarily consciously) one's optimal developmental pathway. Because development itself is ultimately for reproduction, however, I argue as well that the attachment process is ultimately for "choosing" one's optimal reproductive strategy.

In addition to being *for* something, however, adaptations are *relational* as well. In the midst of showing how the attachment process is for reproduction, therefore, I will also address the reverse engineering question of how it is relational. This entails specifying which aspect of a child's environment becomes represented in its phenotype via the attachment process, such that the resulting attachment relationship can be said to constitute a "relation" between the child and this particular aspect of its environment. Expanding on the original ideas of Jay Belsky, Lawrence Steinberg, and Pat Draper (1991), I then argue that the individual differences that typically arise via the attachment process represent the *relationship* between a child's objective reproductive value and his perception of this reproductive value.

My claim, then, is that (1) at any given moment the outcome or output of the attachment process represents the relation between the amount of objective environmental risk and uncertainty facing a child and the state of the child's nervous system, and (2) that children (and adults) experience these particular neuroendocrine states subjectively as Elzanowski's (1993) value experience, which (as we shall see) is the essentially good or bad feeling that is automatically associated with all or most of our models of the past and present and our resulting hypotheses about the future. In the following two chapters, I review evidence that individual differences in attachment experience are relational – i.e., that certain aspects of environmental risk and uncertainty do indeed come to be represented in children's minds – and that these representations are centrally involved in conceiving and evaluating alternative courses of (or hypotheses about) action (as always, not necessarily consciously).

Optimal ontogeny: what is development *for*?

Attachment theory is a theory of the origin and nature of love. More precisely, it is a theory of (1) the origin and development of individual differences in the subjective experience, and internal, mental representation of self and others in close emotional relationships, and (2) the role of these internal models of social relations in subsequent behavior, particularly adult capacity for close emotional relationships in sociosexual and parenting contexts. More precisely still, attachment theory is fundamentally an evolutionary theory of all these things. It was John Bowlby, after all, the founder of attachment theory, who coined the phrase, "the environment of evolutionary adaptedness" (1969:50) to help understand the ultimate function of close emotional relationships in our evolutionary past. This function, he argued, was protection from danger. The subjective experience of such protection – i.e., security – is the essence and ontogenetic origin of love.

While modern attachment theory has strayed somewhat from its evolutionary roots, of all theories of human development it is by far the most compatible with modern evolutionary theory. My approach to human development is thus primarily from the perspective of attachment theory. It goes without saying, on the other hand, that my version of attachment theory is not the mainstream version, for I view it through the lens of modern evolutionary ecology, life history theory, and evolutionary psychology.

One reason why I believe that attachment theory is entailed by an evolutionary perspective on development is that attachment theory seems to have arrived inductively at what current evolutionary models have arrived at deductively. As I explain below, where attachment theory has its "internal working models" and "secure and insecure" models of self and other, evolutionary epistemology and psychology have analogs in "internal models" and "credit assignment."

Internal models and credit assignment
It is no longer remarkable to note that there is more to adaptation than Darwinian natural selection. On the contrary, it is now widely accepted that the process of adaptation has certain formal properties that can be identified in any "complex adaptive system" (Holland 1992), be it evolving species, the immune system, ecological and economic systems, or developing embryos or brains (Dennett 1995; Edelman 1987: Frank 1996; Holland 1992; Plotkin 1994). What all of these complex systems have in common is that they have the capacity to achieve a better fit to, or relationship with, some aspect of their environment (i.e., to *adapt* to it) – with better defined in terms of doing what the system was designed *for*[1] more successfully or efficiently (i.e., with fewer resources, less time, more security, etc.). If it is by virtue of these shared formal properties that all complex adaptive systems do the work of adaptation, then, by the assumption of optimality (i.e., adopting the intentional stance), natural selection – like any other complex adaptive system – should have favored mechanisms or algorithms that embodied these formal properties.

What are these properties? If we know what the work of adaptation logically entails then it may be easier to identify the biological mechanisms that actually do this work in living systems. Holland (1992) maintains that to adapt to changing environments complex adaptive systems must have at least two capabilities: (1) they must be able to predict the future, and (2) they must be able to alter their relationships to the environment according to (i.e., in light of, contingent on) these predictions.

Let us consider prediction first. As we have seen a number of times now, when we look at development from an evolutionary (i.e., reproductive) perspective we expect to find mechanisms or algorithms for reducing uncertainty. For evolutionary epistemologists like Plotkin, life itself is a "knowledge-gaining process" because the essential problem of life is

---

[1] What a system is *for* is what previous adaptations "designed" it to *do*. (Design, remember, does not imply a designer.)

reproduction in the face of the uncertain futures problem – and uncertainty is a knowledge problem. For life history theoreticians like Bonner, development itself evolved *for* reproduction – but when it did it also created the generational deadtime problem, thereby greatly exacerbating the uncertain futures problem. Finally (thanks ultimately to the uncertain futures problem), the trade-off between current and future reproduction is perhaps the most pervasive adaptive problem facing all living forms. It should come as no surprise then that, for Holland, "the fundamental attribute" of all complex adaptive systems is their capacity to form internal models for predicting the future. In a most Popper-like passage, Holland notes that:

> An internal model allows a [complex adaptive] system to look ahead to the future consequences of current actions, without actually committing itself to those actions. In particular, the system can avoid acts that would set it irretrievably down some road to future disaster ("stepping off a cliff"). Less dramatically, but equally important, the model enables the agent [i.e., the complex adaptive system] to make current "stage-setting" moves that set up later moves that are obviously advantageous. The very essence of attaining a competitive advantage, whether it be in chess or economics, is the discovery and execution of stage-setting moves. (1992:25)

There is more to adaptation, however, than models for predicting the future; predicting the future is necessary for adaptation but not sufficient. The reason for this is obvious: the entire point of *having* models of the future is to *use* them for deciding which one offers the best way to avoid a cliff or to approach some future goal. To carry on avoiding cliffs and setting the stage for future good moves as one's environment changes is continually to change one's relationship to that environment (i.e., to track it). Deciding (choosing, selecting) among these continuously updated models of the future means continuously evaluating them. To alter its relationship to a changing environment a complex adaptive system must be able to avoid danger and approach security. In other words, it must be able to detect *good* new moves or directions – it must be able to detect *value*. Again, John Holland:

> Credit [or blame] assignment is necessary because one wants the system, and its rules, to evolve *toward* something. Credit

assignment first requires a sense of what "good" performance is, then it requires a way to pick out and "reward" those parts of the system that seem to be causing good performance. A system that rewards good performance may never become optimal, but it can get better and better (1992:23).[2]

The "something" that one wants the system to evolve toward is the future:

> ... standard theories in physics, economics, and elsewhere, are of little help [for understanding complex adaptive systems] because they concentrate on optimal end-points, whereas complex adaptive systems "never get there." They continue to evolve, and they steadily exhibit new forms of emergent behavior. History and context play a critical role, further complicating the task of theory and experiment. Though some parts of the system may settle down temporarily at a local optimum, they are usually "dead" or uninteresting if they remain at that equilibrium for an extended period. It is the process of becoming, rather than the never-reached end points, that we must study if we are to gain insight. (1992:20)

When we look at development from an evolutionary perspective (viewing it as ultimately *for* reproduction) we therefore expect to find mechanisms not only for more-or-less continuously constructing updated internal models of the future, but also for continuously assigning credit to (evaluating, criticizing) these models. In other words, we expect selection to favor mechanisms for choosing *good* models – both *of* the future and *for* the future. (Models *for* the future are models of action *for achieving* the future; they are strategies.) Or, as I argued in the first chapter, we expect to find mechanisms for representing (however imperfectly) not only certain facts of nature, but also the value that these facts and hypotheses hold for each of us. If the process of adaptation by natural selection works like other complex adaptive systems, then a central part of human development should be about the ontogeny of reproductively relevant *future* detectors and *value* detectors.

If predicting the future requires knowledge of the past and the present,

---

[2] Instead of saying "may never become optimal" I would say that such a system can never become *perfect* – but can become *more* optimal (i.e., it can get better and better at tracking its ever-changing environment). Again, "optimal" does not mean "perfect"; it means "best possible given existing constraints."

then to form better, more rapidly-updated models of the future requires more, better, and more quickly accessed knowledge of the past and the present. If adaptations and life itself are the incorporation and representation of environmental information or knowledge in phenotypes, then it seems possible to characterize the history of life as one of increasing adaptability – i.e., an increasing capacity to predict the future and act accordingly – as Plotkin (1994) and Dennett (1995), among others, have argued. As I mentioned in the preceding chapter, Plotkin identifies three stages in the evolution of knowledge-gaining mechanisms, all of which are versions of his basic GTR heuristic. Dennett, on the other hand, sees four stages in the evolution of algorithms for gaining knowledge, which he describes in terms of "the Tower of Generate-and-Test" (1995:373). This tower (the history of life) consists of four floors, each occupied by creatures with more sophisticated, complex versions of the GTR heuristic than those on the floor below. In Dennett's metaphor, "as each new floor of the Tower gets constructed, it empowers the organisms at that level to find better and better moves [i.e., action that is contingent on the output of better future and value detectors], and find them more efficiently" (1995:373).

The first floor in Dennett's Tower is occupied by Darwinian creatures, who are constituted by matter that is organized by one kind of information – environmental information gained via the original GTR heuristic, in which, as we saw earlier, mutation and recombination generate (G) variability in genes, which, if they pass the test (T) of natural selection, replicate (R) themselves, thereby passing into future generations the information about ancestral environments that they carry. Strictly Darwinian creatures do not have access to this information and thus cannot form models of the future. All they can do is advance hypotheses about the future in the form of copies of their genes that they send into subsequent generations. Indeed, Darwinian creatures *themselves* are "hypotheses" about the future that were advanced by their ancestors. Because strictly Darwinian creatures do not have the capacity to gain knowledge that is *not* in their genes (i.e., information about their current internal and external environments) they cannot respond to environments that change over time periods shorter than a generation (and successful responses by their descendants, if any, is usually a slow, gradual process).

The second floor of Dennett's Tower of Generate-and-Test is occupied by Skinnerian creatures, whose phenotypes are constituted by matter that is organized by two kinds of information: (1) information about past environments, gained via copies of their ancestors' DNA, and (2) information about present environments, gained through simple conditioning. Though constructed like Darwinian creatures, Skinnerian creatures have the additional capacity of responding to environments that change over time frames shorter than a generation because they can alter their phenotypes on the basis of information about the present that is built up through simple conditioning. Conditioning is gaining knowledge through the senses. Conditioning is induction, which is the perception that things are somehow "related" or "belong together." It is *knowing that* if A is true, then so is B. Skinnerian creatures gain knowledge through a version of the GTR heuristic that is faster and more complex than that of strictly Darwinian creatures. First, Skinnerian creatures possess a nervous system that is responsive to environmental input, and so they can generate (G) novel behaviors in novel circumstances. Whatever behavior succeeds – say, in decreasing hunger, thereby passing the "drive reduction test" (T) – will tend to be retained or replicated (R) through the mechanisms of habit formation ("if it reduced hunger once [A = a specific case] then it will do so again [B = a general pattern]"). While conditioning provides a degree of behavioral flexibility and is clearly better than no learning at all, Skinnerian creatures suffer from the inherent shortcoming of all induction: No matter how often some action has worked in the past, there can be no guarantee that it will continue to work in the future.

During evolution, vast numbers of lives and potential lives (reproductive opportunities) were lost because of (1) the slow pace at which Darwinian creatures advanced hypotheses about changing environments and (2) the false generalizations made by Skinnerian creatures. Right now, however, I am concerned with Darwinian and Skinnerian creatures only in so far as they provide a framework for understanding the occupants of the third and fourth floors of Dennett's Tower – the Popperian and Gregorian creatures – for they are the ones who help most to show why we expect evolution to have produced mechanisms for building better, more reproductively relevant future and value detectors during human ontogeny.

The third floor of Dennett's Tower is occupied by Popperian creatures, so-called because they have as their slogan Popper's famous declaration: "we may formulate our hypotheses, and criticize them. Let our conjectures, our theories die in our stead!" Popperian creatures are constituted by matter that is organized by three kinds of information: (1) information about past environments contained in their DNA, (2) information about present environments gained through induction, and (3) information about present environments gained through deduction. Induction is *knowing that* something is the case whereas deduction is *knowing why* it is the case; induction is gaining knowledge through the senses, whereas deduction is gaining knowledge through the mind (Dunbar 1995; Plotkin 1994). Popperian creatures gain knowledge through the mind; they learn to *know why it is* that if A is true, then so is B. Popperian creatures use information about their internal and external environments to construct an internal model of these environments, on the basis of which they generate (G) hypotheses about the best course of action for them to follow. By running each hypothesis through a series of mental operations (e.g., thought experiments) created from their knowledge of *why* the world works the way it does (i.e., their explanatory models), Popperian creatures can (in principle, rationally) *preselect* (T) a course of action in their minds before trying it out in real life. Successful actions are replicated (R) not only in the usual ways, like memory, but also in the form of their informational contribution to even better models of the way the world works. Popperian creatures thus arrive at their strategies for action through practical reason.

The occupants of the fourth floor of Dennett's Tower are known as Gregorian creatures (after the British information theorist Richard Gregory [1981, 1987]). Gregorian creatures are constituted by matter that is organized by four kinds of information: (1) a priori knowledge contained in their DNA, (2) knowledge gained by induction, (3) that gained by deduction, and (4) that gained *culturally*. Gregorian creatures, in other words, gain knowledge by creating internal models of the world out of information *in other peoples' minds*. To build their internal models, Gregorian creatures must therefore first get into other peoples' minds. For this purpose, Gregorian creatures use "mind tools" (Gregory, cited in Dennett 1995:378), which are designed to recognize, retrieve, manipulate, and store information in minds. Mind tools – for example, words, concepts, symbols, metaphors, rules, and recipes – are tools for getting information out of and into minds. (The ultimate mind tool, of course, is a *theory of mind*, which we will get to in the next chapter.) Using these mind tools, Gregorian creatures are able to generate (G) "ever more subtle move-generators [future detectors] and move testers [value detectors]" (Dennett 1995:378). By running each move that has been thus generated (i.e., each future that has been detected, each hypothesis about the future) through a series of actual or simulated mental operations *in the minds of others* (i.e., using language to determine what so-and-so *does* think of some course of

action) or in *virtual minds* of others (i.e., manipulating one's internal
model of another person to determine what so-and-so *would* think of
some course of action), Gregorian creatures can hugely magnify the
power of individual minds to preselect (*T*) the optimal course of action.
The use of language gives Gregorian preselection a quantum increase
over the generative (creative) and evaluative (critical) power of the literally single-minded Popperian creature; in Dennett's words, Gregorian
minds are "virtuoso preselectors" (p. 377). Gregorian models that survive
such broad evaluation are replicated (*R*) in other minds in the form of
culturally constructed knowledge (or Dawkins' [1976] memes).

   If complex adaptive systems require internal models of the future and
credit assignment in order to work (to continue – i.e., to evolve [*R*]), then
it seems right for Plotkin and Dennett to characterize the history of life
(the evolution of adaptations) as one of an increasing capacity to generate
(create) and select among (evaluate) useful models *of* and *for* (reaching)
the future. Further, if adaptations are "biological knowledge," then we
would expect adaptations not only for generating (*G*) hypotheses about
the future and for evaluating (*T*) these hypotheses, but also for *representing* reproductive (*R*) value. This is because reproductive success is the most
fundamental fact of *bios* (i.e., life). Reproductive success is, by definition,
a universal feature of the environment of evolution itself (the EEA of life,
as it were). It is the universal *sine qua non* of all complex adaptive (evolving) systems. *R* is *continuance* – the never-ending "process of becoming"
which "one wants the system, and its rules, to evolve *toward*" (Holland
1992:20, 23).

   When we look at human development from an evolutionary perspective, then, we have reason to think that in some very basic ways it is about
the ontogeny of mechanisms or algorithms for reducing uncertainty by
generating models *of* reproductive value and *for achieving* reproductive
value (i.e., reproductive strategies), for evaluating these models, and then
choosing those that offer the best chance of (1) avoiding stepping off a
fitness cliff and (2) setting the stage for possible future moves that would
have fitness advantages. On this view, the origin of value – the original
and ultimate basis for all evaluation – is reproductive success. Andrzej
Elzanowski put it this way:

> . . . the origin of good and bad feelings seems to be obvious in
> terms of ultimate, evolutionary causes: the negative experience
> or punishment has been associated with the exposure to factors

that decrease fitness and the positive experience or reward has been associated with situations that enhance fitness. (1993:264)

William Cooper (1987) also sees fitness as the ultimate source of value. On the now-familiar assumption that if rational thought is part of life then ultimately it must be explainable in terms of our only scientific theory of life, Cooper argues that "the rules of rationality are not purely intuitive, logical, and analytical at all, but ultimately biological, empirical, and scientific in origin" (p. 396). He begins with Edwards' (1954) definition of rationality: a rational actor "can weakly order [generate models of] the states into which he can get [in the future], and he makes his choice [evaluates] so as to maximize something" (quoted in Cooper 1987:395). He then notes that economists and decision theorists have for the most part simply intuited the nature of this "something" as "utility" (value), but never really bothered, or were able, to define it. He reports, for example, that, whereas Jeremy Bentham defined utility in hedonistic terms of pain and pleasure, modern definitions of utility have actually included "such noncommittal glosses" as "wantabilities" and "desirabilities" (p. 397). For Cooper, subjective probability – the feeling that something will or will not happen – is the basis for all decision theory. The ultimate origin of subjective probability, he argues, is in the objective probabilities that exist as facts of nature that are inevitably associated with reproductive success and failure. Since organisms who achieve long-term reproductive success made objectively good (and sometimes lucky) decisions, then natural selection will tend to favor[3] a "choice function" (decision-making algorithm) that is based on the *subjective correlates of good decisions concerning fitness* (Elzanowski's "value experience"). Therefore,

> ... individual decision making may be viewed biologically as a special form of evolutionary reasoning executed by the individual organism/actor. The decision rules are (as it were) an internalization within the decision maker of the process by which an external bioanalyst might attempt to determine what the decision maker's fittest choice would be ... to the extent these decision processes really do maximize something called "utility," as decision theorists claim, this mysterious utility substance must in some sense reduce to fitness. The same line of thought suggests that the evolutionary process will tend to

---

[3] Perhaps through the Baldwin effect (Baldwin 1896; Frank 1996).

favor modes of individual internal information processing that are analogs of the evolutionary process itself, because their function is to bring about fitness maximization. (Cooper 1987:397)

But this raises the question of how utility – value – comes to be part of an "individual internal information processing" mechanism. If fitness (R, the "state" of continuing) is the ultimate source of value, how are the decision rules that are designed to bring about this ultimate value "internalized within the decision maker"? If reproductive value is the organism–environment contingency that must be represented phenotypically in order to form reproductively relevant models of the past and the present, thereby to predict the future, how is this information about *past and present value* embodied in the organism and projected into the future? To consider these and related questions we now begin the reverse engineering of value. Our first question is, how might an organism detect value?

Emotions as value detectors
The idea that emotions serve as value detectors is an old one. Stoic philosophers, for example, believed that all of the emotions were ultimately varieties of just one, love or attachment, which was the "ascription of a high value to vulnerable 'external goods'" (Nussbaum 1994:370). From love they derived four basic emotions, which they understood as the interaction between this value dimension (good–bad) and a time dimension (present–future). Thus, *present × good* results in "delight"; *future × good* results in "longing" or "appetition"; *present × bad* results in "distress"; and *future × bad* results in "fear" (Nussbaum 1994:386). More recently, Plotkin (1994) has presented an evolutionary epistemological version of the idea that emotions detect value. He views emotions as information about the sources of security and danger in our ancestors' environments that has become represented in us via copies of their DNA. For Plotkin, emotions are not simply irrational messages from our evolutionary past. They mark events

> . . . as being good or bad, those which we should attempt to attain or avoid, those associated with life and those associated with death. The last mentioned, that most fundamental of dichotomies, is the most direct message that we can get from our genes as to what to do, what to avoid or what is worth investing in; but it doesn't have to be as dramatic and stark as

> life and death. Pleasure and pain are signals too, if less intense
> and less dramatic, but ultimately deriving from the approach–
> avoidance or life–death dichotomy . . . Contemporary
> psychology actually postulates the existence of at least six basic
> emotional states (happiness, surprise, sadness, anger, disgust,
> and fear). All must ultimately derive from the fundamental
> dichotomy of what perpetuates genes and what does not . . .
> But whatever the emotion being signalled, one of its functions
> is to tell us what to attend to, what to learn about. (1994:208)

And in fact there is abundant empirical evidence that "we are chronically engaged in ascertaining the goodness or badness of stimuli in our
environments" (Pratto 1994:116).[4] Known technically as automatic evaluation, to "ascertain value" is to unconsciously, involuntarily attach a
valence of "goodness" or "badness" to essentially all stimuli. What this
means is that we can and often do like (approach) or dislike (avoid) people,
things, events, ideas, feelings, etc., on the basis of an unconscious, automatic "prejudging" or "preselecting" mechanism. For a quick example,
consider the work of Corteen and Wood (1972), reported in Pratto (1994).
They first had 36 people perform a task in which they received mild elec-
tric shocks whenever they encountered the names of three particular
cities. Later these subjects were asked to concentrate their attention as
best they could on two tasks: (1) listening to a prose passage being
presented through an earphone to one ear and (2) simultaneously recit-
ing this passage as it was being heard. While this was going on, a list of
words and city names was presented through an earphone to the other,
unattended ear. Subjects' skin conductance, a measure of autonomic
(involuntary) nervous system function reflecting arousal, was recorded
continuously, and variations in skin conductance were related to the
presentation to the unattended ear of the three shock-associated city
names. There were significantly more changes in skin conductance associated with these three city names than the other words and city names.
Afterwards, subjects were asked if they had noticed anything in their
unattended ears. None had. The experimenter then asked them to think
carefully, to try hard to remember if they had heard anything, even if
they could not remember exactly what. Five subjects reported remem-

---

[4] See also Arnold (1960); Bornstein and Pittman (1992); Damasio (1994); Frijda (1993);
Lazarus (1991); LeDoux (1996); Mathews and MacLeod (1994); Niedenthal and Kitayama
(1994); Pratto (1994); Scherer (1993).

bering words, but none recalled any city names. Then the experimenter asked specifically if they heard any city names – and all subjects said no. In sum, subjects implicitly learned (inductively, through the senses) that the three city names "went with" pain. In turn, this unconscious learning produced a physiological response that is associated with emotions and defense. Thus, subjects showed an involuntary, evolved physiological response to stimuli of which they did not seem aware.

From the work of Joseph LeDoux (1989, 1995, 1996) we now know that this automatic "ascertainment of value" is a function of a particular brain module, the amygdala, working closely with the hippocampus. The amygdala is where the emotional component of memories are stored. The hippocampus stores the "where and when" of emotions – information about the context in which they have been experienced. As incoming sensory information about the current environment (internal as well as external) is received, it is processed by the amygdala, which evaluates it as essentially good or bad – or more precisely, as suited or not to elicit fear. In LeDoux's words,

> . . . the amygdala plays a crucial role in deciding whether a stimulus is dangerous or not. Functions mediated by the amygdala are likely to be the neural instantiation of the emotional process known as appraisal, at least for the appraisal of danger. (1995:223)

Automatic evaluations by the amygdala may serve as necessary inputs to emotion. As the storage site for emotional memories, the amygdala processes incoming sensory information, arriving at its evaluation by, in effect, juxtaposing the present environment to the emotional past. It yields a very rapid initial "pre-judgement" of "good" or "bad" on the basis of two kinds of information. The first kind of information is personal experience. When incoming information about the present environment is judged somehow to be "like" old information about the context of personal experience stored in the hippocampus, the amygdala determines the emotional valence attached to this memory and attaches it (inductively) to the incoming information. LeDoux (1996) refers to this kind of information as a "learned trigger" for fear. The second kind of information is genetic information about the cumulative past experience of our ancestors – what LeDoux calls a "natural trigger" for fear. As Plotkin put it, this "is the most direct message that we can get from our genes" – it is about things which are "good or bad, those which we should attempt to attain or avoid, those associated with life and those associated with death" (1994:208). We are thus born with some innate algorithms for sensing what is good and bad. We have, for example, an innate fear of falling (Gibson and Walk 1960) and strangers (Bronson 1972), and an innate affinity for body contact (Harlow 1958) and social responsiveness (Watson 1972, 1985). And because the neural connections between the sensory cortex and the amygdala mature before those between the pre-frontal cortex and the amygdala, all early memories are essentially *only* emotional memories. They are not like explicit, declarative memories, which can be accessed by the prefrontal cortex, and thus brought into consciousness. What is more, because the earliest emotional memories are laid down in the amygdala prior to the development of the hippo-campus and of connections between the amygdala, hippocampus, and the prefrontal cortex they are virtually indelible and inaccessible to con-sciousness. Finally, because the amygdala sends projections back to the very sensory processing systems from which it receives incoming infor-mation about the present environment, these back-projections may allow the amygdala's habitual evaluations (inductive generalizations) of danger to affect perceptions of the present environment. This may be the neural mechanism whereby a sufficient number of early fearful experi-ences predispose children to develop negative, fearful internal models of the future, thereby increasing their wariness.

LeDoux's work is important, however, not just because it reveals the amygdala as the *locus* of automatic evaluation. It is also important because it helps us understand better how we subjectively experience the "good" and "bad" evaluations that it attaches to our perceptions – in other words, how good and bad *value experiences* actually feel. Evaluations of stimuli as "bad" seem unequivocally to be experienced in terms of fear or anxiety. There is a wealth of behavioral and neuroanatomical evidence showing that this is the case, and it is an evolutionarily ancient pattern:

> . . . amongst vertebrates, the neural system involved in detecting danger and producing defence responses is similarly organized in all species studied. This suggests that evolution long ago figured out how to organize the defence system and has continued to use this organizational blueprint. (1995:227)

Life history theory provides a rationale for understanding why the amygdala might be expected to return evaluations of stimuli on an expe-riential dimension of fear (bad) vs. security (good, or at least not bad, or so far, so good) and thus why attachment is all about protection. The reason is that in evolution (as in all complex adaptive systems) the cost of "stepping off a cliff" is always greater than the benefit of "setting the stage" for some future good fitness move. This is because the penalty for failing to avoid a cliff is immediate and severe – death, or other failure to reproduce – whereas the penalty for failing to set the stage for some profitable future move is, by definition, both delayed (making it possible that another opportunity might arise) and not so severe, being an *opportunity cost,* not a direct cost (a failure to increase rather than an actual decrease). Indeed, the demographer Nathan Keyfitz (1977) showed mathematically that the probability of evolutionary extinction is more sensitive to having *few* offspring than it is to having *many* offspring. That is, *lowering* the expected number of surviving offspring by a certain amount *increases* the probability of extinction more than *raising* the expected number of offspring by the same amount *decreases* the likelihood of extinction. Everything else being equal then, organisms that were more sensitive or responsive to threats to their fitness (i.e., risk and uncertainty) than to potential fitness opportunities would achieve greater reproductive success (see also Kacelnik and Bateson 1996; Rubenstein 1982; Seger and Brockmann 1987).[5]

Ultimately, this may explain why people (and animals) are generally *risk-averse* – that is, more concerned to avoid losses than to obtain equivalent gains.[6] Pratto and John (1991) thus propose that automatic evaluations are biased toward negative stimuli. This negative bias is the result, they argue, of natural selection for a preconscious "attention allocation mechanism" by which conscious attention can be directed to environmental stimuli that have already been determined ("prejudged") to be worthy of greater long-term investment of attention through conscious thought. The stimuli most likely to be "worth" this greater investment (i.e., those offering some hope of future benefit) are those holding no

---

[5] This may be why vertebrates evolved a stress-response system which functions well enough with short-term stressors, but which can actually *cause* disease if these stressors become chronic. McEwen (1995) suggests that this unfortunate capacity of our stress-response system to "lead the body down a pathway to disease" when it fails to achieve short-term results shows that "the body is not always wise in its homeostatic or allostatic control mechanisms" (1995:1127). However, if it is always more important to avoid falling off fitness cliffs than to set the stage for future good moves, then it was indeed wise for the body to give priority to short-term stressors.

[6] For example, Ainslie (1992); Kacelnik and Bateson (1996); Kahneman and Tversky (1979), (1984); Kahneman, Slovic, and Tversky (1982); Tversky and Kahneman (1981).

immediate danger. As Pratto (1994) put it, the hypothetical purpose of this mechanism

> . . . is to make the perceiver aware of things in the environment that may require fast responses. If this mental process was indeed selected, then stimuli requiring attention and fast responses were apparently often negatively valenced during human evolution. (1994:134)

Because the EEA of humans was so intensely social, suggests Pratto, we might expect to find that humans were particularly good at perceiving social threats. And indeed there is experimental evidence consistent with the idea of an evolved mechanism for avoiding social cliffs. Hansen and Hansen (1988), for example, found that subjects were substantially faster at detecting an angry face in photographs of a crowd of happy faces than vice versa, finding a happy face in a crowd of people with angry faces. Along similar lines, Leda Cosmides (1989) has presented extensive data consistent with the proposition that humans possess a heightened sensitivity to or awareness of the dangers of the ultimate social threat – "social cheaters" or "free-loaders," i.e., people who fail to reciprocate in social exchanges and thereby do not hold up their end of the "social contract."

Antonio Damasio's (1994) "somatic marker hypothesis" is a good way to summarize the argument that emotions are essentially adaptations for detecting value. In contrast to Plotkin and Cooper, who as we just saw are concerned with adaptationist accounts of rational thought, Damasio, a neurobiologist, is concerned with mechanist accounts of rationality – i.e., the neural mechanisms whereby rational thought is actually embodied or produced. From detailed knowledge of how the workings of their brains affect the ways that healthy and unhealthy people see the world and make decisions, Damasio reasons that rationality inescapably (and adaptively) involves both evolutionarily recent (neocortical) and old (subcortical) brain centers. The capacity for rational thought has traditionally been located entirely in the neocortex, whereas subcortical regions like the hypothalamus, brain stem, and amygdala were believed to be concerned only with regulating basic biological functions. However, it now appears that nature "built the apparatus of rationality not just on top of the apparatus of biological regulation, but also *from* it and *with* it" (Damasio 1994:128).

According to Damasio's somatic marker hypothesis, at the center of every choice or decision, conscious or not, there is a "marker" that represents the body (*soma*) or better, the body's "interests" (i.e., the major components of fitness: survival, growth and development, and the production and rearing of offspring). This marker is the representation in the amygdala of information about (i.e., *fear of*) the dangers that our ancestors faced in our evolutionary past, as well as the feelings of danger that we have faced in our own lives. Virtually in the act of forming (*G*) an image of our future, such images are passed to the amygdala, where they are evaluated (inductively) (*T*) for their "goodness" or "badness" – i.e., their (subjectively) probable impact on our fitness (*R*). For example, virtually in the act of forming an image of, say, a bus rushing toward us just as we step off a curb, that image is passed to the amygdala to evaluate against the databank of dangers faced by our ancestors that is stored there. When the image of this rapidly approaching bus is matched with the innately frightening archetypal image of "large looming object"[7] that is stored in the amygdala, the virtually instantaneous output is "bad" – the powerful visceral sensation of fear that makes us want desperately to avoid stepping off curbs in front of buses (i.e., cliffs). Likewise, virtually in the act of forming an image of ourselves in 20 years if we are willing to set the stage by enduring the sustained effort and sacrifices of, say, 4 years at university, that image is passed to the amygdala to evaluate against a priori images of danger acquired via copies of our ancestors' DNA, as well as a posteriori images of danger that we acquire through our own experience. While our ancestors did not attend university, they surely experienced the loss of long-term projects. And if this image of ourselves in the future were to be matched with a painful emotional memory of the loss of some future that we had previously imagined, then the imagined future benefit of going to university might not balance the very real immediate pain of remembered loss. But if no match is made, and the amygdala returns an evaluation of "good," or at least "not bad," or "not disproved (to be dangerous)," such a "so far, so good" evaluation is then passed on to slower, more complex, evolutionarily more recent processing centers in the neocortex. And, if we have positive emotional memories of having achieved some larger future benefit by having foregone some smaller but immediate benefit, these slower imagining/evaluating processes may elicit a match that serves not as an alarm bell, but as a goal or target.

---

[7] While on-rushing buses were not part of our EEA, our ancestors surely experienced many "large looming objects" in the form of other bodies encountered in rough-and-tumble play and physical aggression.

Thus, once an image of the future has been established as "not bad" it may come to be evaluated as positively "good." As we saw, this is because while it is always immediately disastrous for one's fitness to step off cliffs, the benefits of obtaining some future value can never be of equal certainty or magnitude. This is the essence of the current–future trade-off, which Damasio captured this way:

> When a negative somatic marker is juxtaposed to a particular future outcome the combination functions as an alarm bell. When a positive somatic marker is juxtaposed instead, it becomes a beacon of incentive. (1994:174)

Seen this way, thought, whether it is conscious or not, is rational to the extent that it helps us to avoid stepping off cliffs or to approach one of these beacons. Ultimately, these beacons of incentive are representations of value – reproductive value – in our emotional brain. We experience this value as feelings – Elzanowski's value experience – which we have traditionally judged irrational. We think of alarm bells as loud and jangling, demanding immediate, unthinking action. We think of beacons, on the other hand, as in the distance, in the future, quietly guiding our action, rather than frantically demanding it. Damasio's beacons of incentive, however, are out of our past ("the most direct message we can get from our genes"). They represent the values – security (good) and danger (bad) – that our ancestors experienced. Light from behind us, as it were, reflects on the present and shows us where to go. Rationality derives from, and is ultimately for, continuing, R – the thing of value to be rational *about*.

Gerald Edelman (1992) makes the same point in *Bright Air, Brilliant Fire*. He interprets the emotional brain (the limbic-brain stem system) as the body's "value system." He argues that the neural pathways comprising this system evolved "to match the body," that is, to represent the body's interests in evolutionarily more recent and complex decision-making algorithms:

> The later-evolving cortical system served learning behavior that was adaptive to increasingly complex environments. Because this behavior was clearly selected to serve the physiological needs and values mediated by the earlier limbic-brain stem system, the two systems had to be connected in such a way that their activities could be matched. Indeed, such a matching is a

critical part of learning. If the cortex is concerned with the categorization of the world and the limbic-brain stem system is concerned with value . . . then learning may be seen as the means by which categorization occurs on a background of value to result in adaptive changes in behavior that satisfy value. (1992:118)

On this view, value is ultimately about long-term fitness – *continuing* as part of a complex adaptive system, *staying in* Slobodkin and Rapoport's (1974) "existential game of life." To achieve long-term fitness, organisms must always first avoid short-term disaster: they must avoid dangerous cliffs. Once they have achieved a degree of security, however, they can afford to invest in the future: they can set the stage for long-term fitness projects. From the perspective of evolutionary psychology/epistemology, the capacity to detect danger and security is the capacity to detect value and is a rational way for an organism to approach the future – the beacon of long-term fitness. (I will have more to say about the relationship between value and time in the following chapter.)

But how could this be done? If some adaptationist engineer had the task of building an organism that could detect value, she would have to produce a flesh-and-blood mechanism that could detect and represent (i.e., experience) *security* (good) and *danger* (bad) phenotypically, so that the organism could *use* this valuable information to make decisions about the optimal allocation of its reproductive effort (and do it with limited resources, too). Now is the time, therefore, to explore attachment theory in some detail, for the mechanist heart of this book is the idea that the process of infant–mother attachment is a developmental mechanism for detecting and representing reproductive value. As mentioned, attachment theory is indeed a theory of the origin and nature of love. I believe, however, that what we call love is *value experience*, which ultimately is the phenotypic representation of the organism–environment interactive contingencies that determine reproductive value. As Patricia Crittenden (1997) put it, "attachment is not a theory about happiness; it is about *protection*" (1997a:85–86; emphasis added).

Attachment theory

Attachment theory (Bowlby 1969, 1973, 1980) has roots in psychoanalytic theory, ethology, control systems theory, and World War II. Trained in psychoanalytic child psychiatry, John Bowlby believed that early experience, especially with one's mother,[8] had a powerful effect on adult personality and behavior. Freud himself, after all, had written that the infant–mother relationship was

> ... unique, without parallel, established unalterably for a whole lifetime as the first and strongest love-object and as the prototype of all later love-relations – for both sexes. (1940:45)

This belief was reinforced repeatedly by Bowlby's personal experience, but not for the reasons that Freud might have predicted. Commissioned by the World Health Organization to study the social-emotional development of children orphaned during World War II, Bowlby observed that even when these children had been well nourished, they were still more likely to be anxious and depressed and to develop other emotional or behavioral problems than children who had not experienced such loss. Freudian theory held that the origin of the child's powerful attachment to its mother – and thus the origin of personality development – was in the reduction of the infant's primary drive of hunger. The pleasure of taking in food, in Freud's view, came to be experienced by the child as love for the person providing the food. Because his observations did not square with Freud's drive reduction theory of infant love, Bowlby began searching for an alternative model that could accomodate his growing conviction that infants were born with a primary, autonomous drive to be close to – to be attached to – their mothers.

He found it in the emerging fields of ethology – particularly research by Robert Hinde (1961) and Konrad Lorenz (1935) on imprinting in birds and by Harry Harlow (1958) on "motherless monkeys" – and control systems (information) theory. Because early human infants were helpless for so many months after birth, Bowlby reasoned, their chances for avoiding the various dangers posed by the "environment of evolutionary adapted-

---

[8] I tend to use "mother" instead of "father," "parent," or "caregiver" for reasons of style and because everywhere women seem to have been primarily responsible for childcare. However, I also use "mother" because, as Sara Ruddick (1989) points out, what matters for child survival, growth, and ultimate acceptability as a mate and parent is not *who* does it, but that the *work* of mothering actually gets done. Both mothers and fathers are "mothers," she says, "just because and to the degree that they are committed to meeting demands [of children] that define maternal work" (Ruddick 1989:17). Nor is there any evidence that the sex of the person caring for the child matters to the child or his capacity for secure attachment. I tend to use masculine pronouns to refer to children for reasons of style and the arbitrary reason that I am male.

ness" would have been enhanced by a powerful motivation to remain close to their mothers – in much the way that the survival of Lorenz's goslings was enhanced through their powerful motivation to follow their mothers. With Harlow's demonstration that normal social-emotional development in rhesus monkeys depended on "contact comfort" (physical contact with mother, i.e., being close to her) and not on feeding, the secondary drive interpretion of the infant–mother relationship was effectively demolished. Combining ethology and control systems theory (e.g., Miller, Galanter, and Pribram 1960), Bowlby proposed that through natural selection infants were endowed with the "set-goal" of proximity to mother that functioned to increase infant survival by motivating infants to remain close to their primary source of safety. At the same time, however, because simply avoiding danger is no basis for development, Bowlby proposed as well that through natural selection infants were also endowed with a motivation to use their mothers as a "secure base" from which to explore their worlds – i.e., once security had been established, *to move away from security* to set the stage for development by actively engaging with their environments.

The process of attachment

From such beginnings in the 1950s and 60s – and aided in particular by the contributions of Mary Ainsworth and her colleagues (e.g., Ainsworth 1969, 1979a, 1979b; Ainsworth et al. 1978) – attachment theory today is the predominant theory of infant social-emotional development. What has become crystal clear since its inception is that attachment is a *process*, not a state or a static bond; it is an ongoing, dynamic, interaction between infant and mother in which they cycle in and out of each other's company or attention repeatedly, many times a day, potentially for many years. These cycles of infant–mother interaction are worth closer examination because, as we shall see later, this cyclical process is at the interface of attachment theory and life history theory.

These cycles of attachment begin in early infancy, in what Tiffany Field (1985) called the process of "psychobiological attunement" (see also Field 1994; Hofer 1990, 1994; Pipp and Harmon 1987; Schore 1994; Stern 1977). Being immature and inexperienced with the world and their own bodies, young infants have difficulty modulating their own physiological and perceptual processes. Consequently, they are chronically prone to both overarousal and underarousal, both of which are manifestly upsetting, eliciting increased body movement, fretting, and then crying. The attachment process begins when, through sensitivity and responsiveness to infant signals, mothers provide an external regulating mechanism for these unruly physiological processes that young children cannot yet control. Through appropriate soothing when overaroused and stimulation when underaroused, mothers help their young infants to spend more and more time at an optimal level of arousal. Experiencing his mother's voice, touch, smell, and holding and carrying as she helps him achieve an appropriately higher or lower level of arousal, the infant is believed to form the "expectation" that when he is distressed by hypo- or hyperarousal, his mother will be there to help him modulate these sensations. Such "expectations" are believed to be represented in the infant's brain in the form of synaptic pathways connecting the amygdala, hippocampus, and related structures that mediate the experience of mother as both nonthreatening and a source of protection from his sometimes wild mood swings. In sum, as Allan Schore put it:

> The core of the earliest indelible internalized model of the self in relationship with an emotionally significant other, the substratum of self-identity, contains an expectation, a bias, that the primary attachment object will or will not remain available and accessible at times of hypo- or hyperstimulating affective stress. (1994:316–317)

Later, after children have matured sufficiently to experience fear or anxiety upon being separated from their mothers, the attachment cycle takes a more mature form (see Figure 3.1). This normally occurs in the second half of the first year. Whereas infants separated from their mothers (e.g., by adoption) prior to about 7 or 8 months of age generally establish new attachment relations easily, those separated from their mothers after this age are more likely to react strongly and take longer to establish new attachments (e.g., Yarrow 1967). Although there is little support today for the view that attachment formation is a critical period phenomenon, there is a consensus that the older a child is before starting to form attachments, the more difficult it will be (e.g. Sroufe 1988). Individual iterations of the mature attachment cycle, which may number in the tens of thousands during development, are conceived to begin with the child (say, an eight-month-old) at Bowlby's "set-goal" of proximity to mother. The experience of being close to mother is thought to engender what Sroufe and Waters (1977) term "felt security," i.e., the subjective "value experience" of feelings of safety and protection that constitute his "expectation" or "bias" about his future with his mother. In the terms of cognitive ethology, proximity to mother is said to "release" these feelings of security. In turn, these feelings of security serve as a releaser or trigger for the second phase of the attachment cycle. They give rise to the child's motivation to play or explore, to venture away from mother (psychologically, if not physically), to use her as a secure base from which to engage the world of objects and people. This leads to the third phase, that of separation anxiety. Although there are wide individual differences in separation anxiety, all children eventually show signs of insecurity or fear when they are separated from their mothers, either because they went too far from mother, for too long, or because they encountered something fear-provoking. Because novelty creates uncertainty, too much novelty by itself can be a potent source of fear. Having inhibited the child's inclination to play or explore, his rising anxiety then "releases" his motivation to approach his mother, which initiates the fourth phase of the cycle. This approach may be a literal, physical approach or it may be a symbolic approach. A physical approach reduces both the physical and psychological distance between mother and child, while a symbolic approach reduces just the psychological distance between them. A symbolic approach may be only a quick glance at mother, by which the child reassures himself that she is still there, or it may be an active vocalization or display in an attempt to elicit some overt response from her. The last phase of the attachment cycle is the reunion between mother and child – the way she responds to her child's literal or symbolic approach.

Mothers, of course, also move away from their children, so the preceding description of a "typical" attachment cycle is one-sided. What matters more than who separates from whom, however, are the reasons for such separations, whether they are more-or-less balanced, and especially how they are resolved when mother and child reunite. The attachment cycle is very much a dance of reciprocal approaches and withdrawals. Theoretically (and by some methods, empirically [e.g., Ainsworth et al. 1978]) the reunion phase of the attachment cycle is the nexus of the entire attachment phenomenon. Whether the mother or the infant separated from the other, the critical issue is whether the mother's response renews her child's sense of "felt security." If it does not – and this depends in part on the child's state (e.g., health, nutrition) and temperament as well as other demands on the mother – he may retain for some time the sense of insecurity or fear that led him to seek (or wish for) reunion with mother in the first place. Or, if she receives him roughly, rebuffs him, has

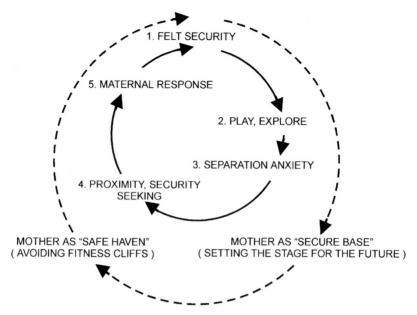

Figure 3.1 A schematic representation of the attachment cycle.

been inconsistent in her responses, or has been intrusive and interfered with his attempts to move away from her to explore (perhaps out of her own fear for his safety), he may become even more afraid and uncertain. He may then be psychologically inclined to defend himself against his feelings of fear and uncertainty, which are inherently unpleasant. But, if her response is sufficiently sensitive and accepting (and typical of her usual response), his sense of security is likely to be renewed and he will be motivated again to move away from mother to re-engage the world, thereby learning more about it – and simultaneously initiating another turn in the cycle of attachment (Bretherton and Ainsworth 1974; Sroufe and Waters 1977; see also Brazelton, Kozlowski, and Main 1974).

Foreshadowing arguments about the links between attachment theory and life history theory to be examined more fully later, it is important to emphasize (following Bretherton 1985) that, for all practical purposes, the attachment cycle is *continuously* active, with the child endlessly oscillating, as it were, between the pull of the environment (when he uses mother as a "secure base" from which to explore) and the pull of mother (when she is seen as a "safe haven" for reducing arousal when the child is frightened or tired from exploring). It is through the child's experience of many iterations of the attachment cycle, day in and day out, for months or years, that an attachment relation develops – and may change. To the extent that the general effect of these iterations is to allay the child's fear and foster his capacity to be "pulled by" (interested in) his environment, the stage has thus been set for the child to enjoy the delayed future benefits of exploring this environment.

Bowlby proposed that on the basis of their attachment experiences children construct "internal working models" of, first, themselves and their primary attachment figure and, later, of their social relations in general. Just as internal models allow complex adaptive systems "to look ahead to the future consequences of current action" (Holland 1992:25), internal working models are generalized *expectations* about "self-with-others," or *trust* (the absence or control of fear) in the benign availability of others to oneself, and in oneself as deserving or worthy of what one expects from others. Long before the cognitive science concept of internal model, however, Bowlby was led to his concept of internal working model in part by Craik's (1943) theory of mental representations, which (rather anticipating Popper) states:

> If the organism carries a small-scale model of external reality and of its own possible actions within its head, it is able to try out various alternatives, conclude which is the best of them, react to future situations before they arise, utilize the knowledge of past events in dealing with the present and future, and in every way to react in a much fuller, safer and more competent manner to the emergencies which face it. (1943:61)

Internal working models are simultaneously affective, cognitive, and perceptual. Representations of past events and perceived alternative courses of future action are thus construed to have emotional dimensions that affect interpretations of the present and the choice of alternative models of and for reaching the future. Once organized, internal working models of attachment tend to operate outside consciousness. Partly for that reason they are resistant, but not altogether closed to change – especially if one's experience also changes (e.g., Belsky and Cassidy 1994; Bretherton 1985; Main 1991; Sroufe 1988).

Not a great deal is known of the neurobiology of internal working models. However, because of (1) the central roles that danger, fear, and protection play in attachment theory, and (2) the amygdala's role in evaluating sensory information for danger, the amygdala is sure to be deeply involved (Crittenden 1997a; Schore 1994; Stansbury and Gunnar 1994). LeDoux's (1989, 1995) demonstration that the amygdala sends projections *back* to the sensory cortices from which it receives its primary data may identify the neural mechanism whereby children who experience too much fear are predisposed to be fearful – i.e., to form negative, distrustful internal working models of their relations with others. Because negative, distrustful internal working models of social relations often amount to self-fulfilling expectations, these back-projections may help to explain why internal working models are resistant to change. Another reason may be simply that the brain is more susceptible to early environmental influences than to later ones. This is because of the "overproduction" of synapses in infancy. The infant's brain is more susceptible to early experience because it has more synapses that experience can affect. Interacting with the environment "validates" the synaptic pathways that represent or instantiate that experience in the brain. Synaptic pathways that are not used are thus not validated, and are more likely to atrophy from disuse. Early experience matters more for development than later experience because by the time later experience arrives there are fewer synaptic pathways available to be validated (Changeux, 1985; Edelman 1987; Rakic 1995). To be sure, the rate at which synaptic pathways atrophy from disuse is slow, and new pathways can be laid down, so, while it may take time, it is possible for internal working models to change – if later experiences are sufficiently different from early experiences. Indeed, on the basis of his observation that early emotional memories are laid down in the amygdala before connections develop between the amygdala and the cerebral cortex, LeDoux speculates that "the role of therapy may be to allow the cortex to establish more effective and efficient synaptic links with the amygdala" (1995:229).

Although Bowlby–Ainsworth attachment theory holds that the psychobiological capacity for attachment is universal and innate, attachment itself is something that only emerges from these cycles of infant–mother interaction during ontogeny. Because infants, mothers, and the environments in which they interact are highly variable, there is a considerable range of individual differences in the patterns of attachment that are generated by these interactive cycles. Based on his observation of this range, Bowlby was convinced that sensitive and responsive mothering is critical for the development of what he believed was "normal," secure attachment and subsequent "normal" social-emotional development.

Individual differences in attachment

A quarter-century of research on individual differences in infant–mother attachment has largely sustained Bowlby's early clinical judgment. Notwithstanding the effects of child temperament and other factors on patterns of attachment (e.g., Crockenberg 1981; Goldsmith and Harmon 1994; Gunnar 1994; Gunnar et al. 1989; Kagan 1994; Kagan, Reznick, and Snidman 1988), there is a consensus that children whose mothers have been generally available, responsive, and accepting are more likely to use their mothers as both a secure base from which to explore and play, and as a safe haven, for comfort and reassurance, when they become upset. Such children are said to be securely attached. On the other hand, children whose mothers have been less available and responsive, or more intrusive or rejecting, are more likely to show an inability or unwillingness to play and explore, or to be comforted by their mother when they do become upset. Such children are said to be insecurely attached. As they grow older they are more likely to become anxious, aggressive, or depressed, or to develop difficulties in close interpersonal relations. Available longitudinal evidence indicates that these patterns are normally stable over at least the first decade in stable families, but they can change, in predictable ways, when the family environment changes (Belsky and Cassidy 1994; Elicker, England, and Sroufe 1992; Sroufe 1988; van IJzendoorn 1995). In low-risk samples, 60–70% of children are typically classified as secure and 30–40% are classified as insecure; even higher insecurity rates (60% or more) are reported in some cross-cultural studies and high-risk samples (Belsky and Cassidy 1994; Campos et al. 1983; Lamb et al. 1985). Most of this research has been based on Mary Ainsworth's (Ainsworth et al. 1978) Strange Situation[9] paradigm, or, more recently, Waters and Deane's (1985) Q-sort method. Both techniques, however, yield dimensions of secure vs. insecure attachment and tend to identify the same children as secure and insecure (e.g., Vaughn and Waters 1990).

In addition to this secure–insecure dimension of individual differences in attachment, research using Ainsworth's Strange Situation paradigm also consistently identifies two kinds of insecure attachment.[10] The first

---

[9] The Strange Situation test is a standardized laboratory procedure for classifying children by their attachment style or organization (secure, avoidant, anxious–ambivalent, etc.).

[10] In addition to the numerous subtypes that have been proposed for each of the 3 main attachment types, 2 additional main attachment types have been proposed as well. However, these 2 additional types have not been as well studied or validated in nonclinical samples as the original 3 and in any event seem to characterize a small number of children (Belsky and Cassidy 1994). I therefore concentrate on the three attachment types originally identified by Ainsworth.

is the *avoidant* pattern, in which children show little or no overt distress at separation from mother and do not seek reunion with her but instead focus their attention on toys and other apparent diversions from mother. In naturalistic observations, mothers of children who are later classified as avoidant are more likely to rebuff or reject their child's bids for attention, especially for physical contact, and/or to intrude insensitively (e.g., abruptly, noncontingently) on their child's ongoing activities. When their children are distressed, mothers of avoidant children may be as likely to *increase* their distress as to alleviate it. The second pattern of insecure attachment is the *ambivalent* pattern. Ambivalent children tend to be distressed prior to separation from mother, difficult to reassure, and seem so preoccupied with their mothers' moods or availability that they are disinclined to play or explore. In naturalistic observations, mothers of children who are later classified as ambivalent are not overtly rejecting but are more likely to be underinvolved with their children, or slow or inconsistent in responding (Cassidy and Berlin 1994; Isabella and Belsky 1991). However, while Strange Situation research consistently identifies these two types of insecure attachment, and there is some evidence that they have different developmental consequences (e.g., Cassidy and Berlin 1994; Main 1990; Shaver and Hazan 1994), their status remains unclear, for neither is predicted by attachment theory (Lamb et al. 1985), and neither is identified by Waters and Deane's (1985) Q-sort methodology.

Bowlby himself, along with many other attachment theorists, believed that sensitive, responsive mothers and their securely attached infants are nature's prototype, and that insecure attachment is, to some extent, abnormal and maladaptive. Ainsworth, for example, argued that

> . . . one major aspect of the environment of evolutionary adaptedness for infant attachment behavior is not merely a mother figure but one who is sensitively responsive to infant behavioral cues. (1979b:5)

Indeed, Ainsworth developed the neutral A–B–C nomenclature (for avoidant, secure, and ambivalent attachment respectively) because she hoped thereby to avoid stigmatizing A and C children or their parents as somehow deviant (Ainsworth et al. 1978). And Sroufe, who argues that the A and C patterns of attachment represent specific adaptations to particular environments, says none the less that "in an important sense they are *mal*adaptations" (1988:25; original emphasis). Moreover, as we will see later, there is evidence from many sources that the insecure attachments – avoidant and ambivalent – are indeed associated with later cognitive, social-emotional, and perceptual difficulties. We will also see that prospective laboratory studies of attachment behavior in bonnet macaques show that environmental stresses experienced by mothers have important consequences for the development of their young, including long-term effects on noradrenergic and serotonergic functions that mediate the experience of fear and anxiety. The attachment process is implicated as the specific mechanism of these maternal effects because the stressed mothers differed from controls in being more anxious and less consistently responsive to their young (Andrews and Rosenblum 1991; Rosenblum and Andrews 1994; Rosenblum et al. 1994; see also Suomi 1991). (I will have more to say about this work in chapter 5.)

Despite the apparent justification, however, evolutionary-minded skeptics have long resisted the implication that so-called insecure attachment is a disorder. Instead, they maintain, hominid infancy was not always as ideal as Bowlby imagined, and such a consistent pattern of individual differences in attachment, with such a high incidence of so-called insecure attachment, might well indicate potentially adaptive alternative developmental strategies rather than pathology.[11] The most complete articulation of this position has been by Michael Lamb and his colleagues, who argue that

> . . . in light of current theory in evolutionary biology, it is not easy to designate certain behavioral patterns as adaptive or maladaptive. Although not all behavioral patterns are equally adaptive, of course, it is clear that there is no single, species-appropriate pattern or template of behavior against which all other patterns can be evaluated. More plausibly, persons are equipped with a flexible repertoire, the selection from which depends on the specific environment in which he or she lives, the behavior of others, and the person's inherent characteristics . . . Viewed from this perspective, it therefore becomes important to specify *how* these alternative patterns may be adaptive under *what* caregiving circumstances. (Lamb et al. 1985:57; original emphasis)

[11] See, for example, arguments by Blurton Jones (1993); Crittenden (1997a); Dunn (1976); Freedman and Gorman (1993); Hinde (1982, 1983); Lamb et al. (1985); Main (1981, 1990); Tronick, Morelli, and Winn (1987).

What is overdue, then, is an evolutionary ecology of attachment organization. We need to understand the socioecological "caregiving circumstances" in which the capacity for the contingent development of so-called secure and insecure attachment – and possibly avoidant and ambivalent as well – would have been evolutionarily adaptive. The first attempt at such a model was proposed by Jay Belsky, Lawrence Steinberg, and Pat Draper (1991), who argued that the attachment process was an evolved developmental psychological mechanism for linking early experience with later reproductive functioning. Since their thinking has been the foundation for much of my own, I will review their model in some detail before presenting my particular life history theory version of it.

The Belsky, Steinberg, and Draper model
In 1982, Draper and Harpending provided an evolutionary interpretation of the "Absent Father Syndrome." Evidence from both Western and non-Western societies has consistently shown that when boys grow up in father-absent households they are more likely than father-present boys to display anger and aggression in a stereotypically confrontational, "hypermasculine" manner, to denigrate authority, and to adopt a manipulative, sexually exploitative attitude toward women. Absent-father girls, on the other hand, are more likely to display an early interest in sexual activity, to denigrate males and masculinity, and to show little ability or interest in maintaining a long-term sexual/romantic relationship with one man. (I describe the absent father syndrome more fully in chapter 5.) Draper and Harpending proposed that these behavior patterns are components of evolved but contingently expressed alternative male and female reproductive strategies. Because of the increasing impact of male parental investment on the survival and ultimate reproductive value of hominid juveniles, they reasoned, the development of human reproductive strategies evolved to be contingent on the presence of an investing male during a sensitive period in early childhood (roughly the first 5–7 years). In the absence of this critical male parental investment children's reproductive value would tend to be low, in which case the optimal reproductive strategy would likely be to reproduce early and/or at a high rate. The routine consequences of father-absence for each sex seem broadly consistent with this proposed adaptive function of favoring the production of offspring over their rearing.

Building on the work of Draper and her colleagues (Draper and Harpending 1982; Draper and Belsky 1990), Belsky, Steinberg and Draper (1991) proposed that the allocation of reproductive effort by adults is contingent not simply on the early presence or absence of father, but on the developmental effects of early psychosocial stress generally working through the attachment system. In brief, their model links (1) early family context, including relations with and between parents, with (2) parents' patterns and styles of interaction with children (e.g., sensitivity, responsiveness), (3) children's attachment organization (i.e., secure vs. insecure), (4) children's age at sexual maturation, and (5) their adult predispositions to emphasize either the production or rearing of offspring. When the early family context is one of stress (e.g., poverty, marital discord), parents are more likely to be preoccupied with their own concerns and thus relatively insensitive or unresponsive to their children. This places the children – especially those who are physically, temperamentally or socially vulnerable – at risk for the development of insecure attachment. Following standard attachment theory, Belsky et al. hold that children with a history of insecure attachment relations are at risk for developing insecure internal working models of themselves and attachment objects. In turn, they argue, these negative expectations of self and/or others will be associated in adulthood with what Skolnick (1986) described as "aloof and detached" or "clingy and dependent" styles in close emotional relations, and with earlier and/or wider sexual/emotional involvement with others. Following a suggestion by Barkow (1984), Belsky et al. also propose that early psychosocial stress is associated with early menarche in girls. In short, the Belsky et al. model holds that the attachment process functions to register early psychosocial stress and to entrain the development of the most appropriate alternative reproductive strategy under stressful conditions. In responding to the stressors in their own environment, parents create an emotional environment for their children that predisposes them to develop the optimal reproductive strategy in the kind of environment that they also inherit from their parents. This results in male offspring who tend to be aggressively competitive and exploit women and female offspring who tend to have children at an early age and difficult, unstable relations with men.

There is growing evidence that the Belsky et al. model captures some important realities of human development. I am going to postpone discussion of this evidence until later, however, because I want first to present an elaboration of their model that I derived from life history theory (Chisholm 1993, 1996a). The gist of my model is that the attachment process evolved to assess certain kinds of risk and uncertainty in children's "caregiving circumstances" and that these assessments function as an index of reproductive value that is represented phenotypically in the form of internal working models. I describe this model more fully in chapter 4, then in chapter 5 I present evidence that is broadly supportive of both the Belsky et al. model and my life history theory interpretation of it – i.e., that individual differences in internal representations of risk and certainty do indeed affect children's and adults' decisions about alternative courses of action in ways that are directly and indirectly related to the allocation of reproductive effort.

Risk, uncertainty, and attachment

Because juveniles cannot reproduce, the most immediate threats to their fitness are not to their reproduction, *per se*, but to the other two primary (and ontogenetically prior) components of fitness – their survival and their growth, development, learning, and all other preparations for reproduction. Because for juveniles the possibility of any future reproduction at all is always absolutely contingent on current survival and growth – and because hominid juveniles in particular are so helpless and take so long to grow – selection may be expected to have favored psychobiological mechanisms whereby hominid juveniles were better able to detect threats to their survival and growth and to respond by avoiding them and/or eliciting protection from others. In other words, because development is ultimately *for* reproduction, strategies for development may be thought of as incipient reproductive strategies.

What were the most predictable threats facing our developing ancestors? While it is increasingly appreciated that the EEA was neither as uniform nor as benign as Bowlby believed (e.g., Edgerton 1992; Foley 1992), it is perhaps not sufficiently appreciated that as each and every one of our ancestors entered the EEA – as newborn infants – the major source of the risk and uncertainty they faced was their *parents* (or their parents' suitors or new mates). Viewed from the perspective of those entering it, in fact, the EEA held certain risks that were surely recurrent and thus quite predictable – but whose *timing* was uncertain. Under such conditions, selection is expected to favor patterns of development that are sufficiently plastic so that the *nature* (i.e., structure, function) of adaptive alternative phenotypes is reliably contingent on, or appropriate to, the predictable risk itself. But because it is the *timing* of these recurrent, predictable risks that is uncertain, the actual *production* (instantiation, development) of locally appropriate phenotypes is expected to be contingent on any environmental cue that reliably indicates that one of these risks is actually impending

(Fagen 1982, 1993; Johnston 1982; Plotkin 1994; Stearns 1982). We saw earlier (pp. 67–68), for example, that when their mothers' food intake is restricted juvenile cats and rats engage in *more* play, thereby enabling them to "squeeze in" more play before they have to forage, prematurely, for themselves. In other words, we expect young mammals to be sensitive to environmental information that enables them to develop in ways that are appropriate to the conditions they will encounter in the future. For reasons to be developed more fully below, we might therefore expect selection to have favored the capacity of our juvenile ancestors to know their parents' moods, motives, and intentions – in short, to know their minds (that is, as we shall see in the next chapter, to have a *theory of mind*).

For Bowlby, predator protection was the ultimate explanation for attachment; in his words, "the function of attachment behaviour is protection from predators" (1969:224). It now seems certain, however, that the major threat to the survival and growth of our juvenile ancestors was not predators but parents. As many have argued, following Trivers' (1974) theory of parent–offspring conflict, the most adaptively significant feature of infants' environments is, and surely always has been, their parents' reproductive strategies (e.g., Bateson 1994; Belsky et al. 1991; Blurton Jones 1993; Draper and Harpending 1982; Hinde 1982; Lamb et al. 1985; Main 1990). More precisely, what matters to juveniles about their parents' reproductive strategies is the way they affect the quantity and quality of parental investment they receive. Viewed from the perspective of life history theory, then, the common individual differences in attachment that we observe today can be interpreted as facultative adaptations to parental behaviors that in the EEA were reliable indicators of what were surely two of the most persistent (and not mutually exclusive) threats to juvenile survival and growth, development, learning, and all other preparations for reproduction: parents' *inability* to invest in offspring and parents' (not necessarily conscious) *unwillingness* to invest.[12]

---

[12] Parental investment may be direct or indirect (e.g., Kleiman and Malcolm 1981). In the former, parental care is received *directly* by the young (e.g., feeding, carrying, grooming). In the latter, it is received only *indirectly* or circuitously, often in the absence of the parent (i.e., resource accrual, group defense). For Hillard Kaplan (1994) this distinction is the one between *care of* and *investment in* offspring, which helps to illustrate how pervasive is the trade-off between current and future reproduction: *care of* offspring tends to maximize their current fitness (i.e., it fosters survival and growth and development right now, in the present) whereas *investment in* offspring sets the stage for increased fitness at some time removed (i.e., it maximizes their potential for health, growth, development, and reproduction in the future).

From time to time throughout human evolution there were undoubtedly some parents who were *unable* to protect or provide for offspring simply because they lacked resources. Without doubt, from time to time there were also some parents who were *unwilling* (not necessarily consciously) to invest because their optimal reproductive strategy was to reduce or terminate parental investment, allocating their resources instead to other offspring with higher reproductive value, or to the production of additional offspring, thereby maximizing current reproduction.

According to the life history model of attachment presented here there is, consequently, no a priori, noncontingent, "normal" pattern of attachment; so-called secure and insecure attachment are both normal. On this view, secure attachment develops today as a facultative adaptation to consistently sensitive, responsive, and accepting parenting, because in the EEA this style of parental investment was reliable evidence that parents possessed both the resources and motivation to protect and provide for offspring for an extended period. Under the conditions of low environmental risk and uncertainty that would tend to support or enable such parental behavior, life history theory predicts that (*ceteris paribus*) the optimal reproductive strategy is likely to be the high-parenting effort strategy of maximizing future reproduction by investing heavily in relatively few offspring. On the other hand, according to this view, insecure attachment (both kinds, if there are two) develops today as a facultative adaptation to what we call insensitive, intrusive, unresponsive, or rejecting parenting, because in the EEA this style of parental behavior was reliable evidence that parents were unable and/or unwilling (not necessarily consciously) to invest in offspring. Under the conditions of high environmental risk and uncertainty that tend to make such parental behavioral styles more likely, life history theory predicts that (*ceteris paribus*) the optimal reproductive strategy is likely to be maximizing current reproduction by investing relatively little in many offspring.

Although we cannot exclude the possibility that the avoidant (A) and ambivalent (C) attachment styles are merely artifacts of the Strange Situation test (e.g., Lamb et al. 1985), they are, as mentioned, widely reported and do seem to have different developmental consequences. It also seems important to distinguish between parents' ability and willingness to invest, because these are among the most fundamental determinants of parental investment. The ability and willingness to invest in offspring are neither dichotomous nor mutually exclusive variables, however, and parents may be both unable and unwilling to invest.

Nonetheless, not only are even very young infants manifestly good observers of their parents' moods and apparent motivation (e.g., Cohn and Tronick 1983; Field 1994), it might be useful for infants to distinguish between motive and opportunity, as it were, because the optimal infant response to "able-but-unwilling" parents would seem necessarily to be rather different from the optimal response to "unable-but-willing" parents. Finally, while attachment theory seems to offer no a priori rationale for the existence of avoidant (A) and ambivalent (C) attachment types, life history theory may: avoidant attachment may represent a facultative adaptation to parental *unwillingness* (not necessarily conscious) to invest, while ambivalent attachment may represent a facultative adaptation to parental *inability* to invest.

In this model, secure, avoidant, and ambivalent attachment patterns have distinct ultimate as well as proximate causes; they are each *for* solving different adaptive problems. In terms of proximate causation, secure children are understood to use their mothers as a secure base from which to explore and play, and as a safe haven, for comfort and reassurance, when they have become fearful, because their mothers have been consistently sensitive, responsive, and accepting. In terms of ultimate causation, however, such consistent acceptance, sensitivity, and acceptance may have been a reliable indicator of his mothers' ability and willingness to *continue* investing in him in the future. To the extent that such consistency was a reliable indicator of the future flow of parental investment to a child, it would also indicate that he had a relatively high reproductive value. Everything else being equal, when the future seems certain – when there is little danger of falling off a cliff – the optimal strategy is to set the stage for future good fitness moves. Ultimately, this may be why secure children engage in more play and exploration (especially social play and exploration) than insecure children (e.g., Belsky and Cassidy 1994; Elicker et al. 1992; Main 1983) – because, as we have seen, play and exploration set the stage for increased adaptability and behavioral flexibility in the future (Fagen 1982, 1993; Johnston 1982).

To insecure children, however, the future is fearsome. In terms of proximate causation, insecure-avoidant children are thought to avoid their mothers out of fear, because their mothers have rebuffed or rejected them. In terms of ultimate causation, however, sufficiently frequent rejection may have been a reliable indicator of a mother's relative unwillingness to invest. The most common ultimate explanation for mammalian females' unwillingness to invest in offspring has probably always been that their better strategy was to allocate resources to already existing children with greater reproductive value, or to the production of additional offspring. The hallmarks of avoidant attachment – low expression of affect and literal avoidance of mother – might thus represent a facultative adaptation to caregivers who, regardless of ability or capacity, were unwilling to invest. For example, Nancy Levine (1987) tells the story of a Nepalese woman in an area where there had traditionally been a strong preference for sons. The woman gave birth to two sons, both of whom survived, and seven daughters, of whom only three survived. Her last child was a girl, and the woman was so enraged at having another daughter that she initially refused to feed it. Other relatives prevailed, however, and she ultimately gave in. Even so:

> The mother's bitterness again surfaced in a refusal to interact with the child or even name her. Instead she has called her daughter a succession of abusive terms, one of which was "Ready to Die." Yet the girl has not died and remains a healthy, if very quiet [avoidant?] child. (1987:292)

Nancy Scheper-Hughes (1992) describes similar (if less overt) rejection of sickly or weak children by chronically stressed, impoverished mothers in the *favellas* of Brazil. And just as human and nonhuman parents today intermittently reject, neglect, abandon, and kill their children,[13] so too, certainly, did our hominid ancestors.

The story is similar for insecure-ambivalent children. In terms of proximate causation, they are thought to be wary of, and preoccupied with, their mothers' moods and intentions because their mothers are under-involved or inconsistent. Although mothers of insecure-ambivalent children do not elicit fear by overtly rejecting their children, their inconsistency causes uncertainty, which is a natural source of fear, as is underinvolvement (e.g., Tronick 1989). In terms of ultimate causation, however, underinvolvement and inconsistency in the EEA may have been reliable indicators of a mother's relative inability to invest. The most common ultimate explanation for mammalian females' inability to invest in offspring has probably always been because their access to resources was limited or uncertain. On this view, anxious, wary preoccupation with mother represents a facultative adaptation for extracting resources (i.e.,

---

[13] See, for example, Boswell (1988); Freedman and Gorman (1993); Gomendio (1991); Hausfater and Hrdy (1984); Hrdy (1977, 1979, 1992); Levine (1987); Scheper-Hughes (1987, 1992); Smuts (1992); and van Schaik and Dunbar (1990).

felt security) from a mother who is irritable and preoccupied herself – with fear, hunger, or exhaustion.[14]

Table 3.1 is a schematic representation of the life history model of attachment being proposed. To develop it more fully I turn now to some examples of the threats and opportunities that parents' reproductive strategies may pose to their offspring. This will illustrate how individual differences in attachment might constitute adaptive responses to common individual differences in parents' abilities or willingness to invest.

Individual differences in attachment as incipient reproductive strategies

All things considered, when environmental risk and uncertainty are low the optimal reproductive strategy is likely to be maximizing future reproduction by investing heavily in a relatively few high-quality offspring. Under conditions of high risk or uncertainty, on the other hand, the optimal reproductive strategy is likely to be maximizing current reproduction by producing many offspring in whom one necessarily invests relatively little. And, as we shall see in chapter 5, there is abundant evidence that when parents today perceive that the environment in which they rear their children is one of low risk and uncertainty – that is, when they are more-or-less confident that they and their children will have an adequate flow of both material and social-emotional resources (including security and time, and reasonable prospects that things will continue as they are) – they find it easier (indeed, "natural") to be sensitive, responsive, and available to their children. There is also abundant evidence that when parents fear that they and their children will not have an adequate flow of material or social-emotional resources they find it less easy to be consistently sensitive, responsive, and available to their children.

---

[14] There may be an additional evolutionary rationale for expecting two kinds of insecure attachment. Even if avoidant and ambivalent children should fear their caretakers for different reasons – unwillingness versus inability to invest – the common denominator is still fear. And, as Marks (1987) has pointed out, vertebrates have evolved just four basic strategies for responding to danger: (1) flight, (2) hiding or freezing, (3) fighting back, and (4) submission. But, for obvious reasons, only two of these response strategies would seem to have much chance of success. Because they are so helpless, vulnerable, and dependent, infants and small children simply cannot effectively fight back against their parents or flee from them, except symbolically. They can, however, *avoid* them – hiding from them a little, not revealing their innermost needs or vulnerabilities, thereby achieving what Main (1981) called "avoidance in the service of attachment" – and they can submit to them, which is quintessentially an *ambivalent* response, for it entails maintaining contact with the very source of fear.

Table 3.1 A model depicting how the three main patterns of attachment organization might result from the interaction between parents' reproductive strategies and children's developmental (i.e., incipient reproductive) strategies.

Attachment classification	Parental reproductive strategy	Child's developmental (i.e., incipient reproductive) strategy
A. Insecure Avoidant	• Short-term • Unwilling to invest • High mating effort • Dismissing, rejecting of child	• Maximize current survival • Avoid rejecting, potentially infanticidal parent
B. Secure	• Long-term • Able and willing to invest • High parenting effort • More unconditionally accepting, sensitive, responsive to child	• Maximize future learning, quality of development • Maintain investment from "rich" parent
C Insecure Ambivalent	• Short-term • Unable to invest • Parenting effort with inadequate resources • Inconsistent, preoccupied but not rejecting of child	• Maximize rate of maturation; minimize age at first reproduction • Maintain investment from "poor" parent

From Chisholm 1996a.

On the view that development is ultimately *for* reproduction, this is not surprising. And on the view that human development is expected to be about the ontogeny of reproductively relevant future detectors and value detectors, this also makes sense. From a life history perspective, the ultimate reason why consistently sensitive and responsive parenting is today associated with secure attachment is that when infants in the EEA experienced consistently sensitive parenting (through their repeated experience of "felt security" in innumerable iterations of the attachment cycle) they also "sensed" (i.e., sensed emotionally) that their environments were low in risk and uncertainty – and that they thus had good reproductive value. The optimal reproductive strategy in such environments is likely to be high parental investment in relatively few offspring. But because infants and juveniles cannot expend reproductive effort, their only avenue to reproduction is through development. The optimal *developmental* strategy (i.e., incipient reproductive strategy) for secure infants would thus be to maximize future reproductive returns on their current growth and development. This may be the ultimate explanation of why securely attached children often do better than insecurely attached children in the realms of physical growth (e.g., Valenzuela 1990) as well as cognitive–perceptual and social–emotional development (e.g., reviews by Atkinson and Zucker 1997; Belsky and Cassidy 1994; Bretherton and Waters 1985; Lamb et al. 1985; Sroufe 1988; Wolkind and Rutter 1985). When their environments are low in risk and uncertainty, parents are more likely to be both able and willing to invest, and so neither child survival nor growth and development are threatened. Under such congenial circumstances, parents and children alike can allocate their resources to maximizing the "quality" of the child's development – i.e., to maximizing future returns on growth, learning, play, and exploration. As mentioned, future returns from present learning or play may accrue via increased behavioral flexibility (Fagen 1982, 1993; Johnson 1982). Future returns from present growth may accrue via accelerated maturation, for when young mammals encounter conditions that are favorable for growth it will generally be adaptive for them to reproduce early. This is because when populations are expanding – as they tend to when the availability of material resources favors growth – individuals who reproduce early have greater long-term fitness because their offspring are born earlier and thus start reproducing earlier themselves (Cole 1954). This may provide an ultimate explanation for why improved health and nutrition almost always lead to earlier menarche (Eveleth and Tanner 1990). (I will have more to say about age at menarche in chapter 5.)

Likewise, the ultimate reason that inconsistent, insensitive, unresponsive, or rejecting parenting is today associated with insecure attachment is that when our infant ancestors in the EEA experienced inconsistent, insensitive, unresponsive, or rejecting parenting (through their failure to experience "felt security" in sufficiently many iterations of the attachment cycle) they also sensed emotionally that their larger environments were high in risk and uncertainty – and that they thus had low reproductive value. From the standpoint of evolutionary psychology, in other words, the subjective experience of fear may be understood as the representation in the phenotype (the embodiment) of environmental risk and uncertainty. All else being equal, the optimal reproductive strategy under such conditions is likely to be to maximize current reproduction by producing many offspring while investing relatively little in each. But again, because immature organisms cannot expend reproductive effort, their only avenue toward reproduction is through development. The optimal *developmental* strategy (i.e., incipient reproductive strategy) for insecure children would thus be to maximize future reproductive returns on their current growth and development. When their environments are high in risk and uncertainty, parents are less likely to be completely able or willing to invest, and so either child survival or growth and development, or both, may be threatened. In such uncongenial circumstances, selection is expected to favor mechanisms enabling the child to make the best of a bad bargain – i.e., to increase his efficiency at eliciting resources and optimizing the critical trade-off between survival and growth and development and other preparations for reproduction.

Given that current reproduction is not an option, which alternative pattern of current growth and development offered the best returns on reproductive effort expended in the future would depend on which of the remaining two major components of fitness (survival or preparations for reproduction) were threatened most, and on the nature of the specific threat to each. For example, as mentioned earlier, when survival is under immediate and severe threat, the optimal strategy may be the complete cessation of growth and development on the chance that conditions improve; taking anything away from current survival would amount to stepping off a cliff. Under other conditions of threat to survival or growth, however, the optimal strategy may sometimes be to grow or mature rapidly, to minimize the total amount of time spent in a vulnerable developmental stage (Janson and van Schaik 1993; see also Bogin 1994, 1995; Rubenstein 1993). For example, Ellison (1990), Peacock (1990, 1991), and Worthman (1993), among others, have each argued that human females rely on information from the environment concerning threats to their health or growth as a basis for adjusting the amount or timing of resources allocated to future reproduction. As we will see in chapter 5, female reproductive capacity is generally delayed or scaled back following episodes of malnutrition, disease, or metabolic imbalance during development. Ellison (1990) hypothesizes that this "feed forward"[15] developmental process might have come about through selection for a mech-

---

[15] So-called because the effects of early stress at time 1 are "fed forward" into the future, affecting reproductive capacity at time 2.

anism for monitoring rates of growth and development. Because rates of growth and development are highly sensitive to nutritional and infectious perturbations, he argues, the rates themselves might have evolved to function as part of a "bioassay," on the basis of which conditions for future reproduction might be (unconsciously) predicted.[16] The same underlying "feed forward" mechanism that accelerates menarche under good conditions may be operating here, in the opposite direction, to delay menarche under poor conditions. (Again, more on menarche later.)

---

[16] Something like this may be the mechanism whereby kittens and rat pups whose mothers have been placed on restricted diets engage in more play, thereby gaining experience appropriate to the conditions they will encounter as a function of their early weaning (above, pp. 67–68).

4   Representing value

> [T]he substitution of the reality principle for the pleasure principle implies no deposing of the pleasure principle, but only a safeguarding of it. A momentary pleasure, uncertain in its results, is given up, but only in order to gain along a new path an assured pleasure at a later time.   Sigmund Freud (1911/1956:223)

> Among personality processes, the most vulnerable seem to be those underlying the ability to establish and maintain deep and meaningful interpersonal relations, and the ability to control impulse in the interest of long-range goals.   Mary Ainsworth (1965:219)

> Some for the Glories of This World; and some
> Sigh for the Prophet's Paradise to come;
> Ah, take the Cash, and let the Credit go,
> Nor heed the rumble of a distant drum!
>   Edward FitzGerald (1809–1883) (*The Rubáiyát of Omar Khayyám*)

Up to now I have presented my life history model of attachment in straightforward biological terms. Adopting the adaptationist perspective I argued first that the attachment process is *for* gaining knowledge about environmental risk and uncertainty in order thereby to gauge one's reproductive value and to adopt the local optimal developmental strategy. Since development is ultimately *for* reproduction, a strategy *for* development is an incipient reproductive (i.e., life history) strategy. Approaching attachment from biology's mechanist viewpoint, I then did a quick reverse engineering analysis of the attachment process to suggest that children gain knowledge of local environmental risk and uncertainty and thus their reproductive value primarily through the effects of "psychobiological attunement" and mutual sensitivity, responsiveness, and acceptance (or the lack thereof) in repeated iterations of the attachment cycle. Extending this reverse engineering to some of the actual neurobiological mechanisms that might be involved, I pointed out that each iteration of the attachment cycle is believed to help "validate" and thus preserve the synaptic pathways that mediate or instantiate the emotional tone (the value experience) engendered by that particular iteration. At least part of our attachment histories appear to be laid down (represented, embodied) in the amygdala and hippocampus where they may subtly and unconsciously yet insistently affect the way we "ascertain value" in close relationships throughout our lives.

In this chapter, however, I take a different tack. While maintaining my joint adaptationist–mechanist concerns, I am now going to look at my model through the lens of cognitive science. Because of recent advances in understanding children's theory of mind, cognitive science (or, better, what LeDoux [1996] calls "mind science"[1]) has developed compelling models of how children understand *intention* – what they and others are *going to do*. Since I believe that a large part of human development is about the ontogeny of reproductively relevant future detectors and value detectors I am necessarily concerned as well with children's understanding of intention, for when you know what someone *intends* to do you have detected the future. Depending on how you evaluate that imagined future, you may then act so as to approach or avoid it. Acting together, models *of* and *for reaching* the future reduce uncertainty. I also argued that during human evolution parents' ability and willingness to invest in offspring were the most important proximate determinants of children's reproductive value. Knowledge of one's parents' ability and willingness to invest would thus constitute extremely valuable knowledge of their intentions. And knowledge of their intentions would contribute enormously to knowledge of one's reproductive value.

We might therefore expect that selection would favor the capacity of juvenile hominids to know their parents' intentions. Accordingly, this chapter is devoted to two topics: (1) the nature and evolution of our ability to detect the future by reading each other's minds, and (2) the phenomenon of time preference, which is the extent to which people devalue or discount the future. Those who discount the future are more likely to value actions that have immediate or short-term pay-offs or consequences. Those who do not discount the future are more inclined to value actions that have delayed or long-term pay-offs or consequences. The crux of this chapter is the suggestion that time preference is an important part of our reproductive strategies and that individual differences in time preference

---

[1] "'Mind science' is the natural heir to the united kingdom of cognition and emotion. To call the study of cognition and emotion cognitive science is to do it a disservice" (LeDoux 1996:39).

are in part facultative adaptations that are produced by an evolved psychological mechanism for attaching reproductively relevant value to the alternative futures that our minds evolved to imagine. What follows is thus an exercise in what life history theory might look like as a theory of mind.

Detecting the future

In this section, I propose that three aspects of mind not ordinarily associated with each other may be different aspects or developmental stages of a single cognitive–emotional adaptation for detecting what is usually the most reproductively relevant aspect of our futures: other people's intentions. In the following section, I suggest that time preference can be thought of as the value that is placed on these images of the future. This value represents objective reproductive value. Reproductive value is an implicit, logical component of the environments of all organisms; it is the objective probability that a given organism in a given environment will leave descendants. Ultimately, emotions are the way that we experience this objective probability – the way that, during development, these objective probabilities become represented phenotypically, which is to say, subjectively experienced (Elzanowski's "value experience").

Internal working models, theory of mind, and Machiavellian intelligence
The three aspects of mind to be considered are: (1) the attachment theoretical concept of internal working model (mental representations of self and other in close emotional relationships), (2) the cognitive science concept of theory of mind, which Simon Baron-Cohen defined as "the capacity to attribute mental states to oneself and to others and to interpret behavior in terms of mental states" (1995:55), and (3) the evolutionary psychological concept of Machiavellian intelligence, which is essentially practical reason in the service of social relations. Building on the work of Nicholas Humphrey (1976, 1984), John Crook (1980), and others, Richard Byrne and Andrew Whiten (1988) proposed that a large part of human intelligence is "Machiavellian," in the sense that it evolved in response to selection for increased social skills in the ecological context of increasingly complex hominid social relations. Practical reason in the service of social relations is in many ways political reason, hence the adjective "Machiavellian." When viewed from the conjoined evolutionary/developmental perspective adopted in this book, internal working models, theory of mind, and

Machiavellian intelligence become different facets of an evolved developmental psychological algorithm for detecting the social future. From this perspective, children's capacity to form internal working models of emotional relationships evolved as part of the basic primate attachment process. In turn, the human capacity to form theories of mind is essentially an evolved elaboration of this basic primate capacity to form internal working models of attachment relations. Finally, the human capacity to form theories of mind – to interpret behavior in terms of our own and others' mental states – is the basis of our species' particular form of Machiavellian intelligence. I will expand on these points one at a time, working backwards from Machiavellian intelligence to theory of mind, then to attachment and internal working models.

Machiavellian intelligence (henceforth simply MI) is the ability to figure out what you, yourself, want, what others around you want, and how your own and others' beliefs and desires determine how you can best avoid stepping off a cliff and set the stage for valuable long-term projects. For Humphrey (1976, 1984) and most MI theorists (e.g., Bryne and Whiten 1988; Crook 1988, 1991; Whiten 1991), this is the primary adaptive function of human consciousness: the ability to be at least vaguely aware of the workings of our own minds enables us to use that self-awareness as a model for predicting and explaining the behavior of others. This ability to predict social behavior is what MI is all about. MI is different from, and more sophisticated or complex than, nonsocial intelligence because, unlike inanimate things, social beings are *reactive*, which means that social intelligence has to be *creative* in order to track and thereby *anticipate* the behavior of others, both opponents and partners.[2] In the words of Whiten and Byrne, the point of MI "is to predict the future on the basis of the past, but what is so special about the social context is that the data on which the predictions are to be based are highly changeable and contingent on one's own actions too" (1988:6).

A truly sophisticated MI would seem to require a theory of mind, for to predict the really interesting behavior of others it would help to have a model for generating such predictions. As Humphrey (1976) noted, the most obvious, readily available model of other minds is one's own. One way to predict the behavior of others would be first to explain one's own behavior, which, in turn, would seem to require attributing beliefs and

---

[2] One cannot help noting that "creative" is an anagram of "reactive." I mention this, of course, only to underscore the role that creativity plays in predicting the future.

desires to *oneself* (i.e., being aware of them) in order to construct the model whereby one predicts the behavior of others. This would make it very important not to confuse self and other. In John Crook's words:

> It would for example be cognitively confusing if an individual could not distinguish clearly between feelings attributed to another through empathy and those arising [in the individual] as a consequence of its own state; the ability to predict an action that would enhance its own condition would then be impaired. (1988:352)

All of this requires a theory of mind (henceforth ToM). ToM is essentially the psychological mechanism whose output is Dennett's (1987, 1995) "intentional stance" – i.e., the apparently universal, innate, and mostly unconscious, algorithm-like assumption that behind every behavior there is an *agent* who *means* or *intends* something by his or her actions.[3] The reason this capacity exists is that in nature agents really do have more-or-less good reasons for behaving. Human agents especially tend to *do* what they *believe* will achieve what they *want*, even if they are not always consciously aware of their beliefs and desires (or actions, for that matter). Because of this natural, biological association of belief, desire, and action, humans are thought to have evolved the capacity for "mind-reading," such that, when one knows any two of one's own or another's belief–desire–action triad, one can, in principle, then infer the one remaining unknown, and thereby predict or explain any agent's belief, desire, or action (Bennett 1991; Baron-Cohen 1995; Fodor 1983; Leslie 1987, 1994, 1995; Premack and Premack 1995).

If MI is figuring out one's best course of action based on predictions about other people's intentions, then ToM is the zenith of MI. But where does ToM come from? If the most important proximate source of risk and uncertainty facing our juvenile ancestors was their parents, as I have argued, then one possibility is that both ToM and MI have their origins in internal working models (henceforth IWMs) of attachment relations. On the view that parents' ability and willingness to invest were important correlates or determinants of their children's reproductive value, then perhaps the best way for children to avoid stepping off a cliff or to set

---

[3] The simplest definition of behavior is "movement." In any event it seems to be the one used by infants, who attribute causal agency to inanimate objects when they seem to move of their own accord (Dasser, Ulbaek, and Premack 1989; Premack 1990).

the stage for future good fitness moves would be to read their parents' minds.

The proposition that MI and ToM both evolved from some basic primate IWM is consistent with the Machiavellian view of attachment presented by Peter Marris (1991). He observes that, in eliciting what they want from their parents (parental investment), children seem to have two main strategies: "making a fuss," as he puts it, and "working the system." By "making a fuss" Marris means the child's assertion of will, which is to display anger. By "working the system" he means "understanding how to comply with the requirements of a relationship to achieve a desired result" (1991:79). Making a fuss and working the system are not mutually exclusive, of course, but, as Marris puts it, "the balance between assertion and compliance in a child's experience of attachment represents a fundamental learning about the nature of order and security . . . Learning to manage the attachment relationship therefore is learning to understand order and control" (1991:79). Understanding order and control is the essence of politics. And according to Trivers' theory of parent–offspring conflict, politics is precisely what we would expect to find in parent–offspring relations if, as he put it, "socialization is a process by which parents attempt to mold each offspring . . . while each offspring [is expected] to resist . . . and to attempt to mold the behavior of its parents" (1974:260).

The attachment relationship is thus nothing if not Machiavellian, and MI proper has its ontogenetic roots in the representations of "order and control" in social relations that are laid down in our early IWMs. Likewise, if ToM is the mechanism that makes it possible to attribute intentions to ourselves and others and thereby to determine our own best course of action, then ToM, too, is fundamentally about attempts to understand and to control social relations, and has its ontogenetic roots in IWMs as well. IWMs, MI, and ToM are *ultimately* (i.e., adaptively) all about predicting the social future in order to avoid stepping off immediately dangerous cliffs and to set the stage for distant but valuable futures. IWMs, MI, and ToM are *originally* (i.e., ontogenetically, historically) all about avoiding the dangerous cliffs indicated by parents' inability or unwillingness to invest and setting the stage for the valuable futures indicated by their continuing ability and willingness to invest. Since the only way that infants can gauge their parents' ability and willingness to invest is by interacting with them, IWMs, MI, and ToM are ultimately and originally social exchange monitors by means of which objective probabilities about possible defection or continuing co-operation are embodied (albeit imperfectly) as subjective expectations about self-with-others. From this perspective, ToM emerges as an evolved, special-purpose "social exchange monitor" of the sort envisioned by Leda Cosmides (1989; see also Scott and Baron-Cohen 1996), but one whose original special adaptive purpose was monitoring social exchange in attachment relationships. Secure attachment, as we have seen, arises from consistent mutual sensitivity and responsiveness in social exchanges between infant and mother. Insecure attachment results from inconsistency in these exchanges, when mother or child "defects" by failing, for whatever reason, to reciprocate with sufficient sensitivity or responsiveness.[4]

As we will see in a moment, there is empirical evidence for the existence of such a "social exchange monitor." However, to set the stage for this evidence it will help first to consider a scenario for the evolution of ToM. Whereas both nonhuman primates and humans are presumed to possess IWMs (Bowlby 1969) and MI (Byrne and Whiten 1988), only humans (and possibly chimpanzees) are believed to have ToM (Cheney and Seyfarth 1990; Povenelli and Preuss 1995; Premack and Woodruff 1978; Tomasello, Kruger, and Ratner 1993). This is consistent with the view that ToM's phylogenetic roots lie in the IWMs of juvenile hominids.

The evolution of ToM

What made the difference for the hominid line? Why do we have ToM and chimpanzees probably do not, or only in rudimentary form? The answer may lie among the factors that are widely believed to underlie the evolution of male parental investment and the family. These include, first, a long evolutionary history of K-selection among primates. As a consequence of this history, our ancestors were already growing more slowly and for longer periods than mammals generally (e.g., Charnov and Berrigan 1993; Gould 1977). Because normal juvenile helplessness was thus prolonged, our earliest ancestors probably already required relatively long periods of parental investment, which, as is the case for most mammals, would have come almost exclusively from females. On top of this, how-

---

[4] Parents are prone to defect when the child has low reproductive value and/or when the parents have high residual reproductive value (i.e., the capacity to invest in additional offspring). Children do not "defect," of course, but sometimes they are hampered in eliciting parental investment or forestalling its termination. Children with difficult temperaments or congenital abnormalities, for example, are sometimes less effective at maintaining their parents' interest. From the parents' perspective, such children may seem to defect or be "defective."

ever, the "obstetric dilemma" (Washburn 1960) resulted in even more help-less infants who took even longer to mature, thus requiring even more and longer parental (i.e., maternal) investment. The obstetric dilemma was the adaptive problem of reconciling two opposing selection pressures, one which had already favored narrowing the pelvis (including, of course, female pelves) as an adaptation for bipedal locomotion, and the other, which began to favor intelligence (perhaps MI in particular), and thus big brains, which led inevitably to infants with big heads.[5] The dilemma was how to accommodate ever-larger newborn crania through a birth canal already narrowed about as much as possible. The solution seems to have been selection for "shorter gestation,"[6] so that the infant could be born before its head grew too large to pass readily through the birth canal (Leutnegger 1974; Martin 1983; Trevathan 1987). The combination of a long evolutionary history of K-selection, the evolution of intelligence, and a relatively short gestation is believed to have resulted in hominid newborns who were extremely helpless at birth and who took many years to mature (Bogin and Smith 1996; Lancaster and Lancaster 1983, 1987).

This extreme and prolonged juvenile helplessness, in turn, is thought to have played a critical role in the evolution of male parental investment and the human family. Because of numerous anatomical and physiologi-cal adaptations females of most mammalian species are able to provide all of the resources that infants and juveniles require for survival and adequate growth and development. There has been no adaptive reason, therefore, for males of most mammalian species to allocate their time and energy to parental investment: there is really nothing they can do. Consequently, sexual selection on mammalian males has generally favored adaptations for allocating time and energy to *producing* offspring (maxi-mizing their quantity) instead of rearing them (maximizing their quality). At some point, however, our juvenile ancestors became so helpless, for so long, that mothers simply could no longer do all the work by themselves; they could no longer provide all the energy, nutrients, security, or infor-mation that their children required. When this happened the typical mammalian male reproductive strategy of maximizing copulations (i.e.,

---

[5] Relative to body size, the brain size of newborn humans is 1.33 times larger than that of great apes (Bogin and Smith 1996).

[6] In fact, selection did not *reduce* gestation length so much as *prevent it from increasing* as much as it might have otherwise, due to general K-selection for longer and slower growth throughout the life cycle. Some estimates are that if human gestation were proportion-ately as long as it is in other primates it would last 21 months (see Gould 1977).

the production of offspring) would have become less effective because hominid females were increasingly unable to provide all the parenting effort required while at the same time maintaining a replacement-level reproductive rate. But if the evolution of increasingly helpless infants and juveniles tended to reduce the fitness of males who attempted only to maximize number of offspring by maximizing number of sex partners, it would also tend to increase the fitness of males who were able and willing to invest more in infants and juveniles, if only indirectly, through their mothers (Trivers 1972). The evolution of prolonged juvenile helplessness meant that, for the first time, hominoid males could have a positive impact on the reproductive value of their offspring. The optimal trade-off between quantity and quality of offspring for at least some males thus began to be biased more toward quality (Dunbar 1984; Kleiman and Malcolm 1981; Van Schaik and Dunbar 1990; Wittenberger and Tilson 1980). Whether or not it was the "initial kick" that got everything started, the evolution of prolonged juvenile helplessness, together with closely related evolutionary changes in male–female sociosexuality (e.g., loss of estrus, increased female choice, the sexual division of labor and sharing), is bound to have been critical for the evolution of the human family.[7]

The selection pressures arising from the evolution of profoundly helpless and demanding juveniles, however, would operate on the juveniles themselves as much as on their parents. In other words, selection would work not only on those in a position to *bestow* parental investment, but also on the capacity of infants and juveniles to *elicit* it. This may be why human infants are motorically highly altricial, on one hand, but on the other are cognitively and perceptually precocial as well (e.g., Konner 1991). While motorically helpless hominid infants and juveniles could not fend for themselves physically, they may have done so psychologically, eliciting parental investment with their nascent Machiavellianism – i.e., using their increasing cognitive and perceptual skills "to understand order and control" (as Marris put it) and "to mold the behavior of parents" (as Trivers put it). One reason, then, why humans have ToM and chimpanzees probably do not, or only in rudimentary form, may also be the reason why humans have a great capacity for male parental investment and the family: just as increased investment was an adaptation for *parents* to reduce the adaptive problems posed by helpless juveniles, ToM

---

[7] For example, Hrdy (1981, 1997); Lancaster and Lancaster (1983, 1987); Lancaster (1997); Lovejoy (1981); Rodseth et al. (1991); Smuts (1985, 1992, 1995); Smuts and Gubernick (1992).

was an adaptation for helpless *juveniles* to adapt to and contain their own helplessness. On this view, ToM evolved from ancestral IWMs of attachment as an especially sophisticated social exchange monitor that helped hominid juveniles to avoid the fitness cliffs posed by parents who might defect (because they were unable and/or unwilling to invest) and approach the future represented by parents who continued to co-operate (because they were still able and willing to invest). Later, as our juvenile ancestors reached adulthood, they could scarcely avoid using their pre-existing IWMs and ToM skills to monitor all of their social exchanges in the same sort of Machiavellian way. IWMs, MI, and ToM may thus be aspects of a single mind tool that makes it possible for Gregorian Creatures to create internal models of their social worlds out of the beliefs, desires, and intentions that they find in their own and other people's minds.

There are two converging lines of evidence that are broadly consistent with this interpretation of ToM: (1) neurobiological evidence that critical features of ToM are localized in the evolutionarily recent prefrontal cortex, and (2) behavioral evidence that individual differences in ToM are related to individual differences in security of attachment and measures of empathy. Before describing this evidence I should mention that the primary diagnostic of children's capacity to read minds is their ability to predict a person's behavior by attributing a *false belief* to that person. This is taken as evidence of ToM because, as Simon Baron-Cohen expressed the idea (first proposed by Dennett 1978), "in such cases it becomes possible to distinguish unambiguously between the child's (true) belief and the child's awareness of someone else's different (false) belief" (1995:70). Except where there is pathology (notably autism, as we shall see), this mind-reading capacity seems to be universal, emerging at around age four (Wellman 1990; Wimmer and Perner 1983).

The neurobiology of ToM
First the neurobiology. Goel et al. (1995) used a brain-imaging technique to identify regions of the brain that were activated when adult subjects were asked to engage in various kinds of mental activity: attending to the visual and semantic attributes of familiar objects, imagining the function of unfamiliar objects, and (the ToM task) imagining what *another* person might think the function of these objects was. They found that the left medial frontal lobe was uniquely activated when the subjects were asked to model (imagine what was in) another person's mind. Consistent with the view that ToM is limited to humans (and maybe chimpanzees),

Preuss (1995) suggests on comparative anatomical grounds that the prefrontal cortex may not even exist in other animals, and that, in any case, the lateral prefrontal cortex exists only in primates and is considerably larger in humans than other primates.

Additional support for the proposition that ToM constitutes a special-purpose social exchange monitor, some critical components of which are located in the prefrontal cortex, comes from the study of childhood autism. The central cognitive–emotional deficit of autism is now conceived as a "defect of empathy" (Brothers 1989) that makes it difficult for autists to understand others' beliefs and desires, and therefore their intentions. An understanding of others' intentions is considered to be the result or "output" of what Alan Leslie (1994) calls ToMM, a "theory of mind mechanism" that produces domain-specific learning about the intentions of "agents." Failure of this mechanism is thought to be the underlying cause of autism (Baron-Cohen 1995; Baron-Cohen, Tager-Flusberg and Cohen 1993; Leslie 1994, 1995). Consistent with this view, when Charman and his colleagues (1997) compared autistic children to developmentally delayed and normally developing children on a range of behaviors they found that, compared to the others, the autistic children were specifically impaired in aspects of behavior that were associated conceptually with ToM. For example, the autistic children were less able or willing to engage in joint attention with other children or to imitate them. Joint attention is conceived to involve ToM because in the absence of some understanding that another child *intends* to look at some object the autistic child has no particular reason to look at it too. Likewise, in the absence of some understanding that another child *intends* or *means* something by acting in a certain way, the autistic child has no particular reason to exhibit that same behavior. When Scott and Baron-Cohen (1996) compared autistic children, mentally handicapped children, and mental age-adjusted normal children on measures of reasoning that did not involve ToM, they found that the autistic children performed just as well as the other children. This means that the autistic children's deficits did not extend to general cognitive skills, but were specific to understanding mental states. In a related study, Baron-Cohen and his colleagues (1994) also found that autistic children were significantly less able than mentally handicapped children to recognize mental state terms, which suggests that this skill is related to ToM. Using a brain-imaging technique, they then found that when normal adult subjects were presented with these same mental state terms there was unique activation in the orbital prefrontal cortex, suggesting that impairments in both the prefrontal cortex and ToM are involved in autism.

The prefrontal cortex is the apparent site of working memory, which is the capacity to hold in mind representations of the world that are necessary to carry out any action. This includes the capacity to hold in mind representations of our own and others' beliefs and desires as a basis for determining our best course of action. As we will see in more detail shortly, this centrally involves the processing of information involved in delayed response tasks – i.e., in *inhibiting* behavior – for, to *plan* a task, to *set the stage* for some future action, it is always necessary first *not* to carry out the intended action or any other that would defeat its purpose (Fox 1991; LeDoux 1996). LeDoux, for example, notes that patients with prefrontal cortical lesions are wrapped up in the present and "unable to project themselves into the future" (1996:177). Pihl and his colleagues also implicate the prefrontal cortex and working memory in the capacity to "project" oneself into the future. They found that, compared to normal controls, boys who had difficulty inhibiting aggression (i.e., were more impulsive) scored lower on tests of both frontal lobe function and working memory (Harden and Pihl 1995; Pihl and Peterson 1996).

The evolutionarily recent prefrontal cortex seems thus to embody ToM. When ToM functions normally it produces human MI, which enables us to know our own and others' beliefs, desires, and intentions (imperfectly, of course) so that we can (sometimes) make good decisions about behavioral alternatives, thereby avoiding cliffs as well as setting the stage for valuable long-term projects. As we have seen, however, the "goodness" of a decision may reside ultimately in its objectively probable impact on reproductive value. In turn, this probable impact on reproductive value may be represented, at least in part, in the amygdala, where, beginning in infancy, automatic evaluation processes attach subjective feelings of security (good) and danger (bad) to essentially all incoming sensory information – perhaps especially images of other people's intentions (i.e., the social future) provided by IWMs and then ToM. To make good decisions, therefore, the prefrontal cortex would seem to need access to information about value from the amygdala. And, in fact, as LeDoux puts it, connections between the prefrontal cortex and amygdala "play key roles in planning and executing emotional actions" (1996:177).

In sum, human MI would seem to consist of (1) ToM (to explain and predict behavior); (2) the prefrontal cortical capacity to inhibit behavior (in order to set the stage for a valuable future); and (3) good connections between the prefrontal cortex and the amygdala (because what makes something valuable or not is subjective value experience, which involves the amygdala and the rest of the emotional brain). As Damasio argues in his somatic marker hypothesis, the emotional brain represents ("marks") the "body's interests," about which the evolutionarily recent prefrontal cortex was selected to make good decisions (i.e., to be rational). It may be difficult then to be fully Machiavellian – to act strategically with regard to one's (body's) interests – without some capacity to delay or inhibit behavior. Certainly, when there is no capacity to delay or inhibit behavior there is no way to act strategically; one can only make tactical responses to events, and cannot influence them by setting the stage for future moves by being creative.

Attachment, ToM, and empathy
The other line of evidence that is consistent with the idea that ToM evolved in hominids as a specialized mechanism for monitoring parents' intentions comes from research relating individual differences in attachment to measures of ToM and, what is perhaps its chief product, feelings of empathy. If ToM evolved out of a basic primate or great ape mechanism for producing IWMs, then this is what would be expected, for empathy clearly involves ToM, which is "the capacity to attribute mental states to oneself and others" (Baron-Cohen 1995:55). To know another's intentions we must know their beliefs and desires; just as language provides a way to know another's beliefs, empathy provides a way to know their desires. For Otto Fenichel, "Empathy consists of two acts: (a) an identification with the other person, and (b) an awareness of one's own feelings after the identification, and in this way an awareness of the object's feelings" (1945:511; quoted in Brothers 1989:11). And, as we have seen, autists are believed to suffer from a "defect of empathy" that is caused by deficits in ToM. What is more, as we shall see, there is considerable evidence that the attachment process is related to individual differences in children's capacity for empathy. The capacity for empathy, then, would seem to be related to the capacity for inhibition, for, to feel empathically what we imagine another person is feeling, it may be necessary first to inhibit our own feelings, if only for an instant.

Peter Fonagy's research group is exploring the relationship between attachment and ToM. They note that most of the research on ToM has come from a social-cognitive developmental perspective that treats the child as an "isolated processor of information engaged in the construction of a theory of mind from first principles" (1997a:52). They argue, on the other hand, that because ToM is inherently an "intersubjective process" measures of interpersonal *affective* development are bound to be related to the children's development of ToM and understanding of emotions (Fonagy 1991; Fonagy et al. 1991). Following Mary Main (1991), among others, they propose an attachment model of the development of ToM in which the mother entrains ToM by "behaving towards the child in such a way that leads him or her to postulate that their own behavior may best be understood through the assumption that they have ideas and beliefs, feelings and wishes which determine their actions and the reactions of others to them" (1997:52). Main and her colleagues (Main 1991; Main, Kaplan and Cassidy 1985) report that both children and adults with secure attachment histories not only give more coherent, elaborate, and accurate narrative accounts of attachment relations than those with insecure histories, they are also better able to reflect upon and perform mental operations on these accounts – what Main calls "metacognition." "In other words," as she put it, "experience with the parents may not only alter the *contents* of the young child's mind, but may also alter *her ability to operate upon these contents*" (1991:129; original emphasis). In theory, because they are not so threatened by their own automatic evaluations of the images that make up their IWMs, children with secure attachment histories find them easier to hold in mind, and so come to have more experience in manipulating these models of attachment relations. As a result, these models may become more complex, sophisticated, and realistic than those of children with insecure attachment histories, whose IWMs contain more fearful images that, like cliff edges, must be avoided.

Putting this idea to the test, Fonagy and his colleagues (1997a) assessed attachment security in 77 British preschoolers and young school-age children, along with their ToM competence (specifically, their ability to predict the behavior of a story character based on knowledge of the character's beliefs and desires). Security of attachment was strongly correlated with performance on the belief–desire ToM task, even after controlling for the effects of the children's chronological age, verbal mental age, and rankings of their social maturity. In another study Fonagy (1996) assessed the adult attachment[8] style of 200 mothers and

---

[8] "Adult attachment" refers to the attachment organization of adults – whether adults are secure or insecure in their emotional relations with others, especially romantic/sexual relations (e.g., Main et al. 1985; Shaver and Clark 1996).

fathers during the mothers' third trimester of pregnancy. When the children were 18 months old, assessments were made of family stress and deprivation as well as parents' metacognitive capacity (i.e., their capacity to reflect upon their own beliefs and feelings). Children's attachment security was then assessed, along with measures of ToM development at several ages. Parents' adult attachment style assessed before the children were born was strongly related to children's attachment style assessed up to five years later. In addition, parents with good metacognitive skills tended to be secure in their attachment relations and, as predicted, had children who developed ToM more quickly.

Support for the idea that attachment history affects ToM is also found when different measures of ToM are used. For example, children who have been maltreated by their parents are consistently found to be at risk for insecure attachment (Cicchetti and Carlson 1989; Cicchetti, Ganiban, and Barnett 1991). In a study of children's spontaneous speech (Beeghly and Cicchetti 1994), maltreated children produced significantly fewer words and types of words referring to their own and others' emotional states than carefully matched nonmaltreated controls. Having fewer words to refer to these mental states, or being less willing to use them, is consistent with the proposition that maltreated children have relatively impoverished and/or painful theories about the nature of other people's intentions or what these intentions seem to imply about their own value to these other people. In a similar study of the relation between attachment security and ToM, but with older subjects and looking at adult attachment, Feldman and Downey (1994) assessed the attachment styles of two groups of young adults who had been exposed to family violence during childhood. One of the groups scored high on a measure of "rejection sensitivity" while the other scored low. Whereas exposure to family violence is typically a risk factor for insecure adult attachment, in this study those who had been exposed to family violence – but had also scored low on rejection sensitivity – were significantly more likely than those who scored high to show the secure adult attachment style. Rejection sensitivity is considered a manifestation of ToM because it is construed as a set of assumptions about other people's intentions toward oneself and/or what these intentions might imply about one's value to these people (e.g., "Other people reject me. Therefore I must be worth rejecting"). In this example, any distinction between IWMs and ToM is hard to see.

If empathic feelings are mediated by ToM (as both the behavior and neurobiology of autistic children suggest), and ToM develops in part through the attachment process, then children with secure attachment histories should be more empathic. Sroufe (1983; Sroufe and Fleeson 1986) and Kestenbaum, Farber, and Sroufe (1989) report that children who were securely attached as infants were judged by their preschool teachers several months later to be more empathic with other children. Likewise, Denham (1994) found that securely attached 4-year-olds were more empathic, both with their mothers and with each other. Because empathy facilitates social interaction, it is important to note as well that securely attached children are regularly found to be more socially competent than children with insecure attachment histories. Schulman, Elicker, and Sroufe (1994) report that preadolescents who had been securely attached as infants were more socially competent with peers than those who had insecure early attachments. Likewise, in a follow-up study of 39 German 5-year-olds who had been classified by attachment style in infancy, Suess, Grossman, and Sroufe (1992) found that overall peer competence was significantly related to attachment history. Moreover, the securely attached children did better on a test of social perception than the insecure children, who were more likely to misattribute negative intentions to others. Troy and Sroufe (1987) also found that children with secure attachment histories exhibit more positive affect and are more socially competent with peers, including less often being a victim or victimizing others. The empathic capacity to enter into the minds of others – to see things from another's perspective – is to have a theory of mind. This ability to see things from another person's perspective may even explain why 19-month-old children with secure attachment histories are better able than insecure children to recognize themselves in mirrors when their noses have been daubed with rouge (Schneider-Rosen and Cicchetti 1984). Finally, because individual differences in attachment have been related to ToM, as we have already seen, it is interesting to note, too, that 3-year-olds who correctly attributed a false belief to another person were judged by their teachers to show more mature social behavior than those who did not (Lalonde and Chandler 1995).

Are securely attached children more empathic because they are better at inhibiting competing feelings that might preclude empathy? In order to be empathic – to feel what another person feels – it may be necessary first *not* to feel what one was already feeling, or might otherwise have felt, if only for an instant. It is not clear how well or fully we can feel two emotions at once – especially when one of them is another's. With only one body, however, it is difficult indeed to *act* on the basis of two different sets of beliefs and desires. As John Crook said, it would be "cognitively confusing" if we could not tell the difference between feelings that we attribute to others empathically and those that arise in us as a consequence of our own unique bodies and experience.

The capacity to inhibit our feelings, or to delay the gratification of acting on these feelings, thus seem to be critical components of ToM and empathy. What is more, from this perspective empathy emerges as somewhat risky. When we see the world (including ourselves, of course) the way that we think another person does, when we take on their beliefs and desires, we inevitably expose ourselves to a degree of risk and uncertainty. First, we risk experiencing any negative feeling that we might attribute to them; we risk feeling their fear, their loneliness, their loss. In addition, to feel their negative feeling we may first have had to give up a pre-existing feeling of pleasure or security, if only for a moment. Second, we risk experiencing our own automatic negative evaluation of the image of ourselves that we might attribute to them; if we attribute to them the belief that we are unworthy, we risk automatically evaluating this image of ourselves as unworthy or dangerous (bad). Third, because of the natural association of belief, desire, and action (or intention to act), when we inhibit our own beliefs and desires in order to take on those of another we may be forced to forego or delay carrying out the action that was implied by these very beliefs and desires that we inhibited. Most of the time this probably does not matter, but, as a general rule, when we delay acting on our beliefs and desires we expose ourselves to uncertainty, for the future is inherently uncertain and the longer we delay action, the less our beliefs may correspond to the reality that they were supposed to represent. Delay exacerbates the very uncertain futures problem that IWMs, MI, and ToM evolved to reduce; in dangerous, uncertain environments delay exacerbates it even more.

Empathy can thus be risky. But this may be the price that Gregorian Creatures have to pay for the capacity to see what is in other minds. By risking empathy we can know something of other people's desires. When we have the capacity to give up some of our short-term security to feel empathically how other people feel, we are better able to deduce their intentions and thereby set the stage for valuable long-term social projects. This may be why securely attached children are more socially competent. Being more secure, they are more likely to learn that their future happiness or security can be improved by a modest short-term effort on their part to act empathically toward others (Zahn-Waxler, Radke-Yarrow, and King 1979). Insecure children, on the other hand, may be less competent socially because they have negative emotional memories of exposing themselves to the risk of finding out what's in other minds, and are more protective of their current feelings of security as a result. If individual differences in attachment are related to empathy, then the attachment process may be implicated as well in the development of individual differences in the critical capacity to inhibit or delay behavior – i.e., in time preference.

Evaluating the future

For organisms to effect the purpose for which they were designed (i.e., leaving descendants), decisions must be made. Ultimately, this is because the resources (energy, security, time, etc.) required to leave descendants are always limited, while selection always presses on regardless for more descendants. From this fundamental tension between the laws of life and the laws of physics emerges the assumption of optimality: the expectation that selection will favor mechanisms (physiological, psychological, developmental, etc.) for optimizing the trade-offs among the components of fitness (survival, growth and development, and reproduction) over the life cycle. To "optimize a trade-off" is to make decisions about how to allocate limited resources so as to produce the best phenotype possible given existing constraints. Thus, as we saw in chapter 2, to understand the phenotype of any organism we need to view it as "a series of *choices* among alternatives, in which the *decisions* reached were those *deemed best* by the designers" (Dennett 1995:230; original emphases). We also saw in chapter 2 that one of the most important or pervasive trade-offs is the one between current and future reproduction. We might therefore expect mechanisms or algorithms for making decisions about the relative value of the present versus the future – i.e., for evaluating the future.

Time preference

One way that people manifest their evaluations of the future is through their time preference. Time preference is the degree to which people prefer to or believe they will achieve their desires (i.e., the benefits or consequences of action) now, more-or-less immediately, or later, at some point in the future. Known as the discount rate in economics, time preference also goes under the names of intertemporal choice, impatience, impulsiveness, self-control, and ability to delay gratification. People who prefer their gratifications to be immediate are said to be impulsive and to lack self-control; they seem not to care about the future and are said thus to discount or devalue it.

For a classic illustration consider the pair of choices shown in Figure 4.1 below. When asked whether they would prefer to receive $100 in 28 days or $120 in 31 days (Choice A), most people chose the larger, delayed option. However, when presented with Choice B – whether they would prefer to receive $100 now, immediately, or $120 in 3 days time – most people chose the smaller but immediate reward. Why the inconsistency? Both choices are between $100 at Time 1 and $120 three days later, at Time 2, and so are equivalent. The answer seems to be that after already waiting 28 days, most people find it easy to imagine waiting just three more for a larger reward. But for most people the prospect of $100 *right now* is more salient, more compelling than $120 after the same three day wait. When tempted with an immediate reward of this sort, most people lose their self-control, and succumb to impulse, acting as if they devalued the future.

Most people, in other words, are predisposed to avoid the uncertain futures problem; they are *risk-averse*: averse to the risks that the future holds. As was mentioned in passing in chapter 3, there is extensive evidence that people and animals alike are generally risk-averse – i.e., more concerned to avoid losses (what assurance do I have that you *really will* give me $120 in three days?) than to obtain equivalent gains (since the

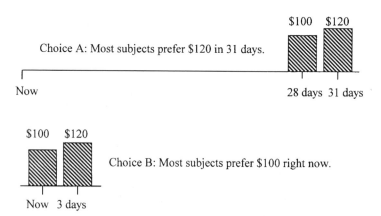

Figure 4.1 The primacy of immediate reward (after Frank 1992).

future is uncertain I will settle for only $100 now).[9] As was also mentioned in chapter 3, the reason that immediate rewards seem so attractive may ultimately be that in evolution, as in all complex adaptive systems, the cost of stepping off a cliff is always greater than the benefit of setting the stage for some future good fitness move. This may explain why the probability of lineage extinction is more sensitive to having *few* offspring than it is to having *many* (Keyfitz 1977). Unless there was a particular reason *not* to opt for some short-term benefit, then, organisms that were more sensitive to immediate costs and benefits than to those in the future would tend to leave more descendants. This is probably the ultimate reason why risk-aversion is "one of the most robust regularities in experimental psychology [and] is apparently part of the hard wiring of most animal nervous systems" (Frank 1992:279).[10]

This is surely the ultimate explanation as well for what Aristotle called *akrasia* – the "weakness of will" that all too often leads us to choose momentary pleasures even when we know their negative long-term consequences. Risk-aversion – i.e., having a short time preference – is thus deeply implicated in our sins of commission: our impulses to have just one more chocolate, one more drink, or (more ominously) to enjoy the rush of adrenalin when we push hard on the accelerator, smash the shop window, or pull the trigger. Weakness of will also leads us all too often to avoid momentary discomforts or insecurities, even when we know we should endure them. Having a short time preference is thus deeply involved as well in our sins of omission: our failure to exercise, to

---

[9] See, for example, Ainslie (1975, 1992); Kacelnik and Bateson (1996); Kahneman and Tversky (1979, 1984); Kahneman et al. (1982); Loewenstein and Elster (1992); Tversky and Kahneman (1981).

[10] This may also explain why, paradoxically, animals seem risk-*prone* for certain kinds of risk. In their review of 59 studies of the effects of risk on the foraging decisions of animals, Kacelnik and Bateson concluded that "when risk is generated by variability in the *amount* of reward, animals are almost always risk-averse [but] when variability is in *delay* to reward animals are universally risk-prone" (1996:402; emphasis added). For example, when pigeons are given a choice of two levers to peck – one of which releases water after a fixed delay of 15 seconds and the other after a variable delay that none the less *averages* 15 seconds – they prefer the variable ("risky") delay. Hard-pressed to explain why animals are risk-averse for amount of reward but risk-prone for delay, Kacelnik and Bateson suggest that risk-proneness for delay might not be an adaptation like risk-aversion for amount, but only "a by-product of the way animals learn" (p. 431). Risk-proneness for delay, however, may be just a special case of overall risk-aversion, for in choosing the variable-delay lever pigeons actually ensure that *half the time* they receive their reward in *less* then 15 seconds. If pigeons were predisposed to value immediate rewards over equal but delayed rewards this would be expected.

save for our children's education, or to use a condom. And *akrasia* is as much a social problem as it is personal. Individual impulsiveness, for example, has been implicated in such pressing social concerns as drug addiction, HIV infection, young male violence, teenage pregnancy, high infant mortality, child abuse and neglect, crime, and low educational attainment.[11]

Short time preference is virtually diagnostic of chronic poverty and inequality. Oscar Lewis (1959, 1967), for example, argued that people who live in the "culture of poverty" are chronically "present oriented." And Edward Banfield noted in *The Unheavenly City Revisited* that the poor have "an outlook and style of life which is radically present-oriented and which therefore attaches no value to work, sacrifice, self-improvement, or service to family, friends, or community" (1974:235). In a similar vein, Sutti Ortiz observed that in the face of chronic uncertainty concerning their ability to market their crops, Indian peasant farmers in the highlands of Colombia preferred to avoid risk rather than seek profit. (Ortiz argues, however, that this is not because they are risk-averse *per se*, but because they lack the information to generate realistic models for obtaining profit: "Habitual behaviour can be a consequence of total inability to formulate an expectation rather than a preference for safety" [1979:77].)

But, as Alan Rogers (1994), Brian Vila (1994, 1997) and others have noted, while we would all clearly benefit from policies for reducing poverty, inequality, drug addiction, teenage pregnancy, etc., such policies are difficult to enact because they appeal to our own *akrasia*: we fail to vote for them precisely because we, too, are weak-willed; they require some immediate sacrifice while offering us only delayed, and hence devalued, benefits. Short time preference is thus also deeply implicated in the social, economic, and environmental degradation brought about by business and government leaders (and those who support them) whose primary concern is short-term gain in the next quarterly report or election. The concept of a "culture of poverty" has been widely criticized on the grounds that it tends to blame poor people for their straitened circumstances by subtly twisting the concept of culture. For example, Eleanor Leacock (1971) argues that the term "culture" is being misused when it is

---

[11] See, for example, Ainslie (1975, 1992); Gardner (1993); Gardner and Herman (1990); Green, Fry, and Myerson (1994); Gottfredson and Hirschi (1990); Lawrence (1991); Logue (1988); Maital and Maital (1977); O'Rand and Ellis (1974); Vila (1994, 1997); Wilson and Daly (1985, 1997); Wilson and Herrnstein (1985).

meant to imply that poor people simply pass their culture (e.g., short time preference) on to their children. In a trivial sense this is true, but only because poverty and inequality give people little alternative. As will soon become apparent, I agree with Leacock's view: to the extent that a culture of poverty exists, it is largely the result of institutionalized inequality.

Even if we are by nature fundamentally risk-averse and impulsive, however, it is critical to understand why we still expect significant age, sex, and individual differences in risk-aversion. Putting it another way, even if risk-aversion is (in Frank's words) "part of the hard wiring of most animal nervous systems," there remain powerful adaptationist arguments for expecting significant differences in the degree to which people are risk-averse. Our bedrock assumption of optimality, after all, obliges us to go beyond what is normal or average and to consider instead the adaptive significance of the entire spectrum of variability in any trait, even "hard wired" traits. Accordingly, let us examine briefly the reasons why we expect three major kinds of differences in time preference: age, sex, and individual.

Age first. It is well known that as a group adolescents and young adults are especially risk-prone; they live "as if there was no tomorrow."[12] Alan Rogers (1994) developed a mathematical model of the evolution of time preference that gives new insights into why young adults are at risk for impulsiveness. His model examines the effects on time preference at various ages of risk of death and parents' choice between (1) consuming some resource themselves (which reduces their risk of stepping off a cliff – i.e., lineage extinction) and (2) investing that resource in their children, grandchildren, etc. (which increases their long-term fitness by setting the stage for good future moves). Rogers found that the optimal discount rate was highest in adolescents and young adults, which suggests that during human evolution the optimal strategy for people at the very beginning of their reproductive careers would generally have been to take risks in order to acquire resources for immediate consumption. Immediate consumption helps to ward off lineage extinction, for at the beginning of any reproductive career the initial fitness challenge is, sooner or later, to *produce* offspring rather than to rear them. In this light, the tendency of young people to discount the future and prefer immediate gratifications is not necessarily irrational.

---

[12] For example, Bell and Bell (1993); Blum (1987); Gardner (1993); Vila (1994); Wilson and Daly (1985, 1997).

Although he started at a rather different place in rational choice theory, William Gardner (1993; Gardner and Herman 1990) reached essentially the same conclusion as Rogers. In Gardner's view, adolescents and young adults are more impulsive than older people for the simple reason that the future is inherently more uncertain for young people than it is for adults. This is so because young people are only just beginning their reproductive careers. Being young, they have had fewer years in which to experience the world, and so have less basis for making predictions about their futures. Moreover, having only just (or not yet) achieved their reproductively mature social–emotional and cognitive–perceptual capacities, their ability to know their own adult sexual, reproductive, and competitive selves is especially limited, and so too their basis for generating realistic, culturally appropriate models of their psychosexual futures. Finally, being young, they generally lack wealth, power, and prestige, and so are handicapped in their capacity to influence their own lives. In short, not only are young people's models *of* and *for reaching* the future generally less accurate, full, and realistic than those of adults, young people also typically lack the *means* to fully implement whatever strategies may occur to them. The future is thus both subjectively and objectively more uncertain for young people than it is for adults. If it is generally adaptive and rational to discount the future under conditions of uncertainty, as everyone seems to agree, then, *ceteris paribus*, it may be rational to discount it more when it is more uncertain – i.e., when one is young.

For Gardner and Rogers, steep discounting of the future by young people is neither character defect nor pathology, but a rational response to uncertainty. And the reason that adolescents and young adults are so risk-*prone* is that, paradoxically, they are in fact risk-*averse*; they *seem* reckless, but it is actually their *aversion* to taking risks that makes them seem this way. It is their aversion to the risks of their uncertain futures that predisposes them to recklessness (see also footnote 10 above, p. 137). Gardner and Rogers both argue that, from the perspective of rational choice theory, *foregoing* the current consumption of a dangerous good (e.g., casting an insult, taking drugs, driving fast, not using a condom, etc.) may be thought of as an investment in the future; by foregoing the short-term security afforded by a momentary pleasure, one buys reduced risk, which constitutes a long-term investment that pays off (but only later) in the form of increased longevity (see also Hill, Ross, and Low 1997). But if the future *actually is* risky and uncertain then it is *not* wise to make long-term investments. When the future is uncertain the value of future consumption decreases relative to that of current consumption. Ultimately, then, young people discount the future more than older people because the future actually is more uncertain for them than it is for their elders.

The second dimension on which we would expect time preferences to vary is sex – and for the same reason that it varies with age: the uncertain futures problem. As a group, young people discount the future steeply because the future is more uncertain for those just beginning to put their reproductive strategies to the test than it is for older people, who have learned more of what works and what does not. For the same reason, we would expect males, as a group, to discount the future more steeply than females: because the future is generally more uncertain for males than for females. This is so because of the way that evolution shaped the sexual division of reproductive labor in mammals. As we have seen, female mammals, as a class, are obliged by their biology to do essentially all of the work of rearing offspring. Through such evolved capacities as gestation, parturition, and lactation female mammals specialize in parental investment, which maximizes offspring quality. The reproductive success of mammalian females has therefore been limited primarily by their capacity to obtain the resources (energy, nutrients, security, time, etc.) that they require for parental investment. On the other hand, because female mammals do the bulk of the work of rearing offspring, they have become a critical *reproductive resource* for mammalian males, who typically do little or no parenting. Consequently, mammalian males have been broadly shaped by selection (sexual selection) to specialize in the other component of reproductive labor – the *production* of offspring, which maximizes their quantity. Because female mammals devote so much time and energy to rearing offspring, the rate at which they can reproduce is lower than the male rate. A mammalian male who mates with only one female therefore reduces his potential reproductive rate to her level. To maximize their production of offspring males have to increase their sexual access to females. As a group, then, the reproductive success of mammalian males has been limited in large part by their capacity to fertilize additional females. A male's capacity to fertilize females has two primary (and not mutually exclusive) components: (1) his capacity to be *chosen* as a sexual partner by females and (2) his capacity to use violence and aggression to *coerce* others to his will – i.e., to coerce females to mate with him and to coerce other males not to oppose his intentions towards any particular female. Sexual selection is therefore expected to have favored the capacity of males to compete with each other – in order to drive each other away and/or to be chosen by females (Daly and Wilson 1983; Emlen and Oring 1977; Hrdy 1997; Smuts 1992; Trivers 1972; Wrangham 1980).

The upshot is that mammalian males are biologically capable of producing more offspring than females. While fewer males than females usually reproduce at all, the most reproductively successful male usually has more offspring than the most successful female.[13] This means that, while the *average* number of offspring is the same for each sex, there is often a large sex difference in the within-sex *variance* in number of offspring. Within mammal species females tend to cluster fairly closely around whatever is the average number of offspring for females in that species. In contrast, while males of that species will be clustered around precisely the same average, they will be less tightly clustered around it; the vast majority of males may not have reproduced at all, while a very few may enjoy astronomical reproductive success. Because it is *possible* for some mammalian males to enjoy astronomical reproductive success – but *impossible* for *any* mammalian female – the benefits of taking risks to increase one's reproductive success are typically greater for males than for females. We therefore expect sexual selection to have favored psychobiological mechanisms for endowing males (especially young ones) with a taste or preference for risky activities. Everything else being equal, males who were thereby more highly motivated to engage in risky activities (like coercing others) would have left more descendants than other males. Ultimately, this is probably why males, as a group, are at greater risk than females for violence against others, for spreading HIV and other STDs, for fathering children they are unable or unwilling to support, and for their own early death from disease, alcohol and drugs, accidents, homicide, and suicide (Archer 1994; Vila 1994; Wilson and Daly 1985). Even in the egalitarian and affluent Netherlands, for example, between 1970 and 1993 men aged 20-29 were almost six times more likely than same-aged women to be injured by violence, and about 2½ times more likely to be involved in all kinds of trauma (see Figure 4.2).

Finally, in addition to age and sex differences in time preference we

---

[13] For instance, according to the Guinness Book of World Records, the most fertile woman who ever lived had "only" 69 children – as against the world's most reproductively successful well over 700. However, given the sexual access to women enjoyed by various despots throughout history, the male record is probably much higher than this (e.g., Betzig 1986).

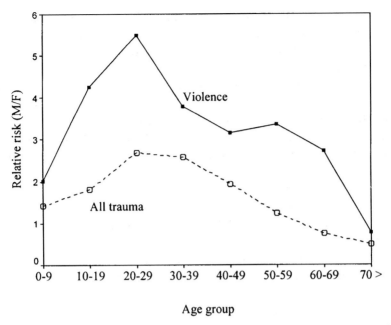

Figure 4.2 The ratio of male/female trauma victims from all trauma and violence. University Hospital Groningen, The Netherlands, 1970–1993 (n = 246,277) (from Kingma 1994).

also expect significant individual differences. Indeed, under some conditions we would expect individual differences to swamp age and sex differences – so that, for example, young people, and even young males, would value the future. Once again, the reason that we expect individual differences in time preference is the reason that we expect age and sex differences in time preference: the uncertain futures problem. Thus, while young people and males may be predisposed to devalue the future because their youth and maleness actually make their futures more uncertain, their age and sex are only risk factors for short time preference and do not ordain it. In other words, what matters more than youth or maleness, *per se*, is the common denominator of *uncertainty* that underlies each. Uncertainty arises from more than age and sex, so uncertainty will differ *among* people of the same age and sex as well as *between* different age and sex groups (see also Hill et al. 1997).

People of the same age and sex may face different kinds or amounts of uncertainty for both intrinsic and extrinsic reasons. People differ from each other intrinsically for genetic, congenital, constitutional, and temperamental reasons. For a particularly relevant example consider the work of Jerome Kagan and his colleagues. They have shown that a major dimension of individual differences in children's temperament is along an axis of "inhibited" (shy, fearful) vs. "uninhibited" (spontaneous, outgoing). These differences can be identified as early as four months and show considerable developmental continuity. The brain regions mediating fear and arousal are more readily activated in inhibited than uninhibited children and there seems to be important inherited variation in arousal threshold, at least at the extremes of the inhibited–uninhibited continuum. Inhibited children may be at risk for uncertain, insecure social relations because they are predisposed to evaluate stimuli as fearful (Kagan 1994; Kagan et al. 1988). Their futures may be inherently more uncertain because they perceive the world through fear-colored lenses.

People who are intrinsically the same (i.e., same age, sex, genotype, temperament, constitution, etc.) can none the less face very different kinds and degrees of uncertainty for extrinsic reasons. The number of extrinsic reasons why people face different futures is vast, but as we will see in more detail in the next two chapters, one of the most pervasive and powerful – at least in industrial societies – is inequality, specifically unequal access to energy, nutrients, security, information, and time. This is what it takes to do the work of life; it is access to these resources that determines our futures. When access to these resources is unequal people face different futures. When access is secure and certain the primary adaptive problem is setting the stage for a better, longer future; when it is insecure and uncertain the primary adaptive problem is having a future at all.

ToM and value

One way to evaluate the future, then, is in terms of its certainty. Ultimately, this may be the only way. If value itself originates in reproductive success (Cooper 1987; Elzanowski 1993; Plotkin 1994), and if the essential adaptive problem is achieving reproductive success in face of the uncertain futures problem (i.e., the General Life History Problem), then evaluating an imagined future in terms of its certainty would make good adaptive sense. The capacity for contingent time preference seems to do just this: as the imagined future becomes more risky or uncertain the present assumes greater value. Since the future is to some extent *always* uncertain, however, humans, like other organisms, are intrinsically risk-averse

– i.e., predisposed to avoid the uncertain future and to choose (select, value) instead actions that we believe (even if unconsciously) will best achieve our immediate desires.

This innate bias in the way that we value our imagined futures seems to be experienced subjectively as the feeling that something good or bad will or will not happen. Elzanowski refers to these feelings as "value experience," which is what "conveys the directional, aversive or appetitive component to the ensuing behavior" (1993:265). In Damasio's somatic marker hypothesis, these subjective feelings of value are the subcortical "beacons of incentive" and "alarm bells" which our neocortical minds evolved to devise rational ways to approach and avoid. On the view that adaptations are the "relationship between the organization of any part of a living creature's body and particular aspects of order in the world outside of that creature" (Plotkin 1994:21), then our intrinsic risk-aversion would seem to be the internal, subjective, phenotypic representation of the external, objective, environmental fact of life that the cost of stepping off an immediate fitness cliff is always greater than the benefit of setting the stage for some inherently uncertain reproductive future. Treating our capacity for rational thought as an adaptation, Cooper argued likewise that "evolutionary processes will tend to favor modes of individual internal information processing that are analogs of the evolutionary process itself" (1987:367). For Cooper, rational thought is a mode of "internal information processing" that works with analogic representations of reproductive success – the central feature of the "evolutionary process itself." From this perspective, just as the aerodynamic forces of lift and drag are represented (imperfectly) in the wings of birds, so, too, is the uncertain futures problem represented (imperfectly) in the psychobiological mechanisms by which we process information to make decisions about behavioral alternatives. Because organisms which achieved long-term reproductive success manifestly made good "decisions" (not necessarily consciously) about the alternatives that were open to them, Cooper reasoned, selection would tend to favor decision-making algorithms in their descendants that worked with subjective representations of what these objectively good past decisions achieved.

For me, then, time preference is an imperfect, subjective representation of one's current objective probability of reproductive success – i.e., one's reproductive value. It is an evolved algorithm for attaching reproductively relevant value to the models of the future that our minds evolved to generate. And if parents' ability and willingness to invest in offspring were important proximate determinants or correlates of children's reproductive value in the EEA, then the future that mattered most would be the social future: parents' intentions toward their children. We would therefore expect these value-attaching algorithms to work intimately with the algorithms for detecting these intentions – i.e., with IWMs, MI, and ToM.

Indeed, if the attachment process is an adaptation *for* entraining the development of the optimal reproductive strategy contingent on local risk and uncertainty (indexed initially by parents' ability and willingness to invest), this is what we would expect. Individual differences in attachment might therefore be conceived as the *relationship* between children's objectively probable reproductive value and the phenotypic manifestations of this value. This value would be represented materially (and imperfectly, needless to say) in the neural pathways that embody what I have referred to (according to their adaptive function) as future detectors and value detectors. The future detector is a mind tool for reading other people's intentions, beginning with one's parents. It consists of IWMs, MI, and ToM and may reside in the prefrontal cortex. It is an example of Plotkin's "secondary heuristic" for gaining knowledge. It works by manipulating representations of other people's beliefs and desires so as to create new information about our current environments: models of (expectations about) other people's intentions. The value detector is another kind of mind tool. It is an "automatic evaluation algorithm" for the internal, subjective, phenotypic representation of one's objectively probable reproductive value. It is embodied in the amygdala and the rest of the emotional brain and works (in the context of social relations) by evaluating models of other people's intentions received from IWMs, MI, and ToM according to innate standards of good and bad (security and danger). These innate standards are old information about our ancestors' environments that has come to us via Plotkin's "primary heuristic" in copies of our ancestors' genes. These innate standards of value are the internal, analogic representations of the central objective feature of the evolutionary process itself, i.e., reproductive success or fitness. Our *experience* of these (imperfect) assessments of our objective reproductive value, however, is Elzanowski's value experience – i.e., the subjective feeling that something good or bad will or will not happen. When this "automatic evaluation algorithm" returns evaluations of security (good) after enough iterations of the attachment cycle, the neuroendocrine pathways that embody positive IWMs of parents' (and then others') intentions are functionally validated and the future seems (subjectively) secure and certain. On the other hand, when too many evaluations of danger (bad) are returned, the neuroendocrine pathways that embody negative IWMs are functionally validated and the future seems (subjectively) dangerous or uncertain. When the future is objectively secure and certain, as we have seen, the optimal reproductive strategy is (*ceteris paribus*) to maximize future reproduction; when it is objectively dangerous or uncertain, however, the optimal strategy is (*ceteris paribus*) to maximize current reproduction. Individual differences in IWMs, MI, and ToM may thus be conceived as subjective representations of children's objectively probable reproductive value that are produced by mind tools for detecting risk and uncertainty – first in our parents' intentions and then in the intentions of others.

We might therefore expect that individual differences in attachment history would be related to individual differences in time preference, and that both would be related to individual differences in the allocation of reproductive effort. To my knowledge there have been no studies of the relationship between early attachment organization *per se* and specific measures of concurrent or later time preference. There is evidence, however, that children who experience risk and uncertainty in one specific kind of early social relationship do indeed devalue the future. In a pioneering study of the source of individual differences in time preference, Walter Mischel (1958, 1961a,b) found that even with SES controlled 7- to 9-year-old children from father-absent households were significantly more likely than father-present children to choose a small immediate reward than to wait a week for a promised larger one.[14] This is a significant finding, for, as we shall see in the following chapter, there is evidence that father-absent children are often exposed to higher levels of psychosocial stress (risk and uncertainty in social relations) and as a result seem predisposed to the early and impulsive expression of sexual and aggressive behavior. While the relationship between explicit measures of attachment and time preference remains to be seen, however, there is already good evidence that the risky and uncertain environments in which children are expected to develop short time preferences are precisely the environments in which children are at risk for developing insecure

---

[14] More than ten years later, the children who had been able to delay gratification were judged more academically and socially competent than the impulsive children. They were also better able to cope with frustration and stress and scored higher on the Scholastic Aptitude Test (Mischel, Shoda, and Rodriguez 1989).

attachments. More important, there is increasing evidence that growing up under conditions of risk and uncertainty in general – and insecure attachment in particular – is associated with the development of reproductive strategies that for all the world seem "designed" to maximize current reproduction. But if we are "designed" to develop our reproductive strategies contingently, on the basis of current estimates about future risk and uncertainty in social relations, this is just what we would expect. It is to this evidence that I now turn.

5   Sex and uncertainty

I can't even imagine what you mean when you ask about being a
teenager. In this neighborhood boys grow up to be men before they are
five. There is no such thing as being a teenager. You're a child, then a
man, and then you die.   Stephen, 19-year-old father in a high-risk
                    neighborhood in a large US city (Burton 1997:211)

I mean we don't have no money so we make up for it with women. I
mean if you going to come into a hundred thousand dollars, you going
to make it. Your friends be envying you. Now, if you don't got nothing,
but you going to have five women, you going to be self-satisfied. It's
just a thing we do. But if you have money, you don't have to be defined
through women.   Eddie, resident of a high-risk neighborhood
                    in a large US city (Bourgois 1995:291)

I love kids. I believe kids are the most wonderful things alive; that's
what made me live until now. Because . . . you know how you love a
mother? You can never love a mother more until you have a baby. I
loved my mother more when I had my first daughter; that's when I
loved my mother more. Because when a baby is born . . . when you see
a baby . . . and you see it so small, you say, that baby can't come and
smack you, and say, "Mommy, don't do this; don't do that." He's so
innocent. And that's pure. And you see so much child abuse, but that
baby doesn't know nothing. It's pure and innocent. That why I still
wanna have twelve.   Candy, mother of five, lives in a high-risk
                    neighborhood in a large US city (Bourgois 1995:216)

Although Bowlby saw from the start that attachment history was related
to adult sexuality, he had no reason to think that the relationship indicated anything but pathology. Without the insights of life history theory
there was no way to see the significance of his empirical observation that
adolescents and young adults who suffered disturbed early family relations were at increased risk for the early or impulsive display of sexual
and aggressive behavior. Writing of these people in his final report to the
World Health Organization, for example, Bowlby noted that "Persistent
stealing, violence, egotism, and sexual misdemeanors were among their

less pleasant characteristics" (1951:380). In the preceding chapters I have tried to show why, in an ultimate, adaptationist sense, we might expect stressful early family relations to be related to later reproductive behavior, and how, through the proximate mechanism of attachment, such early stress might exert its effects. My goal in this chapter is to outline the considerable evidence that disturbed early family relations are systematically related to later reproductive behavior.

I begin with an overview of the human stress response – the way our bodies respond automatically to perceived risk and uncertainty – and the relationship between psychosocial stress and attachment. I then focus on the ways in which family relations act as a vector through which environmental risk and uncertainty affect children's development. This is followed by a brief overview of theory and research on the effects of growing up without a father. The Absent Father Syndrome, as such effects are known, has figured prominently in the history of both psychology and anthropology, and especially in the origin of the first evolutionary model of the development of reproductive strategies by Pat Draper and Henry Harpending (1982). It now appears, however, that the effects of father absence (essentially Bowlby's "persistent stealing, violence, egotism, and sexual misdemeanors") stem not so much from father absence per se, as from a variety of other stressors widely associated with father absence (notably divorce, inequality, and socialization for male aggression). Turning next to what Margo Wilson and Martin Daly (1985) called the "Young Male Syndrome," I examine the role of early psychosocial stress in the development of male reproductive strategies, particularly risk-taking and violence. This is followed with a similar examination of what I shall call the Young Female Syndrome, where I focus first on the determinants of (1) age at menarche and (2) age at first sexual intercourse, and then on (3) the conditions under which early and/or single motherhood might constitute a rational, if not always conscious response to certain kinds of risk and uncertainty in women's lives. At this point I will also explain how a choice can be both rational and unconscious. I then conclude the chapter with a brief look at the handful of studies which have examined the relationship between attachment history and adult reproductive strategies (i.e., sexual, romantic, and parenting behaviors).

Early stress

Early stress and attachment

If the cost of stepping off a fitness cliff is always greater than that of failing to set the stage for some future good move, then there ought to be adaptations for avoiding cliffs. As we saw in chapter 3, the amygdala is precisely that: an adaptation for avoiding cliffs; it is for "detecting danger and producing defence responses" (LeDoux 1995:227). When the amygdala repeatedly detects danger, the hypothalamic-anterior pituitary-adrenal cortex (HPA) system is activated (Aggleton 1992; de Kloet 1991). The HPA system is the heart of the human response to prolonged or chronic stress and is functional in the newborn (Stansbury and Gunnar 1994). When the HPA system is activated it releases glucocorticoids (stress hormones) from the adrenal gland into the bloodstream. The key human glucocorticoid is cortisol, whose primary function is to protect the body from repeated activation of the "fight–flight" response, which is the body's short-term response to stressors. For me a "stressor" is whatever activates the HPA system; "stress" is the activation of the system, resulting in elevated levels of cortisol.

What goes up, however, should come down, for too much cortisol is dangerous. Under conditions of chronic risk and uncertainty, the HPA system is repeatedly activated. This leads to chronically high cortisol levels, which over time can do severe damage that may be irreversible. Persistent activation of the HPA system is implicated in a wide range of disorders such as (1) immune system dysfunction, which increases susceptibility to disease, from cancer to the common cold (McEwen 1995; Cohen, Tyrell, and Smith 1991); (2) cognitive impairment, including the loss of neurons in the hippocampus and other areas of the brain associated with memory (Sapolsky, Krey, and McEwen 1985); (3) gastrointestinal and cardiovascular disturbances (McEwen 1995); and (4) anxiety disorders and endogenous depressive illness (Schulkin, McEwen, and Gold 1994; Sheline et al. 1996). Anxiety (fear of loss) and depression (feeling of loss), in turn, not infrequently lead to self-medication with alcohol, tobacco, and other drugs, which are immediately pleasurable but in the long run tend to increase stress and reduce health even further (e.g., Kushner, Sher, and Beitman 1990). Hyperactivity of the amygdala and resulting chronic high levels of cortisol are also implicated in inhibited growth (Montgomery, Bartley and Wilkinson 1997; Widdowson 1951). While the mechanisms involved are not entirely understood, it is known that children with elevated glucocorticoid levels suffer disturbed sleep (Flinn et al. 1995b; Gunnar et al. 1985) and that growth hormone is released during sleep, and it is thought that the secretion rate of growth hormone falls off when sleep is disturbed (Mascie-Taylor 1991; Preece 1985).

Chronic risk and uncertainty are dangerous, therefore, not just because they increase the probability of death. Even if one manages to beat the odds, repeatedly responding to actual risks and continuously monitoring uncertain ones entails the present consumption of actual resources (e.g., energy, sleep, hippocampal neurons) that would have had a greater fitness pay-off in the form of larger size, better immune function, increased memory, and better mental and physical health in the future. Hominid parents may not have been able to reduce much the objective environmental risks and uncertainties facing their children, but through the attachment system they may have been able to reduce quite a lot their children's internal, subjective representations of these external dangers – i.e., the internal physiological states activated by the HPA system that are experienced subjectively as fear. As Bowlby saw, attachment is all about protection from danger. Taking Bowlby's insight a logical step further, Megan Gunnar and her colleagues (e.g., 1989, 1996; Stansbury and Gunnar 1994) have been exploring the relationship between attachment security and reaction to fearful stimuli by children of different temperaments: those who are relatively fearless (outgoing, uninhibited) vs. those who are more fearful (inhibited, shy, withdrawn). They find that while security of attachment is not related to stress reactivity in the outgoing, uninhibited children, it is in the more fearful children. They conclude that

> . . . secure attachment relationships protect or buffer infants from elevations in cortisol and that these protective effects may be particularly evident for socially fearful or inhibited children . . . Clearly by the 2nd year of life, the neuroendocrine consequences of inhibited, fearful temperament depend upon the security of the child's relationship with the parent who is available to help them cope with threatening events. (Gunnar et al. 1996:200)

Again, while ancestral parents might not have been able to do all that much to lessen the objective risk and uncertainty of the EEA, through their availability, sensitivity, and responsiveness to infant signals they could attenuate their children's subjective experience of fear by "buffering" the phenotypic manifestation of this risk and uncertainty in their children – i.e., by reducing their cortisol levels. Sensitive, responsive mothering in the EEA, then, would have helped our juvenile ancestors allocate more of their resources (e.g., energy, sleep, hippocampal neurons) to growth, development, and learning. Indeed, Gunnar and her colleagues suggest that "one function of the parent–infant attachment relationship is to buffer or protect the developing brain from the potential deleterious effect of glucocorticoid on neural tissue during protracted, postnatal period of brain development" (1996:201). This buffering would constitute a major parental investment in improving offspring quality (reproductive value) in the future (i.e., as adults), which would tend to reduce inter-generational variance in number of offspring and thus to increase number of descendants in future generations.[1]

My point, however, is not that secure attachment promotes growth, development, and learning, for this is well known. My point is that early stress and attachment are deeply intertwined. For Bowlby, as we know, secure attachment was all about protection from danger, and Gunnar and her colleagues have shown that secure attachment buffers children against activation of the HPA system. It also seems not unreasonable to define "stress" as activation of the HPA system, which happens whenever the child perceives danger (a fitness cliff – i.e., something "bad"). On this view, any stressor can activate the attachment system. By the same token, the attachment system itself (i.e., parental behavior, or lack thereof) can be a source of fear, thereby activating the HPA system. This view also suggests that to understand individual differences in attachment it is necessary to consider why children differ in their reactivity to fearful stimuli (e.g., for genetic or congenital reasons). Finally, this view suggests that, in a manner of speaking, all early stress is psychosocial stress, for the psychosocial relations between mother and child can mediate the child's experience with any kind of stressor, including inanimate ones. Nor is emphasizing the interrelations between attachment and the biology of fear and security a novel approach; the view of attachment as "psychobiological attunement" between mother and child is well established (e.g., Field 1985; Hofer 1995; Schore 1994).

---

[1] Language would seem to aid this buffering. Parents with the capacity to get into their children's minds via language could help them to construct mental representations of risk and uncertainty in a way that was less likely to activate the child's HPA system. For example, a meek child might be reassured to learn that someday he would inherit the earth.

This is not to say, of course, that all early stress is *only* psychosocial, or that the distressing effects of early malnutrition and disease are all in children's minds. It is to say only that we are highly social beings and that other people's intentions toward us have always been critical for our survival, growth and development, and ultimate reproductive success. As we saw in chapter 3, Peter Ellison (1990) suggested that because growth rates are highly sensitive to nutritional and disease stress, the rates themselves may have evolved to function as a "bioassay," on the basis of which females might predict (unconsciously, physiologically) the optimal timing of reproductive events (e.g., age at menarche). But when people sicken and die from malnutrition and disease these biological stressors assume an additional, psychosocial dimension. By analogy with Ellison's "bioassay," and building on Belsky, Steinberg, and Draper's (1991) attachment theory model of the effects of early psychosocial stress on reproductive behavior, I suggested that the cognitive–emotional consequences of early psychosocial stress (i.e., insecure IWMs of other people's intentions) may have evolved to function as a "socioassay" on the basis of which the availability, sensitivity, and responsiveness of future social relations might be predicted (Chisholm 1993).

I have two reasons for emphasizing the intimate connection between early stress and attachment. The first is that attachment does not take place in a vacuum. Nor would it need to; in the absence of danger there is no need for protection. No family is an island, apart from the larger socioecology or political economy in which it finds itself. Indeed, the form and functioning of the family is hugely influenced by its larger environment, in particular, as we shall see, by the kind and amount of risk and uncertainty that men and women must shoulder to find acceptable mates and that parents must shoulder to protect and provision their children. This means that attachment theory alone is insufficient for understanding the nature of secure and insecure attachment. It also means that to understand individual differences in parents' behavior we must understand the full socioecological or political economic context in which they are doing the work of mothering. It means as well that we must think long and hard before blaming parents for their children's insecurity.

The second reason for emphasizing the connection between early stress and attachment is methodological. Because there are so few studies (coming later) of the relationship between actual measures of attachment and later reproductive behavior, it is not yet possible to test rigorously Belsky

et al.'s model of the development of reproductive strategies or my particular life history theory version of it. All is not lost, however, for there is
extensive evidence that early stress is also related to later reproductive
behavior. If early stress and attachment are as intimately related as they
seem, then to some extent we can use measures of early stress as proxies
for measures of attachment and thereby at least illustrate the model, if
not test it.

The family as vector for risk and uncertainty

We have seen that in risky and uncertain environments, where extrinsic
mortality rates are high or unpredictable, or where the flow of resources
necessary for bearing and rearing children is low or uncertain, it is often
beyond parents' wealth or power to do much to increase their children's
reproductive value. Under such conditions, the short-term reproductive
strategy of maximizing current reproduction may be the optimal strategy, for by maximizing the probability of having some offspring who survive and reproduce, one minimizes the probability of lineage extinction.
There are just two ways to maximize current reproduction: (1) to start
reproducing at the earliest possible opportunity and (2) to reproduce at
each subsequent opportunity as it arises. Under conditions of chronic
risk and uncertainty, therefore, we would expect to find a young age
at first reproduction and/or a high reproductive rate. In the previous
section, we saw that under such conditions the HPA system is repeatedly
activated and that through the effects of "psychobiological attunement"
secure attachment can buffer children against activation of the HPA
system. In this section, we will review the evidence that chronic risk and
uncertainty make it harder for parents to provide this buffering and
explore some of the reasons why.

Because children in the EEA could not survive or grow and develop
without a large investment of care and attention, from the perspective
of evolutionary ecology it is fair to say that the EEA of children is the
family itself, for throughout our evolution families – including single
mothers[2] – have provided the vast bulk of all the investment that has ever
been made in children. Children are thus not adapted to their parents'

---

[2] There is no male parental investment at all in most mammal species. There is little or
none in most primate species. It is not known when significant male parental investment
appeared in the course of hominid evolution (and it is a variable trait even today). Before
it appeared, however, all mothers were single mothers. I will return to this point later.

environments so much as to their parents themselves. Parents, however, must live (do the work of fitness) in the real world. And when the real world is chronically risky and uncertain parents are not always able or willing (even if unconsciously) to invest in their children. When the real world is chronically risky and uncertain it may be in parents' fitness interest to begin having children at a young age and/or to have many children. But there are costs to everything and no such thing as a perfect strategy. In theory, young age at first birth maximizes current reproduction but at the cost of offspring quality (which maximizes future reproduction). This is because young people are usually less experienced than older people, especially with regard to sociosexual matters (e.g., choosing partners). They also usually have less power, prestige, and wealth than older people. And they also tend to devalue the future. Everything else being equal, young parents have fewer material and emotional resources than older parents. With fewer resources young people are less able to make a difference in their children's reproductive value. All things considered, the less that parents can make a difference in their children's future acceptability as a mate or parent, the more fitness sense it makes for them to have more children, even if they have somewhat lower reproductive value. Likewise, whether or not one starts young, having children at every possible reproductive opportunity also maximizes current reproduction – but again at the cost of children's reproductive value. Whether parents are young or old, resources are still limited, and when there are many children each gets fewer material and emotional resources. Having children at every conceivable opportunity may also entail trading off a degree of concern about a potential partner's suitability as a parent (which usually takes time to assess), perhaps to the point where their capacity for parenting is not the issue at all, but instead only their physical attractiveness,[3] or, indeed, their mere physical presence.

In this way, parents act as vectors through which the risk and uncertainty of their real-world environment is transferred to their children. When the real world is chronically risky and uncertain, parents are not always able or willing (even if unconsciously) to invest in their children because they are anxious about their ability to provide food and security for their families, or about finding, keeping, or leaving a mate. When this

---

[3] Physical attractiveness may give few clues about a potential partner's capacity for parenting, but may say something about the quality of the genes they might contribute to one's offspring (e.g., Thornhill and Gangestad 1993).

anxiety becomes too much or lasts too long, parents may be less able or willing to be consistently available, sensitive, and responsive to their children, especially if the children are weak, sickly, have irritable or inhibited temperaments, or are socially disadvantaged (e.g., by uncertain paternity or other prejudice). Parents may well continue to love their children, but if they are chronically anxious, tired, angry, or depressed it may be harder for parents to buffer their children against HPA system activation. And if the parents themselves have grown up under conditions of chronic risk and uncertainty they may be even less able or willing (even if unconsciously) to invest in children with their time, sensitivity, and responsiveness. If the parents themselves have insecure IWMs of attachment relations, they may find close emotional relations with others difficult to establish or maintain. When parents are unable or unwilling to invest, children are more likely to experience feelings of anxiety, anger, fear, or grief, which are the internal, subjective, phenotypic representations of early stress – i.e., the effects of the external, objective risk and uncertainty in their environments as it has been transduced to them through interaction with their parents.

Marital discord, especially, is intensified under conditions of risk and uncertainty, sometimes with disastrous results for children. Wilkinson (1996) notes that in the UK the top three contributing factors that caseworkers report when registering cases of child abuse are (1) marital problems; (2) debts; and (3) unemployment. But even if it does not go as far as abuse, marital discord is a known risk factor for both insecure infant–mother attachment and early stress. Michael Lamb observes that "of all the findings in the area of socialization, the best validated is the fact that children suffer when there is marital hostility or conflict" (1987:15). Likewise, Steven Wolkind and Michael Rutter state that: "There is ample evidence that several forms of separation, loss, and disturbed family relationships play an important part in the genesis of different kinds of child psychiatric disorders" (1985:51). Davies and Cummings (1994) have recently argued that children view the relationship between their parents egotistically, in terms of their own security (i.e., investment from parents), so that even if the child has had satisfactory relations with each parent, discord between the parents can render his relationship with one or both parents less secure. Reviewing the extensive data on the relationship between marital discord and developmental psychopathology, they conclude that spousal bickering and fighting is a risk factor for insecure attachment: "Children respond not simply to whether or not conflict is expressed but to the implications of conflict for marital relations and, ultimately, themselves" (1994:397).

Children, in other words, respond to marital conflict by generating IWMs of their parents' intentions toward each other and, ultimately, themselves. When these models include images of one or both parents' inability or unwillingness to invest (because they are preoccupied, frightened, angry, depressed, or might leave), they may activate the child's HPA system and be experienced subjectively as fear. This may be why Durrett, Otaki, and Richards (1984) found that mothers who reported higher levels of support from their husbands were significantly more likely to have infants classified as securely attached in the Strange Situation test. In a follow-up study of 5,362 adults born in Britain during one week in 1946, Wadsworth et al. (1990) found that parental divorce (especially before age five) generally had more severe and long-lasting effects than death of mother or father, substantially increasing the risk in adulthood for delinquency, low educational attainment, and smoking (among both men and women), unemployment (among men) or low job status (among women), and high alcohol consumption (among women). Mark Flinn and his colleagues (Flinn and England 1995; Flinn et al. 1995b) have found clear evidence of an association between children's HPA activation and household type on the Caribbean island of Dominica. Although the relationship between household type and family relations in Flinn's study is not known, the simple correlations speak volumes: they found that children living with (1) nonrelatives, (2) stepfathers and half siblings, and (3) single parents without kin support had significantly higher cortisol levels than children living (1) with both parents, (2) single parents with kin support, or (3) grandparents. Moreover, analyses of children's caretaking histories showed that children who experienced severe neglect, parental alcoholism, and/or maternal absence in infancy had distinct cortisol profiles that were suggestive of long-term neurobiological dysfunction. All children with high cortisol levels also showed disturbed sleep patterns, which, as we saw earlier, is implicated in slow growth. It is interesting to note in this context that in a follow-up study of 6,574 people born in the UK during the week of March 3–9, 1958, Montgomery et al. (1997) found that adults who experienced family conflict before age seven were significantly more likely than those who had not to be among the shortest 20% of the adult sample, even after controlling for social class, crowding in the childhood home, sex, and genetic influences on height. In sum, there is abundant evidence that the family is the main vector through which environmental risk and uncertainty affect child development.[4]

It is imperative to point out, however, that "family *process* is much more important than family *structure*" (Wilkinson 1996:166; emphasis added). What matters to children is much more likely to be the social relations within the family (process) than its particular form (structure). The distinction between form and process is important because probably the most pervasive source of risk and uncertainty for families, at least in industrial societies, is poverty and inequality, which usually affect both family process and form. Because of the resulting class differences in family form, some types of families tend to have lower status than others. If poverty and inequality have deleterious effects on child development that society hopes to ameliorate, and if family process and form are confused, then social policy may be misdirected at changing the devalued family *form* instead of reducing the risk and uncertainty that affects family *process* (family relations), which is what exerts all or most of the deleterious effects on children. For example, Wilkinson (1996) notes that, among the developed nations, Japan has one of the most conservative patterns of family structure, with exceedingly low rates of divorce and births outside of marriage and with the vast majority of children being reared in traditional two-parent families. In Sweden, on the other hand, over 50 percent of births are outside marriage. Nonetheless, in terms of the single best measure of overall child health – child deaths under age five – Sweden has the lowest rate in the world, followed by Japan at number two. This suggests that it is not family structure that determines child health.

Family relations (not form) are the primary vector for the effects of risk and uncertainty on children, and, as we will see in more detail in the next chapter, poverty and inequality are major sources of risk and uncertainty. Just as there is abundant evidence of an association between marital discord and increased likelihood of insecure attachment and/or early stress, so, too, is there abundant evidence that poverty and inequality diminish the capacity for consistent and involved parenting. And it is

---

[4] For additional studies of the association between family discord and increased likelihood of insecure attachment and/or early stress see Belsky, Rovine, and Fish (1989); Bretherton, Ridgeway, and Cassidy (1990); Cherlin et al. (1991); Egeland and Farber (1984); Fox, Kimmerly, and Schafer (1991); Friedman et al. (1995); Greenberg and Speltz (1988); Hetherington and Clingempeel (1992); Howes and Markman (1989); Isabella and Belsky (1985); Lundberg (1993); Radke-Yarrow (1991); Wadsworth et al. (1990); Wallerstein (1991).

not just that parents become anxious, depressed, exhausted, and short-tempered when faced with the risks and uncertainties of chronic poverty and inequality. It is also the case that the lack of money, food, time, space, sleep, health, security, education, status/respect, etc. inevitably means that parents have fewer options and that the needs of more people are going to come into conflict, so that the overall potential for discord in the family is raised.[5] There is also evidence that attachment patterns vary according to socioeconomic status, presumably because of the effects of poverty and inequality on mother–infant interaction (e.g., Erickson, Sroufe, and Egeland 1985; Fonagy et al. 1997b; Thompson 1997). It goes without saying that not all families living with poverty and inequality suffer disturbed family relations, or, vice versa, that all wealthy and privileged families have warm and tranquil relations. However, to deny that poverty and inequality make consistently sensitive and responsive parenting more difficult flies in the face of mountains of empirical evidence. It also does a disservice to disadvantaged parents and children by inviting facile explanations in terms of their mental or moral inferiority (e.g., Sennet and Cobb 1993; Shorris 1997).

Finally, although the families in question are nonhuman, the prospective studies of attachment behavior in monkeys by Leonard Rosenblum and his colleagues provide a wonderfully clear picture of how environmental risk and uncertainty affects mothers, and thus mother–infant interaction and the attachment process, and how the effects of insecure attachment in infancy can be lifelong. Rosenblum's group (Andrews and Rosenblum 1991; Coplan et al. 1996; Rosenblum and Andrews 1994; Rosenblum et al. 1994) studies the effects of environmental risk and uncertainty on mother–infant interaction in bonnet macaques by varying the amount of work and uncertainty that mothers must endure to obtain food. This is a far more realistic, natural stressor than perhaps any other in the experimental study of early psychosocial stress. Under conditions of increased risk and uncertainty in food supply mothers have to work hard to obtain food (risking hunger) and are rewarded for their foraging efforts on a variable, unpredictable schedule (uncertainty). Under this variable foraging demand (VFD) condition the mothers are forced to allocate more time and attention to feeding and less to maternal activi-

---

[5] For references, see Conger et al. (1984, 1994); Duncan, Brooks-Gunn, and Klebanov (1994); Egeland, Carlson, and Sroufe (1993); McLanahan and Booth (1989); McLoyd (1990, 1997); Sampson and Laub (1994); Werner and Smith (1992).

ties. As a result, they become more anxious and are less consistently responsive to their infants than mothers whose foraging efforts are always rewarded, even if not fully. Their infants, in turn, show significantly more behavior disturbances while still in close proximity to their mothers and are significantly less likely to separate themselves from their mothers to explore a novel laboratory environment than infants of the constant foraging demand, unstressed mothers. What is even more striking, though, is that the effects of these early experiences persisted into adulthood, over four years later. Adult offspring of VFD mothers are significantly more reactive to pharmacologic agents which elicit anxiety and show higher levels of corticotropin-releasing factor, which is implicated in human affective and anxiety disorders (Schulkin et al. 1994; Sheline et al. 1996). Rosenblum and his colleagues conclude that disturbed early mother–infant relations may affect the long-term development of neurobiological systems involved in the adult subjective experience of security.

The Absent Father Syndrome

Psychologists and anthropologists have long recognized that children who grow up without a father (or surrogate) are prone to develop the so-called Absent Father Syndrome, the essential features of which are the early and/or impulsive (risky) expression of sexual and aggressive behavior. Use of the word "syndrome" to describe the (apparent) developmental effects of father absence is justified by the fact that the behaviors comprising the syndrome ("persistent stealing, violence, egotism, and sexual misdemeanors") are remarkably uniform in the otherwise very different cultural contexts in which it appears. Psychologists know this syndrome primarily from studies of father-absent families in modern industrial societies where they are frequently associated with divorce, teen pregnancy, and lower socioeconomic status and are widely considered an inferior family form. Anthropologists, on the other hand, know this syndrome primarily from studies of father-absent families in many small-scale, nonindustrial societies where they are considered entirely normal if not superior. Cross-cultural studies show that the two most common correlates of father-absence are high levels of local warfare or raiding and polygyny (e.g., Broude 1990; Divale and Harris 1976; West and Konner 1976; Whiting and Whiting 1975). In both modern industrial societies and small-scale tribal societies boys who grow up in father-absent households are prone to the early and/or impulsive display of aggressiveness in the form of physical violence or threats against other males and authority generally and/or sexual aggression against females, ranging from high levels of sexual antagonism and assertiveness to outright physical coercion to engage in sex. And in both modern industrial societies and small-scale tribal societies, girls who grow up in father-absent households are prone to the early and/or impulsive display of sexual interest in men, but coupled with an apparently low ability or willingness to maintain for long a sexual or emotional relationship with one man (e.g., Bereczkei and Csanaky 1996; Draper and Harpending 1982). Mischel's (1958, 1961a, 1961b) finding that both father-absent boys and girls were significantly more likely than father-present boys and girls to choose a small immediate reward than to wait a week for a promised larger one supports the proposition that impulsiveness is a core component of the Absent Father Syndrome.

It may be, however, that the Absent Father Syndrome is misnamed. Whether floridly or subtly expressed, it is probably not the result of father absence *per se*, but of early stress due to anxiety-provoking family relations. Again, what matters to children more than the form of their family is the nature of the relationships in their family. In industrial societies, divorce is a leading cause of father absence. But just as divorce changes family form it also exposes children to increased poverty and pre- and post-divorce marital conflict, both of which are risk factor for early stress. Another major cause of father absence in industrial societies is single motherhood, in which women never marry, or only after bearing and rearing a number of children. As we will see in more detail toward the end of this chapter, however, the chronic political and economic inequality that makes single motherhood a viable family form for increasing numbers of women around the world also increases their children's exposure to early stress. In short, the Absent Father Syndrome seems to be misnamed because, while correlated with father absence, it is probably not caused by it, at least not entirely. In fact, both father absence and the (misnamed) Absent Father Syndrome seem to be caused by a third factor: political or economic risk and uncertainty, which makes consistently sensitive and responsive mothering more difficult, thereby increasing the risk for early stress and insecure attachment.

Prior to Draper and Harpending's (1982) original evolutionary model of the effects of father absence on the development of both male and female reproductive strategies, most psychological and anthropological models of father absence applied only to males. This was because the early or impulsive expression of sexual and aggressive behavior was seen as stereotypical male behavior, something that only males engaged in (or could engage in) and, indeed, for this reason came to be known as "protest masculinity." Protest masculinity was thought to result from father-absent males' insecure gender identity. Growing up without fathers, it was argued, meant that boys had insufficient exposure to adult male role models, while at the same time being perhaps overexposed to female role models, and so were unsure how they should be and act. To defend themselves against the anxiety engendered by this uncertainty they unconsciously adopted a "hypermasculine," stereotypically male style of behavior, seeming, in effect, to protest to one and all (but perhaps too much?) that they really are "real men."

But how does father absence work? Father absence may be correlated with protest masculinity, but what causes the correlation? For what I believe is the best explanation let us examine Gwen Broude's (1990) work more closely. She notes that anthropologists and psychologists have approached the problem differently. Anthropological approaches to father absence have emphasized the political and economic forces that affect gender identity in the form of the status-envy hypothesis. The status-envy theory of protest masculinity (e.g., Munroe, Munroe, and Whiting 1981; Whiting 1965; Whiting and Whiting 1975) holds that father-absent boys perceive that women control valued resources (food, affection, security, etc.) and so identify initially with females. As they mature, however, they discover that in fact it is really men who control these resources and so develop a secondary identity with males. This conflicted "cross-sex identity" (first with females, then males) is resolved, the argument goes, through the ostentatious, defensive display of stereotypically male behaviors. Psychological theories of protest masculinity, on the other hand, have emphasized the simple presence/absence of a same-sex role model as the key variable (e.g., Biller 1981; Lamb 1981). It was thought that father-absence *per se* had a *direct* psychodynamic effect on gender identity and protest masculinity, and not just an *indirect* effect through the promotion of a primary female gender identity. That is, protest masculinity was thought to result from the specific *absence* of a father figure and not simply by default from the resulting exclusive *presence* of mother. Reasoning that socialization is involved in the expression of all behavior, Broude then rank-ordered societies on the degree to which boys were socialized to inhibit or exhibit aggressive behavior, and related this measure both to the degree of father presence–absence and protest masculinity recorded for each society in her cross-cultural sample.[6] Finding a strong correlation between father absence and socialization for male aggression she argued that the conditions that give rise to father-absence also give rise to increased socialization for male aggressiveness, and that protest masculinity is not a protest against a primary female gender identity so much as another manifestation of the aggressiveness which males are encouraged to exhibit. She concludes that

> . . . the connection of father-absence to high levels of sex-typed behavior in men is not a product of primary identification with females in male-dominated societies, nor is it entirely an outcome of the absence of male role models. Rather, the connection exists as an indirect one, explained in part, and perhaps in large part, by the relationship of father's role itself to patterns of aggression training for boys. In particular, the inhibition of aggression is hard to accomplish without the exertions of a physically present male authority. It is tempting . . . to wonder if whether it is the case that, as has been argued by those recognizing the relevance of biology to behavior, boys are simply naturally prone to aggression and related behaviors and that some cultures desire to inhibit these natural propensities and can succeed in doing so if male authorities are available to persuade boys to behave themselves. (1990:120)

Which raises the question, what kind of society might *not* desire to inhibit male aggression? And what kind of society might *not succeed* in inhibiting male aggression even if it so desired? We have seen from the cross-cultural record that two of the best predictors of father-absent households are warfare/raiding and polygyny. To understand this correlation, Divale and Harris (1976) examined the covariation of these variables with several additional demographic, sociopolitical, and gender role variables in a wide range of small-scale, nonindustrial societies. They found a strong correlation between measures of warfare, cultural preferences for sons, sex ratios favoring young males, female infanticide, and higher mortality rates among girls from neglect and malnutrition.

---

[6] A note on method: Broude's measures were drawn from scales developed by other researchers for other purposes. The scales themselves are based on ethnographic and other kinds of data on the world's societies contained in the Human Relations Area Files.

Making the point that two of the most pervasive and consistent threats facing nonindustrial societies have been overpopulation and warfare, they interpret this cluster of traits in terms of a "male supremacist complex," which they suggest has the effect of minimizing population growth at the same time that it maximizes both the number and the aggressiveness of men that can be arrayed in battle against an enemy. In valuing males so much for their aggressiveness in warfare and raiding, Divale and Harris reason, there will tend to be a shortage of women because parents will be less willing to invest in daughters, either killing them at birth, or selectively neglecting them.[7] With a shortage of women and a high value on male aggressiveness and "supremacy" the result is intensified competition between males to acquire wives, resulting in polygyny for a few very competitive older men, and monogamy or no wives at all for less competitive and younger men. This, in turn, leads to increased sexual jealousy, adultery, and antagonism between older and younger men. It also leads to the devaluation of women and increased antagonism between men and women because increased male–male competition, especially between older and younger men, or richer and poorer men, tends to intensify the Young Male Syndrome (see below), which typically reduces female choice regarding sexual and reproductive matters (e.g. Chisholm and Burbank 1991; Hrdy 1981; 1997; Lancaster 1997; Smuts 1992, 1995; Strassman 1997). Antagonism between the sexes and polygyny itself often mean as well that men do not reside with their wives, and thus neither with their children, thereby limiting their ability to inhibit their sons' aggressiveness (even if they were willing) and perpetuating the conditions that lead to the Absent Father Syndrome. Antagonism between the sexes and reduced female choice are also associated with greater mortality among women from a variety of causes (Holloway 1994; Sen 1990; Smuts 1992). This minimizes population growth too, but biases the sex ratio against women even more, thereby helping as well to perpetuate male–male competition, socialization for male aggressiveness, and the male supremacist complex.

In sum, the kind of society that might not desire to inhibit male aggression is the kind that values it for warfare or for acquiring wives. The kind

---

[7] Remember "Ready to Die" (p. 112 above)? She was the seventh daughter in a family of 2 sons and 7 daughters in a society with a traditional preference for sons. "Ready to Die" was so named because her mother was so embittered that her last-born child was another girl. Both of her sons, but only 3 of her 7 daughters lived.

of society that might not succeed in inhibiting male aggression, even if it wanted to, is the kind in which fathers are absent and unable to socialize their sons against aggression. The two kinds of societies are not at all mutually exclusive, of course, but the former may predominate in small-scale, nonindustrial societies, where fathers are absent in solidary military or quasi-military groups of men (i.e., those devoted to or emphasizing dominance, aggression, and hierarchical relations) or with their other wives. The latter may predominate in industrial societies, where political and economic inequalities mean that some men have little to offer as husbands or fathers. Under these conditions women will sometimes do better without husbands, or at least without living with them, which means that the men will not be available to help socialize their sons against aggressiveness. When a society's men suffer high rates of mortality and incarceration there will also simply be fewer of them. I will take up both of these issues in following sections.

To me, the common denominator of the Absent Father Syndrome and Divale and Harris's "male supremacist complex" is protest masculinity ("persistent, stealing, violence, egotism, and sexual misdemeanors"). There has long been a consensus that the underlying causes of protest masculinity are the political and economic conditions associated with warfare/raiding and polygyny. More recently, due primarily to the work of Divale and Harris (1976) and Broude (1990), there has been a shift away from the idea that primary cross-sex identity and female status-envy were the major psychocultural mechanisms involved. Instead, the consensus now seems to be that socialization for male aggression – for males to have a "supremacist complex" – is the principal mechanism whereby warfare, polygyny, and the conditions that give rise to them affect child development.

Approaching this syndrome of "persistent stealing, violence, egotism, and sexual misdemeanors" from the perspective of evolutionary ecology and attachment theory, however, something is still missing. After all, what is the point of aggression? What is aggression *for*? Aggression is for fear. Warfare and raiding are for fear. From an evolutionary perspective the point of aggression (its adaptive function) is to push an opponent off a fitness cliff, or to coerce him into believing that one is near and to include representations of such cliffs in his mental models of what to do next. If an opponent feels that he is on the edge of a fitness cliff, he may be willing to trade off a certain amount of future value for immediate survival; he may submit to aggressiveness and give up, say, his cattle, his money, or his reputation (i.e., future value) for immediate survival. If an opponent feels that she is on the edge of a fitness cliff she may submit to having sex or even becoming a second, or third wife, giving up her choice about the father of one or more of her children (which affects her future – i.e., her reproductive value) in order to have any life at all.

Socialization for aggression is socialization for fear. In the act of socializing their sons for aggressiveness parents are apt to activate their sons' HPA systems; if parents do a good job their sons will surely activate other peoples' HPA systems.[8] It may not be socialization for aggression, then, that underlies protest masculinity so much as the early (and continuing) stress of fear – which is what aggression is for. On this view, protest masculinity is a consequence of early stress, a phenotypic representation of early risk and uncertainty, and a manifestation of an alternative male reproductive strategy that is developmentally entrained through the early stress-fear-attachment system and "designed" by natural selection to maximize current reproduction in the face of uncertainty. Such an approach is bound to help us understand female reproductive strategies as well, for it focuses our attention on early stress and fear in girls' lives, the ways in which women might maximize current reproduction, and what constraints might limit their options. When the Absent Father Syndrome is seen as an outcome of socialization for fear rather than aggression it becomes as relevant for understanding female development as that of males. Combining life history theory and attachment theory provides a potent rationale for postulating that chronic early fear might be part of an evolved developmental algorithm for maximizing current reproduction in *both* men and women. Attachment theory on its own makes no prediction about sex differences in the sequelae of attachment. But if the attachment process is an evolved mechanism for entraining the development of local optimal reproductive strategies, as Belsky, Steinberg, and Draper proposed, and if the history of sexual selection in mammals

---

[8] Elijah Anderson describes how some parents in high-risk American neighborhoods socialize their children for aggression:

> Many parents actually impose sanctions if a child is not sufficiently aggressive. For example, if a child loses a fight and comes home upset, the parent might respond, "Don't you come in here crying that somebody beat you up; you better get back out there and whup his ass. I didn't raise no punks! Get back out there and whup his ass. If you do not whup his ass, I'll whup your ass when you come home." Thus the child obtains reinforcement for being tough and showing nerve (1994:84).

means that men and women reproduce under different constraints (e.g., Trivers 1972), then we would expect to find sex differences in the effects of early stress or insecure attachment. For this reason the next two sections are devoted to the effects of early stress – first on males (the Young Male Syndrome), and then on females (the Young Female Syndrome).

The Young Male Syndrome: coercion

Because sexual selection has obliged female mammals to reproduce via such adaptations as ovulation, gestation, parturition, and lactation, their reproductive success has been limited primarily by their access to the energy, nutrients, time, and security required for these mechanisms to do their adaptive work. Because female mammals are constrained by their anatomy to do all or most of the work that it takes to produce and care for the young, they have become a critical reproductive resource for mammalian males. The reproductive success of mammalian males has thus been limited more by their capacity to gain sexual access to females than by their capacity for parental investment. As mentioned, there are just two (not mutually exclusive) ways in which mammalian males can gain sexual access to females: they can be *chosen* as sexual partners by females or they can use violence and aggression (or threats thereof) to *coerce* others – *females* into having sex with them and/or *other males* into leaving the reproductive field to them alone. Sexual selection, then, is expected to have favored the psychobiological capacity of mammalian males to compete with each other in order to be chosen by females or to coerce females and/or other males to their will. A taste or predisposition for taking risks is thought to be an important component of this psychobiological capacity for male–male competition. Since there is little or no male parental investment in most mammalian species, the basis on which mammalian females choose males is largely or exclusively on indicators of their genetic quality – for example, their size, strength, aggressiveness, willingness to take risks, etc. (e.g., Bateson 1983; Clutton-Brock 1991).

In human beings, however, the story is different. During the course of human evolution our newborns became progressively more helpless and took progressively longer to mature, and thus required progressively more intensive and prolonged parental investment – eventually more than mothers alone could provide. For this reason, sexual selection is believed to have favored the psychobiological capacity (1) of males to *pro-*

vide this extra parental investment (if only indirectly, through the mother) and (2) of females to *choose* males not only on the basis of their size, strength, aggressiveness, and willingness to take risks, but also on their ability and willingness to provide parental investment – the energy, nutrients, time, and security (e.g., protection from danger) required for child survival and optimal growth and development. The evolution of prolonged helplessness in hominid children thus provided a new domain in which males could compete with each other to be chosen by females: their capacity for parental investment. The reproductive field for hominid males was no longer limited to mating competition; it now included parenting competition as well: competition on the basis of individual differences in males' ability and willingness to provide whatever resources females needed to bear and rear children.

This is the likely evolutionary origin of the two-parent family – i.e., with the origin of the role of father. It is also the likely origin of the Young Male Syndrome – not *de novo*, but as an *alternative* male reproductive strategy. Prior to the evolution of the role of father, the primary (or only?) reproductive strategy for hominid males may have been the Young Male Syndrome – Bowlby's "persistent stealing, violence, egotism, and sexual misdemeanors," which might be rendered in the first person as "I know what I want and I want it now, even if it is yours. And what I want is sex." Less colloquially, prior to the evolution of male parental investment, sexual selection seems to have obliged more or less all hominid males to reproduce by using their size, strength, aggressiveness, and willingness to take risks in order to be chosen by females and/or to coerce females into having sex with them and other males to give them a wide berth, to show some respect – i.e., to show fear.

But the role of father and the capacity for male parental investment *have* evolved. We do not know when, and although it may have been common for some tens if not hundreds of thousands of years, male parental investment is variably expressed even today. The degree to which male parental investment is expressed depends on many things, but perhaps the most common determinant of men's capacity to make a difference in their children's lives (i.e., to improve their reproductive value) has been their access to the resources that women require for bearing and rearing children of high reproductive value. This presents a problem, however, for when young men have no resources that might cause them to be chosen by women – that is, when they are poor, have no status, no power, and no prospects – then they may feel (not necessarily consciously) that their only avenue to reproduction is through coercion: coercion of females to have sex with them, coercion of other males to give them power or at least respect, and coercion of anyone with material resources to surrender them. Coercion – the use or threat of force – is a risky business because when pushed to the edge of a cliff many people will push back. But as we have seen several times now, when the future is objectively uncertain it can be rational to take risks. This is the *sine qua non* of the Young Male Syndrome.

In their original formulation of the Young Male Syndrome, Wilson and Daly (1985) used police reports on homicidal conflicts in a large US city to test the prediction from sexual selection theory that a person's willingness to enter into highly risky violent interactions with others should be a function of membership in the age and sex class that experienced the most intense reproductive competition during evolution (i.e., young males), and whose present circumstances were most predictive of reproductive failure (i.e., inadequate or uncertain resource flows, including low probability of future survival). Their analysis of 512 closed cases of homicide supported the prediction: overwhelmingly, participants in homicidal interactions were unemployed, unmarried young men. Although they do not suggest any psychobiological mechanism for doing the adaptive work entailed, Wilson and Daly propose that the contingencies of male sex, relative youth, poverty, and an uncertain future may constitute a developmental "trigger" to increase a person's motivation to engage in risky activities. A certain impulsiveness, they argue, along with a deep desire for "respect" from other males, may form the core of such young men's "taste for risk."

Extending this reasoning further, Wilson and Daly (1997) recently focused on the relationship between objective measures of both environmental uncertainty and the Young Male Syndrome. Using demographic, economic, and crime statistics for 77 neighborhoods in Chicago, they found a negative correlation between life expectancy (with deaths from homicide removed) and homicide rates – meaning that in neighborhoods where the future was objectively uncertain (short life expectancy) men were significantly more likely to kill each other. They also found that measures of economic inequality were also significantly related to homicide rates (greater inequality = more homicide). What is more, they found as well that just as homicide rates go up with decreasing life expectancy, age-specific reproduction goes down (i.e., as life expectancy decreases, women give birth at younger ages). DuRant et al. (1994) have also explored the relationship between future unpredictability and violent aggression. They asked 225 11- to 19-year-old young men living in inner-city housing projects in a large US city to complete an anonymous questionnaire that included items about their use of violence and the degree to which they expected to be alive at age 25. Compared to those who were least confident about being alive at age 25, those who were most confident were significantly more likely to report that they had never used physical violence against other people. In an analogous study, but with somewhat older, mostly middle-class US college students, Elizabeth Hill and her colleagues (Hill et al. 1997) found that self-reported risk-taking (in the realms of safety, sexual behavior, finances, and social relations) was significantly higher in those who believed that they would have short lifespans, even after controlling for the effects of gender and individual differences in predispostions for "sensation seeking." If short life expectancy and economic inequality are taken as evidence of environmental risk and uncertainty, and if high homicide rates (impulsive aggressiveness and risk-taking) and young age at reproduction are taken as evidence of alternative male and female reproductive strategies respectively, then these findings are consistent with the prediction from life history theory that (*ceteris paribus*) when the future is uncertain the optimal strategy – for both men and women – may be to maximize current reproduction.

Because chronic poverty and inequality make consistently sensitive and responsive mothering more difficult they are risk factors for insecure attachment (see above, pp. 151–161). However, because insecure attachment is correlated with increased aggressiveness in boys more than girls (Cohn 1990; Renken et al. 1989; Turner 1991), growing up in a high-risk neighborhood is in itself a risk factor for the socialization of aggression in boys. This is consistent with the proposition that the risk and uncertainty associated with poverty and inequality work through the early stress–fear–attachment system to entrain alternative reproductive strategies. Since males and females reproduce under different constraints, it is also consistent with predictions from sexual selection theory (Trivers 1972). In addition, if the optimal reproductive strategy for adult males in risky and uncertain environments has frequently involved coercion, it might make adaptive sense to increase boys' aggressiveness or impulsiveness so that they can have more of the kind of early experience that teaches the most useful lessons.

But there is more to attachment than behavior. According to the view of attachment presented in chapter 4, attachment behavior has to make sense in terms of subjective, phenotypic representations of objective environmental risk and uncertainty – i.e., mental models of the beliefs, desires, and intentions of attachment figures. How, then, are we to understand the relationship between insecure IWMs of attachment relations and the early or impulsive display of aggressiveness? Although it does not speak directly to the issue of early attachment, Elijah Anderson's (1994) deeply insightful ethnographic description of the Young Male Syndrome in a high-risk neighborhood in a large US city may none the less provide some clues. Describing the propensity for violence among the young men of this community, Anderson observes that:

> An important aspect of this often violent give-and-take is its zero-sum quality. That is, the extent to which one person can raise himself up depends on his ability to put another person down. This underscores the alienation that permeates the inner-city ghetto community. There is a generalized sense that very little respect is to be had, and therefore everyone competes to get what affirmation he can of the little that is available. The craving for respect that results gives people thin skins. Shows of deference by others can be highly soothing, contributing to a sense of security, comfort, self-confidence, and self-respect. Transgressions by others which go unanswered diminish these feelings and are believed to encourage further transgressions. Hence one must be ever vigilant against the transgressions of others or even *appearing* as if transgressions will be tolerated. Among young people, whose self-esteem is particularly vulnerable, there is an especially heightened concern with being disrespected. Many inner-city young men in particular crave respect to such a degree that they will risk their lives to attain and maintain it. (1994:89)

If attachment is about protection, and if insecure attachment results from a sense that attachment figures are unable or unwilling to provide protection, then coercing "respect" and "shows of deference" from others might be one way to relieve the anguish (the subjective experience) of fearful IWMs and an overactive HPA system. Signs of respect and deference (i.e., fear) do for these aggressive young males what consistently sensitive and responsive mothering does for securely attached children: they give "a sense of security, comfort, self-confidence, and self-respect."

The Young Male Syndrome is surely a human universal – in the sense that, given the right conditions, all normal males have more-or-less the same innate capacity to develop it. To the extent that the Absent Father Syndrome and the Young Male Syndrome are really the same thing, then the considerable psychological and anthropological literature on the Absent Father Syndrome suggests that when the conditions are right the Young Male Syndrome is not uncommon. Indeed, if the argument of this book is not far off, the Young Male Syndrome is a facet of an evolved universal capacity that enables males to develop what may be (or have been) the optimal reproductive strategy under risky and uncertain conditions. So far, most of the risky and uncertain conditions that I have described are those found in high-risk neighborhoods in large US cities. This is because poverty and inequality are the most virulent sources of risk and uncertainty in the modern world. They are not, however, limited to large US cities, and we should expect to find a higher incidence of the Young Male Syndrome wherever there are concentrations of chronic poverty and inequality.

One such place is the remote and rugged Kimberley region of northern Western Australia, where Australian Aboriginal people have been living for perhaps 50,000 years. Although in contact with pastoralists, pearlers, miners, and missionaries from the second half of the nineteenth century, the amount of contact was limited until after World War II. Today there are a few small villages in the Kimberley, but the majority of the population of approximately 15,000 people lives in widely scattered settlements of up to a few hundred people each. In terms of culture, ecology, and history nothing could be further from the high-risk neighborhoods of large US cities. What is similar, however, are the afflictions of poverty and inequality, with much the same results for young Aboriginal men. It was to understand these afflictions that Ernest Hunter (1993), an Australian psychiatrist, carried out his multidisciplinary research.

Hunter's primary goal was to understand the dramatic rise in suicide among young Australian Aboriginal men that began in the mid-1980s. To this end, he conducted a study in historical psychiatric epidemiology, recording the cause of virtually every death that occurred in the Kimberley between the years 1957 and 1986 and as much as he could of the circumstances surrounding each death from a wide variety of sources, including medical and legal records and ethnographic interviews with surviving friends and family members, police, etc. Hunter chose this time frame because it included the 15 years before and after the removal of the last legal restrictions on Aboriginal people's access to alcohol in 1972. He was particularly interested in the role that alcohol might play in the history of Aboriginal health and mortality because of its well-known use in self-medication for anxiety and depression and its equally well-known effect of exacerbating the physical, psychosocial and economic stresses associated with inequality and forced acculturation. He was able to show that after alcohol became readily available in 1972 there began a steady increase in the number of deaths from motor-vehicle accidents, other accidents, and young male violence – especially against women. While alcohol surely abetted this rise in violence against women, Hunter argues, the underlying reason was that the impact of forced acculturation and inequality in some ways fell harder on Aboriginal men than women. For example, the traditional domestic role of Aboriginal women was appreciated by white Australian society rather more than it appreciated the traditional hunting and politico-religious role of Aboriginal men. Moreover, welfare payments for children went to their mothers, not their fathers, giving Aboriginal women new leverage in domestic affairs with men. With virtually no work available locally anyway, and little preparation (or desire to leave their families) for jobs in far-away white Australian towns, Aboriginal men and women increasingly had to come to terms with the fact that the men had few resources that made them attractive as husbands or fathers.

Over time the stresses of forced acculturation and inequality, free access to alcohol, and antagonistic relations between men and women exacerbated each other and became chronic. Increasing numbers of parents argued and bickered and separated and divorced because they were chronically anxious, depressed, hurt, and angry. Increasing numbers of parents and other family members died because of stress- and alcohol-related disease, accidents, and homicide. At the same time increasing numbers of the children of these men and women experienced the early stress associated with separation, loss, and strained family relations. This is why, Hunter argues, when the children born after 1972 started to reach puberty in the mid-1980s, there began a steady increase in the developmental consequences of early stress and insecure attachment[9] – essentially "persistent stealing, violence, egotism and sexual misdemeanors." The clearest increase was in violence, especially violence against self

---

[9] In fact, Hunter uses an object-relations model rather than attachment theory to interpret the developmental effects of early stress and strained family relations.

(suicide and self-mutilation) and by men against women, mostly over real or imagined infidelity ("sexual misdemeanors"?). Hunter concludes that:

> It is . . . among the most disadvantaged and powerless that these phenomena, violence to others and to the self, are increasing – among unemployed, heavy-drinking males and similarly vulnerable childless women living at the periphery of the dominant culture. They are members of the first generation to grow up in communities with widespread drinking and welfare dependence. The conflicts over resources occur in an environment that is increasingly dangerous, particularly for Aboriginal women. One hypothetical explanation for the concurrent increase in male violence to women and to themselves is that, in this male subgroup, both behaviors are responses to perceived powerlessness. (1993:191)

To be without power is to be without the means to address the uncertain futures problem. Powerlessness thus magnifies risk and uncertainty, which magnifies fear. But, because the cost of falling off a fitness cliff is always greater than that of failing to set the stage for some future fitness benefit, the optimal strategy in the face of powerlessness may be to let tomorrow take care of itself and to allocate whatever limited resources one has to avoiding fitness cliffs. The first rule of life is like the Hippocratic oath: first do no harm to your reproductive value. From the perspective of evolutionary theory, the ultimate harm to an organism's reproductive value is lineage extinction: failure to reproduce, failure to achieve R – the "state" of continuance. At least in principle, then, when young men are without power, without the capacity to affect their futures, it may be (or have been) evolutionarily rational for them to take even great risks in order to avoid lineage extinction.

This being so, we would expect natural selection to have favored the genetic basis for phenotypic mechanisms that help young males do the actual adaptive work of taking risks in order to maximize current reproduction. Testosterone, the primary male sex hormone, is clearly involved in the frequently risky activities of sex and aggression. Udry (1988), for example, showed that even after controlling for the effects of permissiveness and low church attendance, testosterone levels were significantly related to adolescents' sexual experience, recency of sexual intercourse, and frequency of thoughts about sex. James Dabbs and his colleagues are particularly interested in the relationship between testosterone and both sex and aggression. They recently explored the relationship between testosterone levels and the kinds of crimes committed by 692 prison inmates (Dabbs et al. 1995). Men who had committed personal crimes involving sex and violence had significantly higher testosterone levels than men who had committed property crimes. In another study, Dabbs and Morris (1990) argue that previous studies of the relationship between testosterone and sex and aggression have been limited by small sample sizes and the failure to control for the potentially confounding effects of social class. They suggest, for example, that in low SES neighborhoods the most exciting things for young men to do are often illegal (e.g., stealing cars), whereas in wealthier neighborhoods young men have greater access to activities that are both exciting and more socially acceptable (e.g., driving family cars fast). To address these problems, Dabbs and Morris used a very large sample (4,462) that was representative of American men in race, education, income, and occupation. All had been enlisted men in the US Army and had been followed longitudinally from 1985 as part of a study of the effects of the Vietnam military experience. In addition to its large size, what makes this sample so valuable is that the men's testosterone levels were measured during their induction into the Army. Extensive information relating to the men's sexual behavior, aggressive and criminal behavior, and social class (education and income) since their discharge from the Army was also collected. Half of the men had served in Vietnam during 1965–71, and half had not. However, the potentially confounding effects of service in Vietnam, age, and race on the relationships between testosterone, sex, aggression, and social class were controlled for statistically.

Dabbs and Morris's findings are consistent with the proposition that testosterone is part of the Young Male Syndrome – that it is part of a mechanism for doing the adaptive work of maximizing current reproduction in the face of uncertainty. First, they found an association between testosterone levels and SES: low SES men were significantly more likely than high SES men to have high testosterone levels (i.e., in the upper 10% of the sample). Second, men with high testosterone levels were significantly more likely to have been involved in childhood delinquency, adult crime, hard drug use, marijuana use, alcohol abuse, to have gone AWOL in the Army, and to have had "many sex partners" (10 or more in one year). Dabbs and Morris also found, however, that the relationship between testosterone levels and these outcome variables differed by social class. While low SES men were more likely to have high testosterone levels than high SES men, the relatively fewer high SES men who did have high testosterone levels were *not* more likely to have been involved in delinquency, crime, substance abuse (with the single exception of marijuana use), to have gone AWOL, or to have had "many sex partners." In a later study comparing these same high- vs. lower-testosterone men, Booth and Dabbs (1993) found that the high-testosterone men were also less likely ever to marry, but if they did, they were more likely than lower-testosterone men to separate or divorce because of troubled relations with their wives, extramarital sex, or violence against their wives. Dabbs and Morris conclude that

> . . . testosterone is related to antisocial behavior, is lower among subjects who are higher in SES, and is less strongly related to antisocial behavior among subjects who are higher in SES. Testosterone is thus directly associated with many negative effects. While high testosterone theoretically might lead to prosocial behavior, the present data provide no indication of such redeeming social value. Prior findings emphasize the importance of testosterone in individual confrontations . . . Individuals high in SES tend to avoid individual confrontations, especially physical ones, and to submit to years of schooling. Perhaps the antisocial behavior associated with high testosterone interferes with education, but those individuals who do become highly educated are better equipped to control their antisocial tendencies. (1990:211)

Testosterone has all the earmarks of being part of a mechanism for motivating powerless, basically fearful young men to engage in risky activities that maximize current reproduction. High levels of testosterone seem to increase men's chances of coercing a woman into having sex or of coercing other men into surrendering something of value. The value coerced may be material, like cattle or money, or it may be non-material, like signs of respect or shows of deference. Having coerced sufficient cattle, money, or respect he may then hope to be chosen for sex by a woman. Coercion is pushing opponents to the edge of fitness cliffs and it is a risky business. It is risky because it is fundamentally antisocial; it is done only to opponents and it works against freedom. To the extent that "egotistic" is a synonym for "antisocial," then testosterone is implicated in each of the core features of the Young Male Syndrome: "persistent stealing, violence, egotism, and sexual misdemeanors," which Bowlby understood as the outcome of insecure attachment.

Antisocial people might also be said to lack empathy. Otto Fenichel, remember, defined empathy as "identification with the other person" (1945, p. 171), which is surely a *prosocial* thing to do, for it is only through empathy that we can know what another person is feeling. This makes empathic behavior the unqualified opposite of antisocial behavior. As we saw in chapter 4, children with insecure attachment histories are judged less empathic than those with secure histories and they score lower on ToM tests – i.e., they are less skilled at assessing other people's beliefs, desires, and intentions. If a history of insecure attachment reduces a person's capacity for empathy it may foster a certain impulsiveness, as well. If we have insecure IWMs of other people's beliefs, desires, and intentions then identifying with them only causes us more fear. When we fail to consider other people's beliefs, desires, and intentions we are apt to act without inhibition, as if we did not care how they viewed us – in short, as if we devalued the future. High-testosterone young males are prone to exhibit sexual and aggressive behavior impulsively, apparently without considering their effects on others (or themselves). This may not be entirely irrational, for, as we know, when the future is objectively risky and uncertain the optimal strategy may well be to take risks in order to achieve immediate benefits. Testosterone is essentially a drug for taking risks.

The Young Female Syndrome: single mothering

We come thus to the Young Female Syndrome, for when young women's futures are risky and uncertain it is every bit as evolutionarily rational for them to take risks as it is for young men. However, due to sexual selection, men and women reproduce under different constraints. This means that the nature and degree of the risks that they take will likely differ. Even so, men and women have exactly the same evolutionary rationale for taking risks: When the future is risky and uncertain the primary adaptive problem for both men and women is to maximize current reproduction. If the Young Male Syndrome is an evolved developmental mechanism whereby young men can maximize current reproduction, then we would expect there to be an analogous Young Female Syndrome whereby young women can maximize current reproduction.

Like males, females have just two ways to maximize current reproduction. They can start reproducing at the earliest possible opportunity and/or they can reproduce at each subsequent opportunity as it arises. When girls experience early stress and insecure attachment, therefore, we would expect to find facultative adaptations for early childbearing and/or a high reproductive rate. Because age at menarche and age at first sexual intercourse are major determinants of the age at which childbearing begins, I first look at how each is affected by early stress. This is followed by an evolutionary ecological analysis of the relation between early stress and high reproductive rates in which I will argue that to understand high reproductive rates as an adaptation to early stress we also need to understand why single mothering might be a rational response to risk and uncertainty in women's lives.

Age at menarche
The relationship between early stress and age at menarche is complicated. On one hand, there are three kinds of evidence that early stress in the form of malnutrition or disease acts to *delay* menarche. First, the secular decrease in age at menarche seen across developed nations is usually attributed to improved living standards and nutrition (Tanner 1962). Second, comparisons of age at menarche within countries show that it generally occurs later in rural than urban populations and later in lower-than higher-income groups (Eveleth and Tanner 1990). Third, prospective studies show that girls who suffer malnutrition and/or high disease loads reach menarche later than nonmalnourished, healthy controls (e.g., Khan et al. 1996). Moreover, delaying menarche in the face of malnutrition and disease seems to make adaptive sense; when times are tough it will often be adaptive to delay reproduction until health and nutrition improve. Accelerating menarche when health and nutrition are good also makes sense, for when young mammals encounter conditions that favor survival and growth and development it will generally be adaptive for them to reproduce early. This is because when populations are expanding (as they tend to do when resources are plentiful and health is good) individuals who reproduce early have greater long-term fitness because their offspring are born earlier and thus start reproducing earlier themselves (Cole 1954). On the other hand, as we shall soon see, there is also evidence that at least some kinds of early psychosocial stress act to *accelerate* menarche. But this, too, makes adaptive sense, for the General Life History Problem holds that when the future is risky and uncertain the optimal strategy will generally be to reproduce early, to maximize

the probability of any reproduction at all in the face of high or uncertain mortality.

The answer seems to be that age at menarche is facultatively determined by at least two broad environmental pressures: malnutrition and disease (lack of material resources) seem to delay menarche, while insecurity (lack of social resources) seems to accelerate it. Nor does evidence for genetic influences on age at menarche (e.g., Treloar and Martin 1990) preclude a significant, possibly adaptive role for these environmental influences during development. It is in healthy, well-nourished, unstressed populations that genetic factors account for the greatest portion of the variance in age at menarche (Marshall and Tanner 1986:189). But it is precisely under the conditions of energy imbalance and nutritional stress, or social imbalance and psychosocial stress, that the genetic capacity to adjust age at menarche facultatively would be most adaptive (e.g., Ellison 1990; Chasiotis et al. 1998).

Jerome Barkow (1984), elaborating on Draper and Harpending's (1982) model of father-absence as a "developmental switch" for entraining alternative reproductive strategies, was the first to suggest that such a switch might involve sexual maturation as well, and he predicted that girls from father-absent homes would reach menarche earlier than those from father-present homes. Belsky, Steinberg, and Draper (1991) then recast Draper and Harpending's absent-father model and Barkow's prediction in terms of attachment theory and suggested that the psychosocial stress associated with father absence would work through the attachment system to accelerate menarche. While to my knowledge there have been no studies of the relationship between early attachment *per se* (i.e., using direct measures of attachment organization) and age at menarche, there are now many studies showing that psychosocial stress is related to age at menarche.

Perhaps the first such study was by Jones et al. (1972), who noted that in a sample of lower SES Australian women, those who grew up without their fathers during the first six years of life reported significantly earlier menarche than the father-present women. In another early study, Rona and Pereira (1974) found that lower SES Chilean girls reached menarche significantly earlier than girls of the highest SES. Although neither of these studies had any information about the relationship between early psychosocial stress and SES, their results are interesting because they run counter to the usual finding of an association between low SES and delayed menarche. The findings of Proos, Hofvander, and Tuvemo (1991) also run counter the usual association. Although Proos and his colleagues had no measures of early psychosocial stress, they found that the median age at menarche among 107 Indian girls adopted into Sweden was 11.6 years, significantly lower than both the median for Swedish girls generally (13.0 years) and those reported for Indian girls in India (ranging in various studies between 12.8 and 14.4 years). Five of the 107 girls adopted from India reached menarche before age 9; the youngest was 7.3 years old. Of the girls for whom background information was available (87 or 81%) almost all were adopted from orphanages or foster homes in India. They ranged between 1 month and 11 years old when they arrived in Sweden. Later age at arrival was significantly associated with earlier menarche.[10] Given the well-known association between malnutrition and disease and delayed menarche, it is difficult to understand why these girls – orphans from a relatively poor country – should have early menarche. Proos et al. offer no explanation, but note that the fact that age at menarche was inversely correlated with age at arrival suggests the influence of factors that are "related to the length of residence in the pre-adoptive environment." To be an orphan is to have lost one's parents, and orphanages and foster homes are not always the best places to find new ones. The early experiences of these girls surely included more than a little stress.

In the first study designed specifically to explore the relationship between early psychosocial stress and menarche, Michelle Surbey (1990) found in a large sample of Canadian women that psychosocial stress generally, but in particular that related to father absence, was associated with earlier menarche. In the first test of the Belsky et al. (1991) prediction of an association between insecure attachment and early menarche (but, alas, with only inferential measures of early attachment), Moffitt, Caspi, and Belsky (1992) examined the relationship between early psychosocial stress and menarche in a large sample of New Zealand women who had been followed longitudinally. They concluded that family conflict and father absence in childhood predicted somewhat earlier age at menarche, but they argue that, because of evidence of mother–daughter correlations in age at menarche from other studies, a genetic transmission

---

[10] The longer the girls lived in orphanages and foster homes in India before coming to Sweden the younger they were when they reached menarche ($r = -0.23$; $p < 0.05$). This relationship was even stronger when only those who arrived before age 7 were included ($r = -0.39$; $p < 0.001$).

model might provide a more parsimonious explanation of their findings. (I will return to this point shortly.) In the next study motivated specifically by the Belsky et al. model, Wierson, Long, and Forehand (1993) examined age at menarche in relation to divorce of parents and interparental conflict in 71 girls between the ages of 11 and 18. Girls from divorced families had earlier menarche and those from families in which the mothers reported higher conflict with husbands had significantly earlier menarche. Graber and her colleagues (1995) then reported results from their study of 75 middle- and upper-middle-class, premenarcheal girls between the ages of 10 and 14 who were followed longitudinally. They found that girls who reported lower levels of family warmth and cohesion and who scored higher on a measure of depressive affect reached menarche significantly earlier than the other girls. Although they do not rule out a genetic transmission model, they conclude that the bulk of evidence suggests that "stressful or negative affective situations are accelerating development" (1995:356). And recently, in a study of 380 secondary school students between the ages of 16 and 19 years in southern Italy, Kim, Smith, and Palermiti (1997) report that several measures of family conflict were significantly correlated with early menarche, which in turn was related to younger age at first sexual intercourse. In addition, various measures of family conflict in men were significantly correlated with earlier spermarche, earlier intercourse, and more sexual partners.

Finally, Chasiotis et al. (1998) have made an important contribution to our understanding of the relation between early stress and menarche by making good use of a unique natural (or cultural) experiment: the reunification of Germany after 40 years of division into two very different political and economic systems. With information on age at menarche for 35 mother–daughter dyads in West Germany and 33 mother–daughter dyads in East Germany, along with extensive contextual variables for each family, they were able to examine the influence of both environmental (early stress) and genetic factors (mothers' age at menarche) on the daughters' age at menarche. They found that mother's age at menarche predicted daughter's age at menarche – but only when mother and daughter had similar levels of environmental stress. This was the case in West Germany, where the political and economic system was much the same for mothers and daughters, but not in East Germany, where the mothers grew up under one system, but after reunification experienced a new one, in which their daughters matured. Although absolutely poorer than West German mothers, East German mothers experienced less economic uncertainty (i.e., less inequalty: zero unemployment) than West German mothers. East German mothers also experienced less early stress than their own daughters, who experienced the effect of the collapse of the former German Democratic Republic on their parents.

West German mothers, in other words, passed on to their daughters not only the genes "for" a certain age at menarche, but also more-or-less the same environment in which they grew up. With environmental influences on age at menarche held constant for West German mother–daughter dyads, mothers' age at menarche accounts for more of the variance in daughters' age at menarche. East German mothers, on the other hand, passed on to their daughters the genes "for" a certain age at menarche but did not pass on the same amount of early stress. In fact, the East German mothers passed on to their daughters *more* early stress than they had experienced, and so their daughters reached menarche earlier than they had. In the new, relatively high-stress environment of East Germany, the genes "for" age at menarche that daughters received from their mothers had a different effect than they had in the relatively low-stress (i.e., predictable) environment in which their mothers matured.

This study shows the necessity of controlling for maternal age at menarche when investigating the effects of early stress or any other environmental effect on age at menarche. But the opposite is also true: this study shows the necessity of controlling for environmental effects on age at menarche when investigating genetic effects (e.g., mother–daughter correlations) on age at menarche. For example, Moffitt et al. (1992) and Campbell and Udry (1995) both found significant mother–daughter correlations in age at menarche and cast doubt on any important role for environmental effects. But neither do they take into consideration that along with their mothers' genes, the daughters in their samples also inherited their mothers' environments. Again, as Marshall and Tanner (1986) emphasized, it is in healthy, well-nourished, low-stress populations that genetic factors account for the greatest portion of the variance in age at menarche. It is precisely under conditions of early stress, however, that the genetic capacity to accommodate age at menarche to changing conditions would be most adaptive.

However, because actual reproduction has a greater impact on fitness than the mere capacity for reproduction, there is clearly more to maximizing current reproduction than early menarche. Therefore, we must explore the effects of early stress on all of the determinants of age at first reproduction, not simply age at menarche. Theoretically, even if early stress were found to have no effect on age menarche, this would not require us to abandon our expectation that early risk and uncertainty will be associated with early reproduction.

Age at first sexual intercourse
One obvious additional influence on age at first reproduction is age at first sexual intercourse. In fact, not only is early menarche associated (at least in the US) with early sexual intercourse,[11] but so is the sort of early stress that has been associated with early menarche. A good example is Gail Wyatt's (1988, 1990) work with a large sample of women in Los Angeles. Matching these women on race, income, education, and marital status, Wyatt found no effect of race on age at first consensual sexual intercourse, but did find clear effects for three kinds of early stressors. First, early sex was associated with low socioeconomic status, with daughters of skilled and unskilled workers having first consensual sex between 1 and 2 years earlier than daughters of professional and semi-professional workers. Virtually all studies of age at first sexual inter-course find earlier sex among lower SES men and women (e.g., Kinsey, Pomeroy, and Martin 1948; Kinsey et al. 1953; Weinrich 1977). Second, *consistency* (i.e., predictability, certainty) of household structure, rather than *number* of parents, delayed age at first consensual sex.[12] Women from single-parent, two-parent, or multiple-parent households whose makeup was none the less relatively consistent prior to age 18 had their first sexual intercourse at an average age of 17; women from households whose composition was less consistent had their first consensual sexual intercourse significantly earlier, at 16. Finally, women who experienced the early stress of at least one occasion of contact sexual abuse (fondling, frottage, attempted or completed oral or vaginal intercourse) had their first consensual sexual intercourse fully 15 months earlier than women in the nonabuse group.

In fact, early stress in the form of sexual abuse is often associated with early sexual behavior in women. In addition to Wyatt's work, for exam-

---

[11] See, for example, Bernard (1975); Cvetkovich et al. (1978); Garn, Pesick, and Petzold (1986); Presser (1978); Soefer et al. (1985); Udry and Cliquet (1982); Zabin et al. (1986).

[12] Consistency of household structure here implies a degree of consistently satisfactory *process* (family relations). If the relations between the men and women had broken down then the structure of the household (number of parents) is more likely to have changed.

ple, Alexander and Lupfer (1987) interviewed 586 undergraduate women at a US university and found that fully 25 percent reported that family members or other adult males had "fondled or touched" them when they were girls in a way that made them "feel uncomfortable." Compared to those who reported no such early sexual abuse, these women were very much more likely to have experienced consensual sexual intercourse ($p = 0.0004$) and more frequent intercourse ($p = 0.006$). While several hypotheses have been advanced to explain why early sexual abuse is correlated with early sex and/or a high frequency of sex, most of them are consistent with the proposition that early sexual abuse activates the HPA system. Chronic activation of the HPA system may affect the hypothalamic-anterior pituitary-gonadal (HPG) system, which is the hormonal mechanism that mediates sexual maturation. In effect, then, early sexual abuse would constitute another (albeit highly malignant) member of the category of "early stressor," any one of which might foster early menarche or early sexual intercourse. Herman-Giddens and her colleagues (1988) seem to have been the first to propose this idea. Having noted in their clinical experience that sexually abused girls often seemed physically more mature than same-aged nonabused girls, they hypothesized that sexual abuse might stimulate the release of cortisol, which in turn might trigger precocious puberty.

Trickett and Putnam (1993) also note that the HPA system has well-known effects on the HPG system and that early chronic activation of the HPA system may account for the "widespread clinical impression that early sexual abuse victims show an early onset of puberty" (1993:85). Following this line of reasoning further, Putnam and his colleagues (DeBellis et al. 1994; Putnam and Trickett 1993) have been studying the relationship between early sexual abuse and activation of the HPA system. They have found that, compared to carefully matched controls, sexually abused girls show significantly higher morning cortisol levels up to a year after the abuse was first disclosed to child protective services (and presumably ended). This is indicative of a hyperactive HPA system. As we saw earlier, persistent elevations of cortisol have been implicated in the development of a number of diseases and disabilities, including neuronal loss in the hippocampus and increased risk for anxiety and depressive disorders. As we saw earlier (p. 199) hyperactivation of the HPA system and chronic high levels of cortisol are also associated with disturbed sleep in children. It is thus interesting to note that in their study of the childhood precursors of age at first intercourse for girls, Udry and Van den Berg (1995) found that girls who had frequent nightmares or wet their beds during the first five years of life were significantly younger at first intercourse than other girls. Since nightmares and bedwetting are associated with disturbed sleep – and perhaps elevated cortisol as well – Udry and van den Berg may have provided indirect corroboration of the association between early stress (elevated cortisol) and early age at first sex. Since disturbed sleep is also thought to result in impaired release of growth hormone, they may have explained as well why early maturing girls tend to be shorter than late-maturers (Garn et al. 1986a; Shangold et al. 1989; Wellens et al. 1992).

In sum, when girls grow up under conditions of chronic risk and uncertainty they are likely to experience HPA system hyperactivation, which is implicated in both early menarche and young age at first intercourse. It remains to be seen how attachment history *per se* is related to age at menarche and first sexual intercourse, but to the extent that early stress and the attachment process are deeply intertwined, the question itself becomes more interesting. It is also remains to be seen what factors besides age at menarche and first sexual intercourse might foster early reproduction. There is some evidence, for example, that early menarche may also be associated with higher fecundability for both first pregnancies (Apter and Vihko 1983) and subsequent ones (Cutright 1972; Presser 1978). Nonetheless, since early menarche and young age at first intercourse tend to minimize age at first reproduction, and since the optimal strategy for reproducing in risky and uncertain environments may be to reproduce at the earliest opportunity, these findings are broadly consistent with predictions from life history theory. It is no surprise, then, that the world's most disadvantaged peoples tend to have high reproductive rates, especially among their youngest women. The Alan Guttmacher Institute (1998), for example, provides data for 18 nations on the proportion of births to women between the ages of 20 and 24 who gave birth before they were 18 years old (ranging from 1% in Japan, Germany and Poland to 47% in Bangladesh) and the United Nations Human Development Index (HDI) for each country. The HDI is a number which combines three measures of a nation's quality of life: average life expectancy, years of education, and income. In this sample it ranged between 0.938 (in the USA) and 0.364 (in Bangladesh). The association between early fertility and the HDI is highly negative ($r = -0.87$; $p < 0.001$; see Figure 5.1). This is consistent with the view that when people have reason to expect short lives, little education, and low incomes, young women have high birth

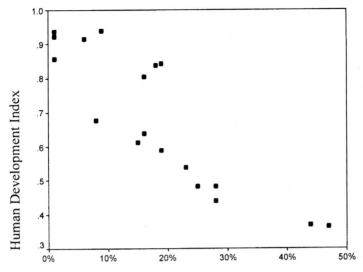

% births to women aged 20–24 who delivered before 18

Figure 5.1 Relationship between the UN Human Development Index and percentage of total births to women aged 20–24 who gave birth before they were 18.

rates (see also Cincotta and Engelman 1997; Kelley and Schmidt 1996; Lancaster 1997).

A rational choice perspective on single mothering
But minimizing age at first reproduction is not the only way to maximize current reproduction. Regardless of when a woman starts reproducing, another (not mutually exclusive) way for her to maximize current repro-duction is to maximize her reproductive rate. David Hamburg (1993), in fact, notes that, at least in the US, women who begin childbearing in their teens also tend to have their children in quick succession. Carried to the hypothetical extreme, this would mean producing children at each and every reproductive opportunity that came along. Actually doing this, however – and having the children survive – is obviously impossible because the rate at which females can produce children is sharply limited by their access to the resources that they are anatomically obliged to invest in bearing and rearing them. When a woman's access to these resources is limited or uncertain, there are only two ways that she can

increase her reproductive rate. The first is to invest less in each offspring. By sacrificing some of her children's reproductive value she might be able to increase her own reproductive rate (see above, pp. 51–61). If children's reproductive value is heavily dependent on parental investment, however, finding the optimum trade-off between offspring quantity and quality may be difficult, especially under risky and uncertain conditions. The second possibility for increasing reproductive rate is to gain access to more resources. Doing so, however, entails the trade-off between direct *care of* offspring and indirect *investment in* offspring – i.e., working *with* children vs. working *for* children (Kaplan 1994; Kleiman and Malcolm 1981). Again, however, if children's reproductive value is heavily dependent on direct parental care, finding the optimum trade-off between direct care of children and obtaining resources for children may be difficult, especially under risky and uncertain conditions. This is the evolutionary ecological origin of the essential quandary of all single mothers: children need food, but having children makes it hard to get food; children need protection, but having children makes it hard to protect them. And the more children you have, the harder it gets. But sometimes it is good (adaptive) to have more children.

Hominids became capable of solving the single-mother problem through the evolution of the psychobiological mechanisms underlying our capacity for social exchange, which enabled mothers to gain access to the resources they require for bearing and rearing children from others (e.g., Irons 1983). The most common social exchange arrangement for solving the single-mother problem has been through the evolution of the psychobiological capacity for the sexual division of labor and for sharing. This is thought to have resulted in the capacity for significant male parental investment, the role of father, the origin of the family, and increased offspring reproductive value (see above, pp. 124–126). However, if the risky and uncertain conditions that make it adaptive for women to maximize current reproduction also make it adaptive for men to do the same, women will not necessarily gain better access to the resources they require by turning to men for their investment. Indeed, when men do not have access to the resources that women require, the best way for women to increase their reproductive rates without unduly sacrificing their children's reproductive value may be to reproduce *without* husbands – i.e., as single mothers. To see why, we need to understand why the choice to be a single mother may be a rational, even if unconscious, response to risk and uncertainty.

Before the evolution of male parental investment, all mothers were single mothers. And before the evolution of male parental investment all males were anatomically obliged to reproduce by using their size, strength, aggressiveness, wits and willingness to take risks in order to be chosen by females for sex and/or to coerce females into having sex and other males into fearing them. For all practical purposes, then, before the evolution of male parental investment, the primary (or only?) reproductive strategy for males was the Young Male Syndrome. The evolution of prolonged helplessness in hominid children, however, created a new arena in which males could compete with each other to be chosen by females: their capacity to provide parental investment. With the evolution of this new male reproductive strategy, the existing, prototypical hominoid male reproductive strategy (i.e., the Young Male Syndrome) was relegated to the role of an *alternative* male reproductive strategy. Likewise, the evolution of prolonged helplessness in hominid children created a new set of criteria by which hominid females could choose males: their ability and willingness to provide parental investment. With the evolution of this new basis for female choice, the existing, prototypical hominoid female strategy of resisting male coercion and selecting males exclusively on the basis of their genetic quality (appearance, size, strength, aggressiveness, and willingness to take risks, etc.) was relegated to the role of an *alternative* female reproductive strategy.[13]

On this view, the Young Female Syndrome is an evolved facultative adaptation whereby young women who find themselves growing up in risky and uncertain environments can maximize current reproduction. The evolution of prolonged helplessness in hominid children led to sexual selection via female choice against the Young Male Syndrome as an obligate male reproductive strategy. At the same time, in the act of choosing males for their ability and willingness to provide parental investment, hominid females also exerted sexual selection against the Young Female Syndrome as an obligate female reproductive strategy. When men today are unable or unwilling to provide parental investment, the Young Male Syndrome is still available as an alternative (if unconscious) strategy. Similarly, when women today find that conditions are risky and

---

[13] To be chosen on the basis of their capacity for parental investment, males are obliged to control whatever resources females require for parental investment. But by controlling these resources males may also be in position to use this very control to *coerce* females into having sex (e.g., Hrdy 1997; Smuts 1992, 1995).

uncertain, and that men have little to offer as husbands or fathers, they can fall back (unconsciously) on the Young Female Syndrome, resisting male attempts at coercion while attempting to maximize current reproduction. One way for them to maximize current reproduction is to take immediate advantage of any reproductive opportunities that may arise. However, this may entail trading off a degree of concern about a potential partner's suitability as a husband or father. When males have little to offer (or there are few of them) and the adaptive problem is to maximize current reproduction, there is no virtue in spending time assessing a man's resource-holding potential or capacity for commitment as a husband/father. Not only does choosing carefully take time, the pay-off to having a good husband/father is in the *future*, in the form of children with higher reproductive value. But when what matters is the *present*, a woman's optimal strategy may be to choose men quickly (impulsively?), perhaps even automatically (unconsciously) evaluating them on the basis of what they *can* contribute to her existing or potential children *right now, without waiting*. This contribution may consist of two kinds of value: (1) the inferred quality of a man's genes (i.e., his looks, charm, size, strength, aggressiveness, willingness to take risks, etc.) and/or (2) whatever resources he may have immediately on hand or that would be quickly forthcoming from or through him.

Like the Young Male Syndrome, the Young Female Syndrome works against long-term monogamy. When the optimal strategy for either sex is to maximize current reproduction, the psychosexual/attachment bonds that develop between men and women are less likely to endure or to be exclusive. Indeed, such bonds may be counterproductive, perhaps especially for women. This is because when a man is unable or unwilling to offer the parental investment that a woman requires for bearing and rearing his children, she gains nothing by maintaining an exclusive relationship with him. At the same time that he fails to provide for the woman and her/their children, he may also compete with them for whatever resources come to hand. In addition, his very presence reduces her capacity for female choice – i.e., her capacity to show interest in other men, to select them as fathers for her children. Any expression of interest in another man (which may be construed simply as seeming to attract it) also runs the risk of exciting the violent expression of the sexual antagonism and jealousy that is so often part of the Young Male Syndrome. Ultimately, this sexual antagonism and jealousy may be due to the uncertain paternity that follows when the optimal strategy for either men or women is to maximize current reproduction (e.g., Daly and Wilson 1988).

Jane Lancaster (1989) makes the same point in her evolutionary model of single motherhood. She argues that female-headed households result not from the *absence* of males (a deficit model of single motherhood) so much as from the positive, creative efforts of women to achieve access to resources for parental investment. Lancaster uses the principles of evolutionary ecology and the cross-cultural record of family types to argue that the recent world-wide increase in single motherhood[14] is largely a rational, if not necessarily consciously planned, response by women to political and economic forces that deprive men of reasonable and predictable access to the resources that women require for bearing and rearing children. From this perspective, single motherhood is not simply the result of men's abdication of responsibility to their wives, girlfriends, and children (i.e., the Young Male Syndrome), but a potentially adaptive, rational response by women to the demands of rearing children without predictable help from the children's fathers under chronically risky and uncertain conditions.

Lancaster notes that one traditional setting in which men are unlikely to provide many material resources for women and children is polygyny. In many polygynous societies, males compete with each other to provide social and political/military protection for several wives while co-wives and networks of female kin effectively do the real work of provisioning households. She also points out that a great many single-mother families are really polygynous families from which the father is mostly absent. Increasingly, however, in both large-scale industrial societies and developing nations, and even small-scale traditional societies,[15] large numbers of men have limited and uncertain access to the resources that women require for setting up households because of inadequate educational resources and the virtual absence of work (e.g., Bourgois 1995; Shorris 1997; Wilson 1987, 1996). Under such conditions, Lancaster argues, facultative polyandry[16] may be a woman's optimal reproductive strategy. By

---

[14] Lancaster refers to studies that suggest a 300% increase in the frequency of female-headed families in the USA since 1970 and that similar trends are occurring world-wide.

[15] For example, Victoria Burbank (Burbank and Chisholm 1989, 1998) shows how changing political and economic conditions have resulted in an approximately 500% increase in the frequency of single motherhood in an isolated Australian Aboriginal community during the 1980s.

[16] Polyandry is a rare form of marriage in which one woman is married to two or more men. Facultative polyandry may be thought of as *ad hoc* or informal polyandry.

maintaining social, economic, and sexual–emotional relations with more than one man, while at the same time refusing to allow any man to live for long with her and her children, she may be better able to insure an adequate flow of resources. By maintaining friendships with a number of men, especially the ones with whom she has had children, a woman reduces the risk of interrupting her flow of resources by spreading the risk among several men. Further, by maintaining friendships with the fathers of her children a woman also maintains her ties to each man's circle of kin, who may provide something of value to their grandchildren, nieces, nephews, etc. Finally, excluding men from their households also enables these women to minimize the potential for male sexual jealousy and to maximize their female choice – their freedom to choose with whom they will have sex, and for what reasons. Although Lancaster does not include the Young Male or Female Syndromes in her model, to the extent that each has been linked to polygyny in the cross-cultural record, they may be linked as well to single motherhood. And, as we have seen, of course, single motherhood itself has been linked with the early stress that may lead to these syndromes

There is growing ethnographic, demographic, and epidemiological evidence to support the proposition that facultative polyandry can be an adaptive reproductive strategy under conditions of risk and uncertainty. In poor communities in the Dominican Republic, for example, some women live in traditional two-parent, monogamous households, while others live in female-headed households and practice facultative polyandry. When these women and their families were compared on a number of biomedical variables, it was found that the women in the female-headed households had more children, healthier children, fewer pre- and post-natal medical complications, more children surviving to age five, more protein per caput in their children's diet, and better psychological health (Brown 1973; cited in Lancaster 1989). In a similar study, William Dressler (1982) found that single mothers practicing facultative polyandry had significantly lower blood-pressure than women in other kinds of families. Analogous findings from other parts of the world suggest that single motherhood may provide a way to maximize reproductive rate without sacrificing too much offspring reproductive value (e.g., Burbank 1988, 1995; Burbank and Chisholm 1989, 1998; Mencher and Okongwu 1993). Linda Burton (1990) and Carol Stack (1974), among others, also observe that single motherhood frequently occurs in a context of three or more generations of women in extended families, which gives young women access to the extended family's resources, especially help in child care. Single motherhood in these circumstances carries less cost for both young women and their children than it might if the women were living with their husbands/boyfriends in more "traditional" but socially isolated nuclear families. As we shall see a bit later, however, that single mothers occasionally do better than married mothers does not mean that single motherhood is wrong, irrational, or maladaptive on the more frequent occasions when they do worse.

Arline Geronimus (1987, 1994, 1996) has done important pioneering work on the socioecology of early childbearing in the US. Her conclusions support the proposition that in the face of risky and uncertain futures it is not inherently irrational for women to begin having babies early and often. The crux of her argument is that, well before they have children, many chronically poor women have already been deeply affected by the cumulative effects of early stress – by the literal embodiment of risk and uncertainty. As we saw earlier, chronically high cortisol levels have been linked to immune system dysfunction and increased risk of disease; loss of neurons in brain areas involved in memory; gastrointestinal and cardiovascular disorders; anxiety, depression, and the associated increased risk for substance abuse. Geronimus argues that under such conditions early, rapid childbearing may maximize reproductive opportunities; delaying or slowing reproduction only allows these stressors and disease processes more time to work their deleterious effects. Younger mothers may thus be healthier mothers – at least healthier than they would be if they postponed childbearing. They are also more likely to leave descendants, for in time these deleterious effects can kill. Using data from the US Census and birth and death certificates, she shows that the percent of first births to teenage mothers is higher in communities where life expectancy is low (Geronimus 1996). In their recent study of the relation between age-specific fertility and mortality in 77 Chicago neighborhoods, Wilson and Daly (1997) found the same thing: the highest rates of early childbearing were concentrated in those neighborhoods which had the highest mortality rates. And, in her study of teenage childbearing as an "alternative life-course strategy" in multigenerational African-American families in the US, Burton (1990) reported that 91 percent of the women in her sample did not expect to live to be 60 years old – despite the fact that actuarial figures put the life expectancy for African-American women considerably higher.

In part because of Burton's finding of an association between expected lifespan and teenage childbearing, I used questionnaires to elicit recollections from 136 middle-class American university women aged 19–25 about early psychosocial stress, their sexual histories, and how long they expected to live (Chisholm 1999). Several measures of early stress (mostly strained family relations) correlated with both expected lifespan and age at first sex. Multiple regression analyses suggested that early stress affected age at first sexual intercourse primarily through its effects on expected lifespan – i.e., after controlling for the effects of early stress on age at first sexual intercourse, expected lifespan still had a significant independent effect of age at first sex (thus: early stress → shorter expected lifespan → younger age at first sex).

Delaying or slowing reproduction also allows the cumulative effects of early stress on women more time to kill their babies. Comparing African- and European-American neonatal mortality rates for children of mothers between the ages of 15 and 34 and over, Geronimus (1987) also found that at all maternal ages African-Americans suffer higher rates of neonatal mortality. But, whereas African-American women aged 24–26 lost their babies at a rate 2.68 times higher than European-American women, 16-year old African-American women did significantly better, losing babies at a rate "only" 1.22 times higher than 16-year old European-American women. In risky and uncertain environments the optimal age for childbearing is expected to be younger than in safe and predictable environments.

Finally, delaying or slowing reproduction also allows the cumulative effects of early stress more time to kill men as well as mothers and babies. By maximizing current reproduction, young women may also maximize their chances to benefit from their choice of men. This is because when conditions are risky and uncertain for women, they usually are for men as well, and the longer women delay childbearing, or slow its pace, the more men will die. McCord and Freeman (1990), for example, used demographic data to show that in Harlem, a high-risk area of New York City, the death rates for both sexes and most ages were higher than in Bangladesh. In fact, they found that a boy born and raised in Harlem has less chance of living to age 65 than one born in Bangladesh. For both men and women under 65, the relative risks in Harlem compared to the rest of the US were highest for homicide and alcohol- and drug-related deaths. These mortality figures reflect the overall effects of inequality, risk and uncertainty, chronic stress, and the Young Male Syndrome throughout the lifespan. They also show how the number of men available as suitable husbands for women is low and decreases with age. Even if men do not die from drugs, homicide, and alcohol, as they age they are more likely to show other effects of accumulating stress and disease processes, including being in jail. By having their children early in their reproductive careers, women in high-risk environments may have more opportunity to exercise their choice of fathers for their children. And, even if men survive, of course, a major determinant of single mothering in high-risk neighborhoods is the absence of work, which means that many men simply do not have access to the resources that women require for reproduction (Burton 1990; Phoenix 1993; Wilson 1987, 1996).

The reason that many chronically poor women begin childbearing early and/or have their babies fairly rapidly, often as single mothers, may thus reflect, as Arline Geronimus put it, their "strategic considerations" concerning perceptions that they "face not simply a shorter, but a far more uncertain lifespan" (1996:346). "By deciding to become teen mothers," she says, "young women in some persistently impoverished populations may be planning for the kind of future they have every reason to expect" (Geronimus 1996:346). Kristin Luker (1996) makes the same point, arguing that for many disadvantaged young women there is no reason *not* to begin or continue childbearing. For young women who are already disadvantaged, the extra burden of a child is a small, marginal, short-term cost with some immediate benefits. Having a child entails few opportunity costs; if there are no jobs, having a baby scarcely jeopardizes an income. On the other hand, having a child gives the immediate benefit of a new child to love. (As Candy put it in the epigraph at the beginning of this chapter, "you know how you love a mother? You can never love a mother more until you have a baby.") Nor may having a child now entail losing any perceived future benefit. Having grown up in the midst of risk and uncertainty, she may devalue the future. She may even find it hard to imagine being alive in the future. Such perceptions might not be entirely subjective. Early and frequent childbearing, therefore, may be a rational, even if unconscious, response to restricted horizons and the absence of hope.

Which brings us finally to the question of how a choice can be rational without being conscious. Following Cooper, Elzanowski, Damasio, and Plotkin, I argued in chapter 3 that rationality derives from, and is ultimately for, fitness – the "state" of continuance. Rationality is an adaptation for achieving fitness; fitness is the ultimate thing (i.e., value itself) to be rational *about*. But in order to be rational about fitness it must first be represented internally, phenotypically. These internal representations of fitness (reproductive value) can then be used to evaluate (select among) alternative models of the future. This capacity to choose makes it possible to approach the future rationally, according to an objective principle: the internal, imperfect, subjective representations of objectively good fitness moves made by our ancestors. These internal representations of objective value are experienced subjectively as emotions (Elzanowski's "value experience"), which, as we know very well, are often unconscious. Indeed, some emotions appear *always* to be unconscious (e.g., those involved in automatic evaluation). For Cooper, the foundation for all decisions is the subjective feeling that something good or bad will or will not happen. Ultimately, then, all decisions go back to a "choice function" which works with representations of value that may very well be unconscious.

These representations of value (emotion) derive from and represent fitness, which is continuance. To continue, as Holland argued, all complex adaptive systems must be able to see into the future in order to do two things: to avoid stepping off fitness cliffs and to set the stage for future good fitness moves. To do these jobs rationally, both cliffs and future good moves must be represented internally, phenotypically, so that they can be used by the "choice function" to evaluate models of the future. When an environment is objectively risky and uncertain (filled with cliffs), these internal, phenotypic representations of value are more likely to be experienced subjectively as insecurity – fear of loss – the subjective feeling that something bad will happen. When an environment is objectively risky and uncertain it may well make fitness sense (be rational) to maximize current reproduction. If the subjective feeling that something bad will happen predisposes young men and women to the early and impulsive display of sexual and aggressive behavior, then such feelings may be part of a rational (even if unconscious) mechanism for avoiding fitness cliffs.

This evolutionary psychological notion of unconscious rational choice supports the "revisionist" view of teenage childbearing, which is simply the view (of Geronimus, Lancaster, Luker, and others) that early childbearing is not necessarily irrational or maladaptive. Frank Furstenberg (1991) criticizes this position on the grounds that "no existing evidence shows that disadvantaged women *believe* that early childbearing will produce healthier babies" (1991:135; original emphasis). But, as we just saw, rationality does not require a conscious "belief" that one course of action is better or worse than another. To paraphrase Pascal, the amygdala and HPA system have inherited reasons that the cerebral cortex knows not.

Furstenberg also criticizes the revisionist position on the grounds that teenage childbearing manifestly does not always improve the lot of the mothers or their children:

> That many teenage mothers and their families respond resourcefully to the challenge of managing motherhood is undeniable . . . But it is a far leap from this observation to the assertion that early childbearing is an *adaptive* pattern that *improves* the circumstances of economically disadvantaged minorities . . . How would teen mothers themselves look upon the Geronimus thesis? Do they think that teenage childbearing *contributes* to their chances of success in later life? More importantly, do they think that it *improves* the prospects of their offspring? . . . If early childbearing is in fact *desired* and its costs are minimal, then policies and programs aimed at postponing parenthood are surely misguided. (1991:135; emphasis added)

The problem with this criticism (not counting the rationality/conscious thinking issue dealt with above) is that *adaptive* does not necessarily mean "improve" or "contribute to making better." It can mean as well "avoid making worse." As we know, there is more to fitness, and thus adaptation, than setting the stage for a better tomorrow; there are also cliffs to be avoided (especially in risky environments). Early pregnancy may not be "desired," in the sense that it may not be the *best imaginable* reproductive strategy. And there may well be considerable costs associated with early reproduction (as we will see in the final chapter). But this does not mean that early reproduction is not still the optimal strategy for many young men and women in risky and uncertain environments. When the future is objectively risky and uncertain, and young men and women lack the resources to make much difference in their children's futures, their *best available* alternative strategy may be to avoid a fitness cliff. This may involve a "craving" for the kind of immediate security provided by "gaining respect," "having women," and "having babies."

Attachment and reproduction

The central feature of the Belsky, Steinberg, Draper model of the development of reproductive strategies (and therefore my life history theory version of their model) is that the attachment process is a mechanism for entraining the development of the local optimal reproductive strategy. If so, individual differences in attachment history should be related to individual differences in reproductive strategies. We have already seen that individual differences in early stress do seem to be related to various aspects of adult sexual function and behavior, in both men and women. However, while there are good reasons for thinking that early stress and attachment are intimately related, the fact remains that to my knowledge there are as yet no studies of the relationship between early attachment and adult reproductive behavior that use any direct measures of early attachment. Until such studies start appearing, we will have to make do with the few studies that exist of the relationship between *adult* attachment and adult reproductive behavior. Again, while these studies are insufficient to adequately test the Belsky, Steinberg, and Draper model, they do allow some cautious inferences about the effect of early attachment on sexual and parenting behavior, and help to illustrate the model more fully.

As we saw in chapter 2, the General Life History Problem is a model that predicts the optimal allocation of resources to reproduction based on the assumption that there is a trade-off between current and future reproduction. If the attachment process evolved at least in part as a mechanism for entraining the development of the local optimal reproductive strategy, then individual differences in the effects of attachment on reproductive behavior should reflect this current–future trade-off. Simpson and Gangestad's (1991) finding that their Sociosexual Orientation Inventory revealed two independent dimensions of sexual attitudes and behavior – for both men and women – is consistent with this expectation. One dimension reflects what might be called "sex drive" (degree of desire for frequent intercourse) and the other reflects degree of desire for "uncommitted" sex or number of different sexual partners. In turn, there is some evidence that desire for uncommitted sex may be related to attachment history. Hazan and Shaver (1987; Kobak and Hazan 1991; Shaver and Hazan 1994) found that patterns of romantic love in heterosexual couples were related to their adult attachment style – their present IWMs of romantic/sexual relations – and to their recollected patterns of attachment to their parents.[1] Men and women were judged to have been securely attached in childhood if they reported memories of warm relationships with their parents and between their parents. Those so judged were more likely to describe their important adult love relationships as happy, friendly, and trusting. Significantly, they also reported *fewer* and *more committed* (i.e., longer-lasting) relationships than men and women thought to have experienced insecure attachment. The men and women who seemed to have suffered more early emotional stress were apt to describe their adult love relationships in terms indicative of fear of intimacy, more extreme emotional peaks and valleys, jealousy, love as obsession, and *extreme sexual attraction* (Hazan and Shaver 1987:515). Similarly, Brennan and Shaver (1995), using Simpson and Gangestad's (1991) Sociosexual Orientation Inventory and a measure of adult attachment, found that avoidant attachment predicts more indiscriminant sexuality. And when Baldwin et al. (1993) gave their subjects a series of hypothetical, "if–then" scenarios involving patterns of social relations with romantic partners, those who were judged to have had secure attachment histories were quicker to identify words representing positive interpersonal outcomes, whereas insecure subjects were quicker to identify negative outcome words. This is consistent with the notion that attachment history affects expectations about romantic/sexual relations

Using the Belsky et al. model to investigate the role of "childhood adversity and environmental risks" on adult romantic/sexual relations, Elizabeth Hill and her colleagues (1994) showed empirically that a variety of measures of early stress (e.g., poverty, parental divorce, abusive punishment, etc.) were good predictors of adult attachment style (i.e., secure vs. insecure) and adult romantic/sexual behavior. They found, for example, that insecure adults were less likely than secure adults ever to have been in a love relationship – but that if they had ever married or cohabited, they did so at a younger age and after a shorter courtship. They also found that attachment history affected men's and women's love relationships differently: secure men had *longer* love relationships than insecure men – but secure women entered love relationships when they were *older* and after a significantly *longer* courtship than insecure women. This is significant because while attachment theory makes no predictions about sex differences in patterns of attachment, life history theory expects them (e.g., Trivers 1972). Hill and her colleagues interpret their findings in explicit life history terms, arguing that their results are consistent with the proposition that early environmental risk and uncertainty "fosters short-term rather than long-term mating strategies" (1994:323).

The life history theory view of attachment presented here suggests that there is no a priori, "normal" pattern of attachment – that secure and insecure attachment styles (and possibly others) are both normal in the sense that they represent the normal working of an evolved mechanism for entraining the development of locally optimal reproductive strategies. On this view, the normal functioning of the mechanism is highly dependent on information from the past in the form of DNA. But to function adaptively, to do its adaptive work, the attachment mechanism must also work with information from the present, because it is only by juxtaposing information from the past and the present that one can predict the future. Predicting the future is what attachment is all about: predicting what other people are going to do (manipulating their beliefs and desires to work out their intentions) in order to estimate the amount of risk and uncertainty one is likely to face in the future. On the basis of this "knowledge" of the future, one can begin following the developmental trajectory leading to the most appropriate reproductive strategy for that particular future.

We might expect, then, that individual differences in adult reproductive strategies would show relatively low heritability – because the adaptive job of the evolved mechanism that produces individual differences is to match the individual to its particular environment. Waller and Shaver's (1994) recent behavior genetic analysis of patterns of adult romantic attachment supports this prediction. Using a twin-family study research design, Waller and Shaver examined the heritability of particular "love styles" using Hendrick and Hendrick's (1986) Love Attitude Scale (LAS). While there remain questions about measurement and interpretation, the LAS is thought to capture dimensions of behavior or attitude that might be expected to vary with reproductive strategy (sample item: "My lover and I were attracted to each other immediately after we first met"). Subjects were 838 adult twins and 153 of their spouses from the California Twin Registry. Waller and Shaver found that, in contrast to most other attitude dimensions and personality traits, genetic factors accounted for essentially none of the variance in love styles. They conclude that

> . . . shared experiences, not shared genes, account for twin
> similarities in love attitudes. And the correlation between
> spouses' love styles, which we showed cannot be attributed to
> attitude convergence, indicate that love attitudes influence
> mate selection . . . Hence, an orientation toward romantic love
> that may have been learned during childhood can eventually

affect adult relationship outcomes. (Waller and Shaver
1994:272)

There is evidence that attachment history affects parenting behavior as
well as adult attachment. Several studies have shown significant relationships between mothers' recollections of their own childhood attachment relations and objective measures of the way they interact with their
own children. Main and Goldwyn (1984) found that women who were
judged to have had relatively insecure attachment histories were significantly more likely to have children classified as insecure in the Strange
Situation test. Likewise, Ricks and Noyes (cited in Ricks 1985) found that
mothers of infants classified as secure in the Strange Situation reported
significantly more positive recollections of their parents than did mothers of insecure children. And, as we saw in chapter 4, both Main et al.
(1985) and Fonagy et al. (1997a) found that parents (both mothers and
fathers) who were judged secure in their adult attachment relationships
generally were significantly more likely to have secure infants.
Approaching the issue in a different way, Rholes et al. (1997) report that
in a sample of 638 university students who had never been married, those
who were classified as insecure in their adult attachment styles had
significantly more negative expectations about children and their capacity to be parents than those who were classified as secure.

There is also evidence that early psychosocial stress, broadly defined,
is related to later parenting behavior or attitudes. Hall, Pawlby, and
Wolkind (1979) found that women who reported disruption (divorce,
death, or long-term separation) in their families of origin were significantly
more likely to be unmarried and to have been a teenage mother.
Moreover, in naturalistic observations of these mothers interacting with
their own children, they talked to, looked at, and touched their babies
significantly less than other mothers. They seemed relatively indifferent
to their babies and, indeed, spent more time in a separate room away
from their infants than did other mothers. Another kind of evidence that
early stress affects parenting behavior adversely comes from studies of
the intergenerational transmission of child abuse. In a particularly clear
prospective study, for example, Egeland, Jacobvitz, and Papatola (1987)
worked with a sample of American women who had been selected for
their high (statistical) risk for abusing their children. They found that
70 percent of the women who had been abused as children themselves
(physically and/or sexually) ultimately mistreated their own. Similarly,

Constantino (1996), compared the adult attachment styles of single mothers whose children were abnormally aggressive to a carefully matched control group of single mothers whose children were less aggressive. He found that all of the mothers of the aggressive children were classified as insecure, while only one mother of a nonaggressive child was so classified. And Moncher (1996) found that single mothers with an insecure adult attachment style scored significantly higher than secure single mothers on a set of measures for assessing risk for child abuse.

In sum, while the evidence is limited, it is none the less consistent with the main prediction of Belsky, Steinberg, and Draper's model. On the face of it, insecure attachment does seem to predispose both men and women toward an "uncommitted" style of romantic/sexual behavior. This, in turn, would seem to be consistent with the hypothetical adaptive function of a strategy for maximizing current reproduction – that is, the production of offspring. But, because limited resources must always be allocated amongst competing fitness needs (components of fitness), it follows that, if insecure attachment predisposes people to put more of their resources into the *production* of offspring, they can only put less into *rearing* offspring. Because of the assumption of optimality, we expect there to be a trade-off between the production (quantity) and rearing (quality) of offspring. Therefore, in order to test the Belsky, Steinberg, and Draper model more completely, and to integrate attachment and life history theories more fully, we urgently need more information about the relationship between attachment history and adult sexual and parenting behavior.

6   The cost of continuing

The search for a universally applicable account of the quality of life has, on its side, the promise of a greater power to stand up for the lives of those whom tradition has oppressed or marginalized. But it faces the epistemological difficulty of grounding such an account in an adequate way, saying where the norms come from and how they can be known to be the best.   Nussbaum and Sen (1993:4)

Evolutionary Humanism is necessarily unitary instead of dualistic, affirming the unity of mind and body; universal instead of particularist, affirming the continuity of man with the rest of life, and of life with the rest of the universe; naturalistic instead of supernaturalist, affirming the unity of the spiritual and the material; and global instead of divisive, affirming the unity of all mankind.
                                                    Julian Huxley (1964:77)

Now, as each of the parts of the body, like every other instrument, is for the sake of some purpose, viz., some action, it is evident that the body as a whole must exist for the sake of some complex action.
                                                    Aristotle (384 - 322 BCE)

For evolutionists, the only candidate for Aristotle's "complex action" is reproduction. The complex action for the sake of which all bodies exist is fitness; fitness is the complex work that must be done to leave descendants. Like all complex adaptive systems, adaptation by natural selection is about R, continuance, staying in the "existential game of life" (Slobodkin and Rapoport 1974); it is about the "process of becoming, rather than the never-reached end point" (Holland 1992:20). The purpose of this final chapter is to explore some of the implications of the fact that bodies exist for the sake of continuing – even in the face of appalling costs.

To continue becoming (to evolve), complex adaptive systems must solve the uncertain futures problem. They must be able somehow to predict the future and detect value (assign credit and blame). The capacity to predict the future allows the system to identify potential danger and security; the capacity to detect value allows the system to alter its relationship to its environment (adapt to it) according to these value predictions, thereby avoiding cliffs and setting the stage for future good moves. In living systems adaptations consist of matter that has been organized by different kinds of environmental information embodied by the GTR heuristic. This information is the *relationship* between the organism and its environment, and it is *for* doing the work of fitness in that environment. For evolutionary epistemologists, adaptations are thus "biological knowledge" (Plotkin 1994); they are information about the environment that has become represented in the organism's phenotype, thereby enabling the organism to do fitness work. The organism itself is a kind of prediction – a proposition about future environments – advanced by its ancestors.

Information reduces the uncertain futures problem; better information reduces it more. If reproducing in the face of uncertainty is the quintessential problem of life, Plotkin (1994) and Dennett (1995) are right to characterize the history of life as the increasing capacity of organisms to generate (create) and test (criticize, evaluate, select) useful models of and for reaching the future. For an evolutionist, then, it is appropriate to try to understand human development in terms of the ontogeny of affective–cognitive mechanisms for acquiring and creating more and better information with which to predict and reach the future. This is why I began thinking of the attachment process as a developmental mechanism for children to embody information about value (local risk and uncertainty) in order thereby to entrain the development of their optimal reproductive strategies. Inspired as well by Belsky, Steinberg, and Draper (1991), it occurred to me that because one of the most pervasive sources of risk and uncertainty for our juvenile ancestors was their parents' ability and willingness to provide parental investment, MI and then ToM evolved from the basic hominoid IWMs of attachment relations as mechanisms for predicting the social future – i.e., as algorithms for children to generate theories about first, their parents', and then other people's beliefs, desires, and intentions. On this view, IWMs, MI, and ToM are social exchange monitors for detecting cheaters. Cheaters are defectors from the social contract. Fundamentally, then, IWMs, MI, and ToM are adaptations for detecting social risk and uncertainty. Where objective risk and uncertainty are high, the early subjective experience of insecurity is likely to be more common. Everything else being equal, when objective risk and uncertainty are high, the optimal reproductive strategy is likely to be to maximize current reproduction. Indeed, the subjective experience of insecurity may constitute the internal, phenotypic representation of objective, external risk and uncertainty, and be the trigger for, or early manifestation of, an evolved alternative strategy for maximizing current reproduction.

There is, however, no such thing as a perfect strategy. Nothing in life is free. Reproduction has costs. The inescapable work of life requires resources, which are always limited. Trade-offs are thus inevitable. The impossibility of reconciling the conflicting ends and means of life is the rationale for the assumption of optimality. We expect that natural selection will tend to favor traits (adaptations) that allocate limited resources among the different components of fitness (the work of survival, growth and development, and producing and rearing offspring) in the way that results in the most descendants. Evolution is driven not by differential survival or growth and development, but by the differential production of descendants. But *not* just in the next generation; complex adaptive systems are all about continuing *indefinitely*. It follows that people, like all organisms, are not evolved to maximize health, wealth, happiness, lifespan, vigor, power, prestige, beauty, love, sex, truth, honor, reason or anything else, but to have descendants, which is continuation. It follows, too, that if people find themselves in risky or uncertain environments that threaten their capacity to leave any descendants at all we should not be surprised to find that their limited resources are not always allocated to improving their health, wealth, happiness, lifespan, vigor, etc. – or even that of their children. On the contrary, because adaptation by natural selection is all about continuance, we should expect that when people lack the resources to limit risk and uncertainty or to make a difference in their children's reproductive value they will be more likely to grow and come to behave (most of the time probably quite unconsciously) in ways that maximize current reproduction (or did in the EEA) – even at the cost of appalling health, poverty, despair, and shortened lives.

When risk and uncertainty are extreme, it may be (or have been) evolutionarily rational to pay extreme costs or take extreme risks for a chance to leave descendants. This means that under extreme conditions the optimal reproductive strategy may be one that, in fact, entails or magnifies pathology (what I regard as the opposite of well-being: pain, despair, shortened lives, etc.). This looks like a grim fact of nature. As we saw in chapter 3, for an evolutionist, value itself originates in fitness. At the edge of a fitness cliff, *badness* (danger – i.e., pain, despair, shortened lives) thus becomes, if not *goodness* (security – i.e., continuance), then at least *better* than failing to continue (stepping off the cliff and out of the game of life).

At the extreme edge of a fitness cliff, the optimal path to goodness (continuance) may involve extreme reproductive costs. And, indeed, we saw in the previous chapter that both theory and considerable data suggest that, barring frank disease and malnutrition, the world's most disadvantaged peoples often have high rates of reproduction, especially among their youngest women.

This chapter is about the implications for therapy, practical reason, and ethics that arise from this grim fact of nature: the fact that under extreme conditions optimality entails pathology; that sometimes pathology is normal and natural, if not adaptive; that sometimes frightful pathology is the cost of continuing. First, I illustrate this point by examining some of the costs of early reproduction in women.[1] This is to make clear how it is that a reproductive strategy can entail or exacerbate pathology yet, in principle, still be the optimal strategy. Second, after showing how and when pathology is likely to be a cost of reproduction, I turn to the new discipline of evolutionary medicine, where the sometimes subtle distinction between adaptation and pathology virtually defines the field. Adaptations are for doing the work that needs to be done to leave descendants. If increased pathology is the cost of reproduction – something that makes reproduction possible – then is pathology an adaptation? If the trade-off for reproduction under conditions of risk and uncertainty is reduced survival, is a short life an adaptation? Well, no, the costs and trade-offs of reproduction are not adaptations for they do not actually *do* any fitness work. But sometimes (for example, when conditions are risky and uncertain) the only way that the work of leaving descendants *can* be done is to take resources (time, energy, security, etc.) away from survival, growth and development, or rearing children and allocate them instead to *producing* children, early and/or often. Sometimes this is the only way to avoid a fitness cliff.

After a brief introduction to evolutionary medicine, I raise the possibility of an evolutionary public health. For me, an evolutionary public health would use the principles of evolutionary ecology, life history theory, and parental investment theory as a basis for preventing pathology in the first place. It is here that my argument becomes an exercise in Huxley's evolutionary humanism. It is here that it becomes an essay on the use of evolutionary theory as a rational, scientific basis for a theory of value and an ethical stance that aims to be therapeutic by increasing practical

---

[1] Because more is known about the cost of early reproduction in women than in men.

reason. My contention is this: in suggesting that the ultimate function of life is reproduction – that value itself originates in reproduction (fitness, continuance), not health, wealth, or happiness – evolutionary theory specifies the target at which we should aim. This target is the complex action for the sake of which bodies exist: indefinite continuance. This seems to me an objective fact of nature; to me, value is a fact of nature. And the only way that we have been able to sense this particular fact is emotionally, as personal, subjective value experience. When enough early value experience is positive or secure, this contingent environmental fact becomes represented in us, in part, as the moral sense: the capacity to discern that one image of the future is better (right) than another (wrong) and to "strongly evaluate" that future such that we feel Taylor's "demanding commitment" to move toward it. On this view, the moral sense is the emotional experience of a powerful attachment to someone or something into the future; it is "love over time." It is the subjective value experience of a strong evaluation of an image of a person or thing in the future, such that defection from that person or thing is inconceivable. (And, as we saw in chapter 4, children with secure attachment histories do, indeed, tend to be more socially competent and to score higher on tests of ToM and empathy then insecure children.)

What is more, evolutionary theory may point to a method for approaching this target (the "never-reached end point"). This method is the moral injunction first, to do no harm and second, to nurture future time preference. It is the inner command to avoid fitness cliffs and then to set the stage for achieving future value, first for oneself, and then for others. This means reducing objective risk and uncertainty. If people, like other organisms, are naturally predisposed to maximize short-term reproduction in the face of risk and uncertainty – even at the cost of decreased health, wealth, happiness, lifespan, etc. – then an evolutionary public health or an evolutionary humanism would seize on this fact of nature and work to maximize value (i.e., to increase health, wealth, happiness, lifespan, vigor, etc.) by reducing risk and uncertainty. Minimizing objective risk and uncertainty would tend to maximize subjective feelings of security, which, in turn, would tend to nurture future time preference, thus making the future seem more valuable, thereby fostering long-term projects. As we saw in chapter 2, minimizing intergenerational variance in fitness in the long run results in more descendants than maximizing current reproduction.

But how should we go about reducing risk and uncertainty? Since inequality is arguably the major source of risk and uncertainty, at least in post-EEA societies (e.g., Boehm 1993, 1997; Erdal and Whiten 1994, 1996; Knauft 1991), certainly one way to proceed is by reducing inequality. I defend this proposition first by examining evidence from several sources that inequality is the ultimate cause of a wide range of pathologies. I then focus on Amartya Sen's (1980, 1992, 1993b) splendid question, "equality of what?" By way of explicating Sen's answer, I compare my evolutionary approach to value to his influential argument that value inheres in people's "capability to achieve valuable functionings" (1993b:31). In the capability approach, as this position is known, value derives not from income, wealth, goods, resources, or utilities, but from people's *capability to use* such goods and resources to achieve "functionings" that "intrinsically matter" to them. What intrinsically matters to people, on Sen's view, is a fuller realization of what a human life *can* be. In other words, hope – the expectation that a person is capable of becoming or doing something *in the future* (say, living to old age). But if people feel that they have no future then their capability to achieve valuable functionings is curtailed. For this reason, Sen maintains that public policy should be aimed not at creating equality of income, wealth, goods, resources, or utilities, but at "equality of shortfall" – i.e., equality in the degree to which people fall short of achieving a fuller realization of the functionings that they have reason to value. Working primarily with Martha Nussbaum's (1995) interpretation of Sen's valuable functionings, I argue next that the evolutionary theoretical and capability approaches to value are not only compatible, but, indeed, enhance each other's rationale for valuing equality and freedom. Nussbaum makes the point that what intrinsically matters most to humans – next to having a life at all – is their capability of crossing the threshold from "human life" to "good human life" (i.e., their hope of doing so). I shall attempt to make the point that crossing Nussbaum's threshold is the same as, or would result in, crossing the evolutionary ecological threshold from maximizing current reproduction to maximizing future reproduction – i.e., from avoiding fitness cliffs to setting the stage for future good fitness moves.

Evolution and well-being

Evolutionary ecology would suggest that, in the end, inequality leads to ill health because the "complex action" for the sake of which bodies exist is not well-being or health but producing descendants (continuance).

However strongly we may value well-being, in the face of prolonged risk and uncertainty, as value comes to reside more and more in managing to leave any descendants at all (just "having a life" and avoiding fitness cliffs), the present looms larger, the future ebbs, hope wanes, and *akrasia* flows (and not necessarily maladaptively, either). We have seen that chronic risk and uncertainty are hazardous not only because they increase our risk of death, but also because repeatedly responding to actual risks and continuously guarding against uncertain ones entails the present consumption of resources (e.g., energy, sleep, hippocampal neurons) that would have had greater fitness pay-offs in the future (if only we had had a "good life" and been able to set the stage for the future). Our bedrock assumption of optimality demands that we look for the trade-offs associated with reproduction. This is true under any circumstances, but if we are interested in health and well-being it is especially true for reproduction on the edge of fitness cliffs. As we shall see below, when the optimal strategy is to maximize current reproduction (e.g., under conditions of chronic risk and uncertainty) resources allocated to this fitness task cannot be allocated as well to maximizing one's own survival, growth and development, or future reproduction, or that of one's children.

The cost of early reproduction
While early stress is clearly not the only cause of early menarche, evidence presented in chapter 5 suggests that it may be one cause. To the extent that early menarche is part of an evolved alternative strategy for maximizing current reproduction in the face of risk and uncertainty, then we would expect to find associated costs or trade-offs that reduced early maturers' capacity for future reproduction (through reduced survivorship and/or offspring quality).

And indeed we do. Stanley Garn and his colleagues (1986b) showed in a sample of more than 16,000 women that while early-maturers are only a little shorter than late-maturers, they weigh 4 kg more, are 30 percent fatter, and almost twice as likely to be obese. Shangold et al. (1989) and Wellens et al. (1992) report similar results, but found as well that late-maturers were significantly taller than early-maturers. Obesity, of course, increases the risk for several morbid conditions, including diabetes mellitus, hypertension, coronary heart disease, and some cancers (Solomon and Manson 1997). Brindley and Rolland (1989) propose that the common denominator is chronically elevated glucocorticoid levels. As we saw in the previous chapter, chronically high levels of cortisol (the major glucocorticoid) decrease immune function, which increases susceptibility to disease. However, elevated glucocorticoids also increase blood glucose levels, which results in increased insulin secretion. Brindley and Rolland suggest that the combination of elevated glucocorticoids and increased insulin secretion predispose the body to deposit fat and atherosclerotic plaques. This might help to explain why early menarche is associated with obesity: because early stress (elevated glucocorticoid levels) leads to *both* early menarche and a tendency to promote fat deposition. Also, as noted in the previous chapter, children with elevated glucocorticoid levels tend to suffer disturbed sleep. Since growth hormone is released during sleep, children with chronically elevated glucocorticoids may suffer disturbed sleep and thus be exposed to lower levels of growth hormone and end up shorter as adults. Regardless of the specific mechanisms though, if early menarche predisposes women to obesity and obesity increases mortality risk, then reduced survivorship due to obesity is an intrinsic, physiological cost of maximizing current reproduction through early menarche. What is more, early menarche also entails prolonged exposure to estrogen, a known risk factor for breast cancer (e.g., Apter and Vikho 1983; Apter, Reinila, and Vikho 1989; Kelsey, Gammon, and John 1993; Vogel 1996). The trade-off for early reproduction, then, may be reduced well-being and shortened life – i.e., lower reproductive value.

Unfortunately, however, the costs of early reproduction are sometimes borne by children as well as their mothers. The assumption of optimality leads to the prediction that when a woman's optimal reproductive strategy is to maximize current reproduction (quantity of offspring), there will tend to be a trade-off in the form of smaller or otherwise less healthy (lower-quality) offspring. In remarkable accord with this prediction, Theresa Scholl and her colleagues (1989) have shown that early menarche is associated with significantly increased risk of low birthweight (through intrauterine growth retardation rather than short gestation). And this is so even after controlling for the well-known effects on birthweight of maternal age, prepregnancy weight, weight gain during pregnancy, smoking, lack of prenatal care, and gestation length. Low birthweight babies gain weight slower than heavier newborns (Garn 1985) and low birthweight is a powerful predictor of infant mortality (e.g., McCormick 1985; Newman 1987). Another cost of being able to bear children early may thus be having children of relatively low reproductive value.

That young women who reproduce early may have lower reproductive value[2] as a consequence seems to make sense. After all, they have done hard reproductive labor, often under difficult conditions. Moreover, if they pay the full price, it is likely to be some years after they have given birth. But how could it make sense for them to produce children of low reproductive value? How could it be adaptive to produce low quality offspring? Wouldn't it always be better to produce fewer, but heavier and healthier babies?

As we have seen several times now,[3] no, it would not. When parents lack the resources to protect their children from risk and uncertainty, or to have a significant positive impact on their children's reproductive value, their most pressing adaptive problem is to avoid lineage extinction. All things considered, in risky and uncertain environments the best way to avoid fitness cliffs is to have offspring early and/or often. But, because resources are limited, especially under risky and uncertain conditions, having offspring early or often means that it is difficult to make each one healthy and strong. However, this may be relatively easier for younger women than older women, for the latter will have been exposed to the cumulative effects of risk and uncertainty longer than the former (e.g., Geronimus 1987, 1994, 1996). Anyway, in risky and uncertain environments, even healthy babies do not automatically have higher reproductive value than their weaker siblings. Therefore, parents who withheld food, love, and attention from several children in order to improve the reproductive value of just a select few would tend to have fewer grandchildren than parents who were more even-handed. On the other hand, in risky and uncertain environments, weak, sickly, and socially vulnerable babies usually have lower reproductive value than their siblings. Therefore, parents who withheld food, love, and attention from the weakest in order to improve the reproductive value of the others would tend to have more grandchildren than more even-handed parents. While withholding food, love, and attention from vulnerable children is surely never easy, it may be (or have been) evolutionarily adaptive (see chapter 3). Parents who were willing to make this sacrifice would also tend to have more descendants to whom they could pass on the cultural

---

[2] Technically, lower *residual* reproductive value, i.e., lower expected future reproductive output. By reproducing early a woman may achieve a degree of reproductive success. In doing so, however, she may reduce her capacity to have additional children.

[3] See especially pp. 51–61.

knowledge not only that it was appropriate to make such sacrifices, but when and how as well.[4]

It is a grim fact of nature that optimality sometimes entails pathology, that children sometimes pay the costs of continuing. It is a grimmer fact still that sometimes they continue to pay throughout their lives. When parents have no alternative but to reproduce on the edge of a fitness cliff, and their children are small, weak, or sickly as a result, that is the cost of continuing. But when the developmental effects of being born small, weak, or sickly are lifelong, then children, and even grandchildren, may keep on paying the cost of continuing. There is increasing evidence, for example, that low birthweight and stress during pregnancy are risk factors not only for morbidity and mortality in infancy and childhood, but in adulthood as well. Working with longitudinal data and large samples, David Barker and his colleagues (e.g., Barker 1992, 1997; Clark et al. 1998) have shown that several major disorders of adult life (coronary heart disease, hypertension, diabetes, etc.) are determined in part by patterns of growth *in utero*. When fetal growth is disturbed by maternal malnutrition or stress, they argue, organ systems undergoing rapid differentiation at the time may be permanently affected, often with deleterious "sleeper" effects that may not be evident for years or decades.

It seems, in other words, that there is no statute of limitations on the costs of continuing, of being born small or unhealthy. These continuing costs, however, are more likely to be exacted in risky and uncertain environments, where, by definition, the flow of resources (including, as always, security) is low and unreliable. Unfortunately, it is under precisely such conditions that the optimal reproductive strategy is likely to be to reproduce early and/or often, which increases the risk for being born small and unhealthy. The upshot is synergy between risky and uncertain environments and unhealthy or otherwise vulnerable children. This positive feedback sets the stage for intergenerational continuity in both environmental risk and uncertainty and vulnerable children. For example, in a recent follow-up study of 1,758 inner-city American children born between 1960 and 1965, Hardy and her colleagues (1997) found that the effects of early childbearing were still evident in the children 27 to 33

---

[4] Again, bear in mind Nancy Scheper-Hughes' (1992) eloquent *Death Without Weeping*. She describes how chronically impoverished mothers in Brazilian shantytowns have adapted culturally to the grim necessity of withholding investment from some weak and sickly children so that other children may live.

years later. Even after adjusting for maternal education, parity, poverty status, and the child's race and sex, when compared to the adult children of the youngest mothers (≤18 years), those of the older mothers (≥25 years) were significantly more likely to have (1) graduated from high school, (2) been independent of public financial support, and (3) delayed the birth of their own first child until they were at least 20 years old.

There is also good evidence of a synergistic interaction between early psychosocial stress and failure to thrive, in which even adequately nourished children fail to gain weight (Drotar 1991; Monckberg 1992; Widdowson 1951). And Marta Valenzuela (1990) found that 93 percent of a sample of low-income, chronically underweight toddlers were insecurely attached, compared to 50 percent of a sample of low-income toddlers of normal weight. She suggests that undernutrition and insecure attachment interact and that secure attachment may enable children to make better use of whatever nourishment is available. In a similar vein, Nyström Peck and Lundberg (1995), with data on the 4,574 participants in a longitudinal study of living conditions in Sweden, found an independent effect of early "dissension in the family" on adult stature. While smallness at birth contributes to short stature in adulthood, the effect is exacerbated by early stress. Likewise, in an attempt to "unpack" the well-known retarding effect of low social class on child growth (and thus adult height), Montgomery et al. (1997) examined longitudinal data on 6,574 men and women born in Britain during one week in 1958. They found that children who had experienced family conflict (as inferred from Health Visitors' reports of "domestic tension, divorce, separation or desertion") were significantly more likely to fall into the bottom fifth of the height distribution at age seven, even after controlling for social class. And even after controlling for the effect of undernutrition on body size in a poor urban community in the US, Karp et al. (1989) found that children reported to have been abused were 16.6 times more likely than non-abused children to show signs of wasting (weight for height < 5th percentile).

Finally, although neither looked at the interaction of low birthweight and early stress, at least two studies suggest that the developmental effects of early psychosocial stress can be lifelong – indeed, they can shorten life. In the first, Wadsworth et al. (1990), using data from a stratified sample of 5,362 Britons whose health and development were studied longitudinally since 1946, found that parental divorce or separation before the age of six generally had a greater negative impact on adult well-being than death of mother. Even after controlling for class, those whose parents divorced or separated were significantly more likely to have engaged in delinquent behavior, to have low educational attainment, and to smoke. Men whose parents divorced or separated were more likely than other men to have a history of unemployment. On the other hand, women whose parents divorced or separated were more likely than other women to have problems with alcohol. In the second study, of psychosocial and behavioral predictors of longevity in Americans, Freidman et al. (1995) found that divorce of one's parents during childhood was associated with shorter lifespan – by about four years.

In sum, when the probability of producing any descendants at all is sufficiently low or uncertain, the optimal reproductive strategy will often be to maximize current reproduction. And if the trade-off for doing so is reduced survival or offspring reproductive value, then that is just the cost of continuing. Evolution is about producing descendants, not well-being. Under conditions of chronic risk and uncertainty, therefore, optimality can diminish well-being and entail pathology. Such pathology can last a lifetime as well as shorten it. Such pathology can also render people more vulnerable to the early stress caused by the very conditions of risk and uncertainty that entailed their pathology in the first place. Obviously, this sets the stage for a potentially vicious intergenerational cycle of risk and uncertainty, maximization of current reproduction, and concomitant reduced well-being and increased pathology. People everywhere seem to value well-being. If the goal of medicine is to increase well-being – but if evolution is about producing descendants, not well-being – then effective therapy is ultimately contingent on knowing how evolution works. We arrive thus at the new field of evolutionary medicine.

Evolutionary medicine

Evolutionary medicine is based on the premise that it is not merely possible, but, indeed, necessary and responsible to use evolutionary theory to generate therapeutically relevant insights. In this section, I will first illustrate how evolutionary thinking can contribute to therapy. I will then attempt to expand our notion of what constitutes therapy in hope of steering a branch of evolutionary medicine in the direction of "evolutionary public health" (Chisholm 1995b).

Western medicine has been based largely on induction and reductionism. Induction in medicine is the patient building up of general principles about health and disease from innumerable observations of the molecules, cells, tissues, organs, behavior, and beliefs of healthy and unhealthy people in particular environments. Reductionism in medicine is explaining health or illness in terms of (reducing it to) the nature or condition of people's beliefs, behavior, organs, tissues, cells, and molecules in their particular environments. From the perspective of evolutionary medicine, all of this is necessary for effective intervention and prevention. For even greater well-being, however, it is not sufficient, because both human beings and their diseases have evolutionary histories. Evolutionary theory enables us to go beyond standard induction and reductionism because it provides a powerful basis for explaining in principle why particular organisms and *diseases* exist and how they came to be the way they are. Evolutionary medicine is about exploring the implications for therapy (intervention and prevention) of understanding the processes of adaptation that produce the evolutionary histories that culminate in a particular person, presenting with a particular complaint, at a particular place and time. On this view, anyone presenting for treatment should be viewed not only as a unique person with a unique developmental and medical history, nor only as a representative of a particular culture or social group with its own unique cultural and medical history, but also as a member of the human species, with its own unique evolutionary and disease histories.

The insight that diseases have their own evolutionary histories is a central part of evolutionary medicine. The essence of evolutionary theory is the assumption that the traits we see in living forms are ultimately explainable in terms of the process of adaptation by natural selection. The essence of evolutionary medicine, therefore, is the assumption that even pathological traits and conditions are the product or by-product of adaptation by natural selection. For a straightforward example, consider Williams and Nesse's (1991; Nesse and Williams 1995) observations about two of the body's most common responses to infection: elevated body temperature and the sequestering of iron. Whereas the standard view has long been that both are symptoms of disease, the emerging evolutionary view is that they are evidence instead of the operation of an evolved pathogen defense mechanism. The distinction here between pathology and adaptation (i.e., disease and defense against disease) is the one made by Nesse (1991) between "defect" (disease) and "defense." When fever is viewed as part of a disease, it makes sense to prescribe analgesics to bring it down. However, when viewed as part of an evolved defense mechanism (for mobilizing white blood cells to fight infection and inhibit bacterial growth) the optimal therapeutic strategy may be watchful waiting.

Prolonged high fever can cause its own damage, of course, but in many cases it may be appropriate to encourage the body's natural defense mechanisms, for by artificially lowering body temperature the physician may inadvertently prolong the disease to which the elevated temperature is the evolved adaptive response (Doran et al. 1989). Likewise, just as temperature goes up during infection, iron levels typically drop, as iron becomes more tightly bound to protein and is removed from circulation by (i.e., sequestered in) the liver. From an evolutionary medical perspective, however, the optimal therapeutic strategy may again be watchful waiting, for sequestering iron in the liver means that bacteria and parasites cannot so readily use it for their own survival, growth, and reproduction. Again, while prolonged low hemoglobin levels can themselves cause problems, the too-early prescription of iron supplements may prolong the disease to which low hemoglobin levels are the evolved response (Weinberg 1984).

Although neither of these researchers used evolutionary theory to arrive at their conclusions (i.e., they worked inductively), adding evolutionary theory to medicine enables us to explain in principle why elevated body temperature and iron sequestration exist – as adaptations for defense. Bringing an evolutionary perspective to medicine compels us always (1) to question our assumptions about normality and pathology, (2) to recognize that such questions have important therapeutic implications, and (3) to accept that it is impossible to define normality and pathology usefully without specifying a particular environment, including its history. Evolutionary ecology is the study of how the history of interactions between organisms and their environments directs the process of adaptation by natural selection.

While pathogens and parasites have been a constant presence in the EEA of humans (and long before), the increasingly crowded, complex, and competitive industrial environments that we have created for ourselves in just a few hundred years bear little resemblance to the environments in which our primate and mammalian ancestors evolved for millions of years. Yet, in terms of basic biology we may differ from them scarcely at all. To avoid confusing "defect" and "defense" in modern humans, therefore, it is critical to keep in mind the possibility that what looks like pathology today might, in fact, have been adaptive in some ancestral environment. As George Williams expressed this idea, "symptoms indicative of harm should always be distinguished from those indicative of the victim's efforts at recovery" (1996:150). But, as we have seen, because evolution is ultimately about *continuance*, not health, we should distinguish between symptoms indicative of harm and those indicative of the victim's efforts not so much at recovering health, but at *reproduction* – that is, his or her efforts at continuance, at avoiding fitness cliffs.

What we understand as pathology ("symptoms indicative of harm"), then, may indicate instead the victim's efforts at reproduction – for example, the early and/or impulsive display of sexual and aggressive behavior. The amount of risk and uncertainty that an environment holds largely determines whether the optimal reproductive strategy is to maximize current or future reproduction. This is the General Life History Problem (pp. 51–61 above): Beyond some point, increased reproductive effort in the short-term is expected to decrease number of descendants in the future, either through the current consumption of resources that would have had greater fitness returns in the future, or by reducing parents' probability of survival into the future. But, if the future is sufficiently risky and uncertain – if parents are poised on the edge of a fitness cliff – then their optimal strategy may be to maximize current reproduction at any cost. After all, what do they have to lose? The amount of risk and uncertainty that an environment holds is determined by access to the resources that organisms require to do the work of fitness. If the flow of energy, nutrients, security, information, and time that is required becomes too low or erratic, then people will begin to die. Mortality rates and regimes (e.g., patterns of age- and sex-specific mortality) will therefore index local environmental risk and uncertainty. Everything else being equal, when the future is risky and uncertain the optimal reproductive strategy is to take whatever resources are available and quickly convert them into offspring. The cost of doing so may be reduced well-being for both parents and offspring. But, from an evolutionary perspective, this may be a cost that parents cannot afford *not* to pay. Extinction, as they say, is forever.

If mortality rates and regimes index local environmental risk and uncertainty, then (according to the model being proposed), through the process of attachment, the subjective "value experience" of past loss (grief, sadness) and of future loss (fear, anxiety, loss of hope) will represent or embody environmental risk and uncertainty. The apparent ontogenetic link between early psychosocial stress/insecure attachment and the early and/or impulsive display of sexual and aggressive behavior may thus make adaptive sense. From an evolutionary perspective, value inheres in long-term fitness (indefinite continuance). Long-term fitness is maximized under conditions of low risk and uncertainty, which, over time, minimizes intergenerational variance in reproductive success. The repeated early subjective experience of security represents or embodies low environmental risk and uncertainty and promotes, through future time preference or hope, long-term projects aimed at future good fitness moves. On the other hand, the repeated early subjective experience of grief and fear represents or embodies high environmental risk and uncertainty and promotes, through the absence of hope, short-term projects aimed at avoiding fitness cliffs.

This might explain why (as we will soon see) morbidity and mortality rates are better indicators of well-being than measures of wealth, viz.., because morbidity and mortality rates reflect environmental risk and uncertainty better than measures of wealth. The total or per caput amount of goods, resources, utilities, or real income that exists are not good measures of the *relative absence* of wealth, nor especially of people's *capability to use* whatever wealth exists to achieve functionings that "intrinsically matter" to them. Measures of morbidity and mortality, on the other hand, "tell us about the impact which the social organization of material life has on human subjectivity" (Wilkinson 1996:54). Or, as Amartya Sen expressed the same idea, "an important part of the capability approach lies in moving us away from the space of commodities, incomes, utilities, etc., on to the space of the constitutive elements of living" (1992:50). For Sen, one of the most important "constitutive elements of living," one that "intrinsically matters" a great deal to most people, is living itself – i.e., simply continuing to live, simply having a life at all. Making the point that wealth is far from the only or best measure of value, Sen notes that:

> Economics is not solely concerned with income and wealth but also with using these resources as means to significant ends, including the promotion and enjoyment of long and worthwhile lives. If, however, the economic success of a nation is judged only by income and by other traditional indicators of opulence and financial soundness, as it often is, the important goal of well-being is missed. The more conventional criteria of measuring economic success can be enhanced by including assessments of a nation's ability to extend and to improve the quality of life ... Mortality data can be used to evaluate policy and to identify vital aspects of economic deprivation in particular nations and in specific groups within nations. (1993a:40)

For an evolutionist, morbidity and mortality rates are better measures of value than wealth alone because they are better measures of environmental risk and uncertainty. As we shall see below, inequality is a major source of morbidity and mortality. By definition then, inequality is also a major source of risk and uncertainty. If maximizing current reproduction is the optimal reproductive strategy in risky and uncertain environments, and if maximizing current reproduction in such environments entails or exacerbates pathology, then a health policy informed by evolutionary theory would work to improve well-being by reducing inequality.

Inequality and pathology
While most people know that poverty is linked to poor health, few know why. Few appreciate that today it is rarely poverty *itself* that is the problem, but rather poverty's familiar companion, inequality. To show why this is so I will examine more closely the relationship between inequality and health that I outlined in the previous chapter, beginning with Richard Wilkinson's (1996) important work. Wilkinson's message is that among developed nations it is not those with the greatest total wealth or per caput GNP that have the best health, but those with the smallest income differences between rich and poor – i.e., the greatest equality. He uses extensive historical demographic, economic, and epidemiological data to show that just as societies go through a demographic transition (from high fertility and mortality to low fertility and mortality), so, too, do they go through an "epidemiological transition." Prior to this transition, death rates are high overall and infectious diseases are the leading cause of death. After the transition, death rates decrease and cancers and degenerative diseases become the leading causes of death.

The underlying cause of the epidemiological transition is increased lifespan due to rising living standards. People live longer primarily because of reduced infant and child mortality due to improved health and nutrition. Once a country has achieved some threshold of total wealth or per caput GNP, however, further increases no longer result in increased lifespan. This is due mostly to the positive correlation between wealth and inequality. With greater wealth there is a greater danger that it will be distributed unequally. (Certainly when there is no wealth there is no inequality.) After the epidemiological transition, therefore, there is typically a change in the social distribution of disease such that relatively poor people tend to suffer higher morbidity and mortality than those with greater wealth.

Wilkinson argues that this is because inequality *itself* is bad for health.

And he masses extensive evidence to support his position. Philmore, Beattie, and Townsend (1994) demonstrated that death rates were four times as high in the poorest 10 percent of electoral wards in northern England as they were in the richest 10 percent. And we saw in the previous chapter that in New York City's Harlem the death rate at most ages was higher than in rural Bangladesh – indeed, men in Harlem had less chance of living to age 65 than Bangladeshi men (McCord and Freeman 1990). Wilkinson also reports that in Brazil, where wealth inequalities are as great as they are anywhere, infant mortality rates vary between 12 and 90 per 1,000 live births – *in the same city.*

But by what mechanisms does inequality affect health? Wilkinson notes first that the relationship between inequality and mortality is nowhere near as strong between countries as within them. The reason is that most countries have gone through the epidemiological transition and reached the threshold where further increases in wealth have no appreciable effect on between-nation differences in mortality. Within countries, however, what affects health and lifespan is relative socioeconomic position. Wilkinson then cites research showing a powerful correlation (r = 0.86; p = 0.001) between life expectancy at birth and the total personal income received by the poorest 70 percent of families in a number of industrial societies. What this means is that in countries like Norway and Sweden, where the poorest 70 percent of families received a larger share of total income than in other countries, life expectancy is higher than in the least egalitarian countries in the sample (the US, Britain, and West Germany). Likewise, he cites research showing that among the 50 US states there is a strong inverse correlation (r = −0.62; p < 0.001) between age-adjusted death rates from all causes and the percentage of total household income received by the poorest half of each states' population (i.e., states with the most unequal income distribution have the highest mortality rates). When only death rates from homicide are considered the correlation is even stronger (r = −0.72; p < 0.001).

The effect of inequality on health is not, however, confined to differences between only the very poorest and very richest. Wilkinson cites another study in the US (Davey Smith et al. 1996a) in which 300,685 white men were followed longitudinally for 16 years. They were then grouped into 12 income categories according to the median family income for the zip (postal) code area in which they lived. Income was regressed against age-adjusted mortality rates in each group. There was a powerful inverse association between mortality rates and median family income (see Figure

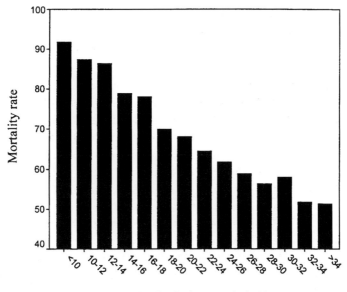

Median family income (in $1000s)

Figure 6.1 Age-adjusted mortality rate (deaths per 10,000 person-years) among 300,685 US white men by median family income of postal-code areas in which they lived.

6.1). Moreover, the same inverse association was apparent in a sample of 20,224 African-American men who had been part of the same study – even though they lived in zip code areas with substantially lower median family income than the white men (Davey Smith et al. 1996b; see Figure 6.2).

Having implicated relative income differences within countries as part of the mechanism whereby inequality affects health, Wilkinson then reviews evidence as to why it is not so much the common correlates of inequality that cause ill-health as inequality itself. He concludes that socioeconomic differences in health cannot be explained away in terms of (1) biased measurement, (2) selective social mobility (i.e., sick people are downwardly mobile), (3) genetic differences, (4) inequalities in access to health care, and/or (5) health-related behavior (poor diet, lack of exercise, smoking, etc.). Socioeconomic differences in health must therefore be due in large part to differences in socioeconomic status. He notes that:

> Although research on these health differences within countries has been undertaken almost exclusively to tell us more about

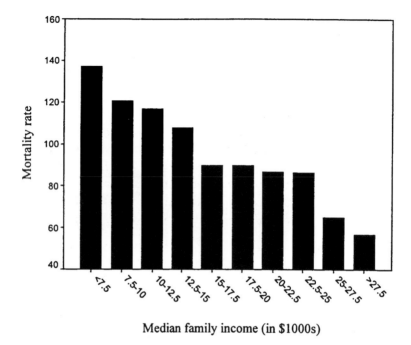

Median family income (in $1000s)

Figure 6.2 Age-adjusted mortality rate (deaths per 10,000 person-years) among 20,224 US black men by median family income of postal-code areas in which they lived.

health and its determinants, what comes out of it may be more important for what it tells us about society. The fact that in almost any of the rich developed societies people lower down the social scale may have death rates two to four times higher than those nearer the top, seems to give us a fairly blunt message about the nature of modern society. But to understand the message clearly we need to know more about why social position is so closely related to health . . . Increasingly it looks as if some of the most important parts of this relationship involve psychosocial and emotional effects of objective features of the social structure. (1996:54)[5]

---

5 Wilkinson's "emotional effects of objective features of the social structure" are what I think of as the subjective, phenotypic representation ("value experience") of external, objective risk and uncertainty.

Other studies of health inequalities reach the same conclusion. Adler and her colleagues (1993) argue that on top of the direct effects on health of greater exposure to pathogens, those lower down the SES ladder also suffer indirectly, through complex developmental psychosocial pathways:

> Exposure to greater stress in childhood reduces the likelihood that children will develop "resilience" and increases the chances that they will develop depression and helplessness, characteristics that have been linked to increased risk of disease . . . Differences related to SES in health-damaging behaviors and exposures to adverse physical and psychosocial conditions differentially place those lower on the SES hierarchy at risk of disease and premature mortality. (Adler et al. 1993:3143)

Likewise, using a model not unlike the one advanced in this book, Charlton (1994; Charlton and White 1995) maintains that "[r]esource differentials lead to stratified health outcomes owing to the differential capacity of individuals and groups to realise 'universal' psychological aspirations of a broadly 'health promoting' nature" (Charlton and White 1995:235). The essence of this "universal psychological aspiration," Charlton argues, is the capacity of individuals or groups to increase the margin between their resources and their needs so that they can maximize long-term benefits. When this margin is sufficiently large people can afford to invest in (set the stage for) the future, which includes good health. Health, in other words, is not nature's default condition. (Reproduction is.) While Charlton's model is not explicitly an evolutionary (reproductive) one, he sees clearly that when people grow up in risky and uncertain environments what resources they have must be allocated preferentially to avoiding fitness cliffs, which, as we have seen, predisposes to later ill health. As Charlton and White put it,

> . . . long-term 'investment' is predicated upon short-term security, and any economic or social policies which tend to reduce the insecurity of individuals and/or groups might be expected to have health-promoting consequences. Conversely, the actively risk-seeking patterns typical of some social groups (such as teenage gangs or drug users) may perhaps prove to be a consequence of their higher rate of health discounting, whereby present pleasure or peer-group status outweighs any future health considerations. (1995:240)

While Amartya Sen has been less concerned than Wilkinson and others with the proximate mechanisms whereby inequality affects health, his far-reaching studies of the "economics of life and death" (1993a) none the less implicate a critical role for psychosocial processes. For example, he notes (1992) that whereas the per caput GNP in Costa Rica is only one-twelfth that of the USA, life expectancy is the same (75 vs. 76 years). And, whereas the per caput GNP in the poor Indian state of Kerala is considerably less than that of India as whole, life expectancy is over 70, very much greater than the Indian average of 57. Sen attributes these auspicious islands of health in their seas of relative poverty to Costa Rica and Kerala's widespread public education, comprehensive social epidemiological and personal health care, and subsidized nutrition. He also attributes the vast differences in female mortality rates around the world to inequalities in women's access to education, health, and nutrition programs. He notes first that women tend to live longer than men – that is, when they receive adequate health care and nutrition.[6] As this is the case in most of Europe and North America, overall sex ratios in these regions are around 1.06 (women per man). In parts of the developing world, however, women receive less adequate care and nutrition and so die earlier, resulting in many fewer women per man (e.g., 0.94 in China, Bangladesh, and West Asia, 0.93 in India, and 0.91 in Pakistan) (Sen 1992, 1993b). And, in Kerala specifically, where commitment to education and health for women is as great as it is for men, the ratio of women to men is about 1.04 (against India's overall 0.93) and women can expect to live 73.0 years while men live to 67.5 (Sen 1992, 1993b). The fact that women live longer than men in Kerala does not indicate that women's longevity has been achieved at the expense of shorter lives for men. Rather, it means that both men and women of Kerala are living about as long as they are intrinsically (naturally) *capable* of living.

The measures that Sen identifies as critical for helping people achieve intrinsically valuable functionings (e.g., a full lifespan) work in two ways: widespread public education, health care, and subsidized nutrition have both physiological and psychosocial effects. First, they instill concrete skills, reduce disease loads, and increase the intake of protein and calories. At the same time, however, they also maximize the internal, subjective experience of security by decreasing external, objective risk and uncertainty. As we well know by now, risk and uncertainty constitute danger (bad), which is contrary to security (good). This is why social position is so

---

[6] See, for example, Waldron 1983.

closely related to health: because inequality increases risk and uncertainty by separating people from each other, by reducing social cohesion and thus social security. As Wilkinson put it,

> . . . absolute income will affect health through the direct physiological effects of material circumstances, whereas relative income involves *inherently social elements* in the causal process[7] . . . The powerful influence which relative income seems to have suggests that it is not so much a matter of what your circumstances are in themselves, but of their standing *in relation to others*: of where they place you in the overall scale of things, and of the impact which this has on your psychological, emotional, and social life. (1996:113; emphases added)

The relations in which humans evolved to stand with others, Wilkinson maintains, were those of direct exchange. In early human societies, essentially all social relations were between equals. Even if they so desired, no individual was able to rise above others, to seem better than others, to treat others disrespectfully.[8] This was because no individual could afford to risk alienating others and have them withdraw from exchange relations. Social security and life itself were utterly dependent on the reciprocal exchange of everything of value. Therefore, just where people placed each other in the overall scale of things would inevitably have a major impact on their psychological, emotional, and social life. Placement beyond the pale of exchange relations would entail extreme risk and uncertainty. This view of the political economy of our hunter–gatherer ancestors is widely accepted by anthropologists and is well documented in small-scale tribal societies today (e.g., Boehm 1993, 1997; Erdal and Whiten 1994, 1996; Knauft 1991; Sahlins 1972; Woodburn 1982).[9]

---

[7] This is not to imply that "direct physiological effects" are not involved in the "inherently social elements in the causal process." The distinction that Wilkinson makes here is similar to the one between Peter Ellison's (1990) "bioassay" (rates of growth and development embody early nutritional/disease risk and uncertainty) and my "socioassay" (psychosocial stress embodies early social risk and uncertainty – through the direct physiological effects of insecurity, as outlined above, pp. 151–155).

[8] This does not mean, of course, that all people were equal in every way. It does mean, however, that by and large, despite their differences, all members of a band were equally *important*. This entails treating people with equal respect (e.g., Chisholm 1996b).

[9] In light of our hunter–gatherer past, I expect that most evolutionary psychologists and anthropologists today would also agree with Wilkinson that "we may not be psychologically well adapted to inequality and individualism" (1996:150).

Knowing how we stand in relation to others inherently involves knowing other people's beliefs, desires, and intentions (as we saw in chapter 4). On the basis of how people behave toward us, we generate images of their intentions. These images are thought to be automatically generated by the ToM mechanism – the apparently innate, algorithm-like assumption that when people behave toward us in a certain way they must have certain beliefs and feelings about us. If people behave badly toward us – thereby activating automatic evaluation mechanisms that return a value of danger (bad) more than security (good) – then we seem intrinsically predisposed to make sense of their behavior by attributing to them the belief that we are worthy of bad treatment or the desire to treat us badly. If we accept their beliefs or desires as real (and children are especially prone to do so), then we cannot help but accept an image of ourselves as standing in a dangerous (bad) position relative to them. This is the essence of psychosocial stress. To perceive danger (badness) is to perceive risk and uncertainty. Chronic risk and uncertainty are dangerous not only because they increase the probability of death, but also because repeatedly responding to actual risks and continuously monitoring uncertain ones consumes limited resources and raises cortisol levels. This, we know, can shorten lives. Through both direct and indirect routes, then, inequality – risk and uncertainty – increases the frequency of loss. This is why sensitivity to loss (death and its side-effects) would be an evolutionarily rational basis for the contingent development of alternative reproductive strategies: because loss is a good indicator of risk and uncertainty. Wilkinson said it this way:

> Perhaps the easiest way of seeing intuitively what the socioeconomic differences in death rates mean, is to imagine two people, each with a similar-sized circle of friends and relations – let us say fifty personal contacts – but living in separate rich and poor areas. For every death that occurs among the circle of friends of the person in the rich area, the person in the poor area will know of two, three or even four times as many deaths among his or her circle of friends. (1996:57)

Knowing how we stand in relation to others also inherently involves exchange relationships. The first exchange relationship is that between mother and infant. The development of attachment depends entirely on the exchange of value (security) between mother and infant. Attachment theory is quintessentially an exchange theory. To receive a gift is to perceive value (security). The attachment relationship is the prototype of the gift/counter-gift relationship described by Mauss (1924/1969). The perception of social value induces us (through ToM) to assume that the giver believes we deserve such gifts or desires to treat us well. If we accept these beliefs and desires as real (and children are especially prone to do so), then we feel that we stand in a good (secure) relation to the giver. Wilkinson seems implicitly to recognize the kinship between attachment and exchange theory:

> The exchange systems through which we are brought together as individuals in society not only build into us powerful assumptions about how we are related to one another but also appear to tell us how social or self-interested our basic nature is. (1996:141)

If the principal social danger is defection from the social contract, and if the attachment system is the foundation for social exchange, then on the argument presented in chapter 4 ToM may be seen as a mechanism for monitoring social exchange as a basis for generating models of other people's intentions, thereby to detect potential defectors. If we experience too many defections (too much loss) we seem naturally predisposed to assume that others desire to treat us badly or that we are unworthy of equal relations with them. If we believe that they want to harm us, we may hate them; if we believe that we are unworthy of them, we may hate ourselves. Either way we face an insecure (risky and uncertain) future that we are apt to devalue. When we devalue the future, we are apt to become less social and more immediately self-interested. Our capability to achieve valuable functionings is thus diminished. We are not completely free then to set the stage for the future or maximize long-term fitness.

Functions, freedom, and fitness

In *Inequality Reexamined* (1992), Amartya Sen presents a logical theory of value. In the preceding pages, I have tried to show that the logic of evolutionary theory identifies fitness (continuance) as the origin and essence of value. In this concluding section, I shall outline Sen's thinking about value and attempt to show that our approaches converge and have similar implications for a science of value and ethics.

Sen notes first that all ethical theories agree that to have a good society there must be equality of *something*. They differ, however, on just what it is that should be equal. For some, equal income is paramount, while for others it is equal rights, responsibilities, opportunities, utilities, or something else of value (e.g., "health, wealth, happiness, lifespan, vigor, power, prestige, beauty, love, sex, truth, honor, reason . . . "). Nor is deciding which equality is most important an empty pastime, for "the judgment and measurement of inequality is thoroughly dependent on the choice of the variable (income, wealth, happiness, etc.) in terms of which comparisons are made" (Sen 1992:2). Therefore, because some inequalities are the source of a great deal of pathology, as we have just seen, the answer to Sen's question, "equality of what?" quite literally has life and death implications. In asking "equality of what?" Sen helps to illuminate the more fundamental question of "*why* equality?"

Sen approaches "equality of what?" with another question: is it possible that competing notions of value (income, rights, opportunities, utilities, etc.) are just surface manifestations of an irreducible core that they all share? He argues yes: one common denominator of all possible answers to the question "equality of what?" is the "capability to achieve valuable functionings" (1993b:31). Focusing on capabilities, he maintains, helps us to distinguish between our means and ends. It takes us away from our concern with income, wealth, commodities, rights, opportunities, etc. on to the ends to which they are simply means – that is, "on to the constitutive elements of living," on to what value is *for*:

> Living may be seen as consisting of a set of interrelated "functionings," consisting of beings and doings. A person's achievement in this respect can be seen as the vector of his or her functionings. The relevant functionings can vary from such elementary things as being adequately nourished, being in good health, avoiding escapable morbidity and premature mortality, etc., to more complex achievements such as being happy, having self-respect, taking part in the life of the community, and so on. The claim is that functionings are *constitutive* of a person's being, and an evaluation of well-being has to take the form of an assessment of these constitutive elements. (1992:39; original emphasis)

A good society for Sen is not simply one in which people are content with their lives, but one in which they are truly free to choose and pursue the futures to which they aspire. In many parts of the world people have been wasted by traditions of poverty and prejudice (inequality, risk and uncertainty) for so long that if they are content it is only because they know of nothing better; they are content because they lack the information to generate models of alternative futures. On Sen's view, theirs are not good societies, for if people lack knowledge of alternative futures they are not free to pursue them. But simply knowing about alternative futures is not enough. If out of fear and insecurity people devalue futures that they know exist, they are equally incapable of pursuing them.

Sen favors social arrangements that equalize people's capability to choose and attain valuable futures – or, more precisely, people's chances of *falling short* of their aspirations. Maximizing everyone's positive attainment is good, but equalizing (and minimizing) everyone's negative shortfall is better because it addresses more directly the problems of inequality. If poor people have shorter lives than wealthy people, they fall short of the years that a human is manifestly capable of living. Allocating resources preferentially to minimize poor people's longevity shortfall reduces inequality. Allocating resources equally to maximize everybody's longevity attainment simply maintains the unequal status quo. This is because, just as a rising tide floats all boats, extending everybody's lifespan by the same amount increases average lifespan without changing the shape of the lifespan distribution. What is more, if the wealthy are already living as long as people are intrinsically capable, then they have a greater capability than the poor to use their allocation to pursue goals other than a longer life – such as setting the stage for future good moves instead of merely avoiding premature death.

But what are these "constitutive elements of living" on to which value is supposed to take us? What is value *for*? This is a critical question because if our judgments and measurements of inequality, and thus our well-being, depend on an "assessment of these constitutive elements," as Sen argues, then we must be altogether clear about what they are. I am thus indebted to Martha Nussbaum (1995) for her understanding of Sen's "constitutive elements." "The basic idea," she says, "is that we ask ourselves, 'What are the characteristic activities of the human being? What does the human being do, characteristically, as such – and not, say, as a member of a particular group, or a particular local community?'" (1995:72). She analyzes these "doings" (functionings) in terms of two thresholds:

> . . . a threshold of capability to function beneath which a life will be so impoverished that it will not be human at all;

and a somewhat higher threshold, beneath which those
characteristic functions are available in such a reduced way
that, though we judge the form of life a human one, we will
not think it a *good* human life. (1995:81; original emphasis)

Nussbaum sees a "human life" as one that possesses the absolute minimum capabilities that we would even *recognize* as human. A person who
lacks the capability to function in a way that we regard as human falls
below the threshold of a human life. By way of example she suggests that
limited capabilities such as those that obtain at the very end of some
lives, when some people lose all sensation and consciousness, might
make a life not worth living. Or when a child is born so severely damaged,
with total sensory incapacity and an utter incapability of recognizing or
relating to others, it might have a life not worth living. Note well that
judging a life to be "not human" says nothing about how we should treat
people with such lives. Indeed, if we do not treat them as well as we can,
we may judge *ourselves* not to have a "good human life." Evaluating a life
as not human simply establishes a set of capabilities as valuable because
they are the irreducible minimum. Such an evaluation constitutes "a
ground floor or minimum conception of the good" (1995:80). A society
that is capable of keeping its people above the first threshold but fails to
do so, or actually pushes them below it, is manifestly not a good society;
indeed, it is an inhuman society.

However, a person can be nourished well enough to maintain some
minimum quality of life without being so well nourished that she is capable, say, of maintaining a pregnancy or continuing to nurse. A person can
be secure enough to maintain life itself without being so secure that she
is capable of generating realistic images of the future for herself or her
child. A person can be trained well enough to earn a living without being
educated well enough to read for enjoyment or additional learning.
Nussbaum sees a "good human life" as one that possesses the minimum
capabilities that we would *accept* for a human. Life below the first threshold is inhuman – not even recognizable as a human life. Life below the
second threshold, however, while recognizably human, is not a good life,
and therefore not acceptable as long as people are capable of doing
better, capable of crossing the second threshold to more valuable "beings
and doings."

Like Sen, Nussbaum acknowledges that precise definitions of the "beings
and doings" that constitute a good human life are difficult and should be

sought only through the widest possible consensus. She none the less offers as a rough guide a list of general capabilities (which I have abridged slightly):

1   Being able to live to the end of a human life of normal length . . .
2   Being able to have good health; to be adequately nourished; to have adequate shelter; having opportunities for sexual satisfaction, and for choice in matters of reproduction . . .
3   Being able to avoid unnecessary and non-beneficial pain . . . and to have pleasurable experiences.
4   Being able to use the senses; being able to imagine, to think, and to reason – and to do these things in a way informed and cultivated by an adequate education, including, but by no means limited to, literacy and basic mathematical and scientific training. Being able to use imagination and thought in connection with experiencing and producing spiritually enriching materials and events of one's own choice; religious, literary, musical, and so forth . . .
5   Being able to have attachments to things and persons outside ourselves; to love those who love and care for us, to grieve at their absence; in general, to love, to grieve, to experience longing and gratitude . . .
6   Being able to form a conception of the good and to engage in critical reflection about the planning of one's own life . . .
7   Being able to live for and to [sic] others, to recognize and show concern for other human beings, to engage in various forms of social interaction; to be able to imagine the situation of another and to have compassion for that situation; to have the capability for both justice and friendship. Protecting this capability means, once again, protecting institutions that constitute such forms of affiliation, and also protecting the freedoms of assembly and political speech.
8   Being able to live with concern for and in relation to animals, plants, and the world of nature.
9   Being able to laugh, to play . . .
10   Being able to live one's own life and nobody else's. This means having certain guarantees of non-interference with certain choices that are especially personal and definitive of selfhood, such as choices regarding marriage, childbearing, sexual

expression, speech, and employment. . . . Being able to live
one's own life in one's own surroundings and context. This
means guarantees of freedom of association and of freedom
from unwarranted search and seizure . . . (Nussbaum
1995:83–4).

In the capability approach, value inheres in people's capability to achieve
inherently valuable functionings (e.g., the items above). Therefore, the
best way to assess the quality of life is not to focus on the *means* of life
(wealth, resources, income, etc.) but on the inherently valuable functionings that constitute the *ends* of a *good* life. For Nussbaum it follows, then,
that

> . . . the central goal of public planning should be the *capabilities*
> of citizens to perform various important functions. The
> questions that should be asked when assessing the quality of
> life of a country are . . . "How well have people of the country
> been enabled to perform the central human functions?" and,
> "Have they been put in a position of mere human subsistence
> with respect to the functions, or have they been enabled to live
> well?" In other words, we ask where the people are, with
> respect to the second [threshold]. And we focus on getting as
> many people as possible above the second threshold.
> (Nussbaum 1995:87; original emphasis)

But how does a "goal of public planning" follow from an understanding of human "capabilities to perform various functions?" How does a
value (goal) follow from a fact? For Nussbaum, the fact that humans have
certain intrinsic capabilities to function entails the moral command
(value) to nurture these capabilities because the capabilities *themselves* are
intrinsically valuable:

> The basic intuition from which the capability approach starts,
> in the political arena, is that human capabilities exert a moral
> claim that they should be developed. Human beings are
> creatures such that, provided with the right educational and
> material support, they can become fully capable of the major
> human functions, can cross the first and second thresholds.
> That is, they are creatures with certain lower-level capabilities
> . . . to perform the functions in question. When these
> capabilities are deprived of the nourishment that would

transform them into high-level capabilities that figure on my
list [above], they are fruitless, cut off, in some way but a shadow
of themselves. They are like actors who never get to go on
stage, or a musical score that is never performed. Their very
being makes forward reference to functioning ... I claim that
just as we hold that a child who dies before getting to maturity
has died especially tragically – for her activities of growth and
preparation for adult activities now have lost their point – so
too with capability and functioning more generally: we believe
that certain basic and central human endowments have a
claim to be assisted in developing, and exert that claim on
others, and especially, as Aristotle saw, on government ... I
suggest, then, that in thinking of political planning we begin
from this notion, thinking of the basic capabilities of human
beings as needs for functioning, which give rise to correlated
political duties ... It is the gap between potential humanness
and its full realization that exerts a moral claim. (Nussbaum
1995:88–9)

Thus, if people are capable of living to old age, then we ought to help
them do so. If people are capable of good health, then we ought to treat
them therapeutically. If people are capable of avoiding pain and having
pleasurable experiences, then we ought to assist them in both functions.
If people are capable of using their senses, of imagining, thinking, and
reasoning, then we ought to nurture these capabilities. If people are capable of crossing the second threshold, from human life to good human
life, then society should help as many as possible to do so. Why? Because
a good human life is constituted by certain elements that are "important
in themselves" (Sen 1993b:33). "It is in asserting the need to examine the
value of functionings and capabilities as opposed to confining attention
to the *means* to these achievements and freedoms (such as resources or
primary goods or incomes) that the capability approach has something to
offer" (Sen 1992:46; original emphasis). Value, in other words, inheres in
certain functionings, certain *ends*, that constitute – or can constitute – a
human life. The fact that humans are intrinsically capable of certain
functionings exerts a moral claim to nurture these capabilities. The first
threshold exerts the moral claim first to provide a safe haven, to do no
harm, to avoid fitness cliffs by maintaining at least the "minimum
conception of the good." The second threshold exerts the moral claim to

provide a secure base for growth, to nurture play and exploration, to set the stage for the future.

Perhaps the most basic of all human capabilities is the freedom to pursue alternative futures. In Sen's words, "functionings belong to the constitutive elements of well-being. Capability reflects freedom to pursue these constitutive elements, and may even have . . . a direct role in well-being itself, in so far as deciding and choosing are also parts of living" (1992:42). In so far as humans have the capability to choose and pursue alternative futures, then they should be free to do so, for in the capability approach practical reason and freedom are deeply intertwined and inherently valuable; they are "important in themselves" and "intrinsically matter" to humans, "characteristically, as such," as ends.

Practical reason and freedom are also valuable in the evolutionary approach, of course, but not quite so intrinsically. From an evolutionary perspective, value originates in fitness and exists as a fact of nature, as does the human capability for value experience. On this view, the fact that humans have the capability for practical reason and freedom entails the moral command (Taylor's "demanding commitment") to nurture these capabilities – not because they are "important in themselves," but because they are evolved *means* to the ultimate "end" of life, which is long-term fitness or continuance. Both the capability and evolutionary approaches hold that value inheres in life's ends, not its means (income, resources, commodities, etc.). For an evolutionist, however, the capabilities that constitute a good human life are not ends that are "important in themselves," as they are in the capability approach. Instead, in the evolutionary approach the *achievement* of these capabilities is an indication that a person is roughly on track for the ultimate "end" of life, which is continuance, staying in the existential game of life. If value experience is the (imperfect) phenotypic representation of the organism × environment interactions that determine one's reproductive value, as I argued in chapter 3, then over time the capability for value experience would function as a mechanism for tracking change in one's reproductive value. Actually achieving some valued capability would effect the phenotypic representation of an increase in reproductive value – i.e., positive value experience. This indicates so far, so good; one is still in the existential game.

In the evolutionary approach, then, health, wealth, happiness, lifespan, vigor, power, prestige, beauty, love, sex, truth, honor, reason, etc. are not ends in themselves but are only means for avoiding fitness cliffs or setting the stage for the future. There might at first appear to be some tension between the ways that the capability and evolutionary approaches value practical reason and freedom. The capability approach sees them as valuable ends (capabilities) in themselves, whereas the evolutionary approach sees them as valuable means to the ultimate end of continuance. I think, however, that this is a difference that does not make a difference, for both approaches have the same implication for ethics. In the capability approach, the gap between "potential humanness and its full realization" exerts the moral claim to bring as many people as possible over Nussbaum's second threshold. Likewise, the evolutionary ecological gap between avoiding fitness cliffs and setting the stage for future good fitness moves would seem to exert the equivalent moral claim to help as many people as possible set the stage to maximize future reproduction.

And here is why. In the capability approach, certain "functionings belong to the constitutive elements of living," and should therefore be nurtured. In the evolutionary approach, however, the "constitutive elements of living" are the complex actions for the sake of which bodies exist: the complex adaptations ("functionings") that are *for* survival, growth and development, and, ultimately, the production and rearing of descendants. Therefore, from an evolutionary perspective, what political planning should aim at are the capabilities that maximize the number of people who are capable of approaching the future by setting the stage for it, for this maximizes the number of descendants in arbitrarily distant future generations. If value itself comes from fitness, then political planning should be aimed at bringing as many people as possible to functionings that maximize long-term fitness. This unquestionably entails nurturing practical reason and freedom. For, as we saw in chapters 1 and 2, the most generic adaptive problem is risk and uncertainty, and, above all other human capabilities, practical reason and freedom are *for* solving the problems of risk and uncertainty. Remember, the definition of practical reason is when "we understand an environment [and] can . . . effect our purposes in it" (Taylor 1993:218); being *able* to effect our purposes (when we are capable of doing so) includes the *freedom* to do so. The claim here is that our ultimate purpose is that for the sake of which our bodies exist: long-term fitness. According to our present understanding of the environment of evolutionary adaptedness of life itself, when any organism faces a fitness cliff its optimal reproductive strategy (*ceteris paribus*) will be to maximize current reproduction – even in the face of appalling costs. Because the cost of falling off a fitness cliff is always greater than the benefit of setting the stage for some future good fitness move, people at the edge of a fitness cliff have nothing left to lose. It would therefore be evolutionarily rational for them to pay horrendous costs for even the barest chance at continuing. And, as I believe the evidence shows, when people have faced too much risk and uncertainty for too long they are prone to the early and/or impulsive display of sexual and aggressive behavior. This often entails increased pathology and shortened lives. It may be a brute fact of nature that this is just the cost of continuing in the face of chronic risk and uncertainty.

But, if this is a brute fact, I think it leads to an unbrutish value: political planning should give preference to reducing the security shortfall of those at the edge of fitness cliffs. If it is an evolutionary biological fact that maximizing current reproduction is the optimal reproductive strategy at the edge of a fitness cliff – but that doing so can exact appalling costs in the form of well-being and longevity shortfalls – then we ought to allocate resources preferentially to reduce the risk and uncertainty that constitute the fitness cliff.

This is both rational and ethical. It is rational because it is consistent with practical reason: making our way and effecting our purposes. Reducing environmental risk and uncertainty helps people to "have a life." It minimizes activation of the HPA system, cortisol levels, and the subjective value experience of insecurity (danger; bad). Over time, this leads to improved health and reduces the early and/or impulsive display of sexual and aggressive behavior. In the capability approach, improved well-being and more thoughtful, concerned, or compassionate sexual and aggressive behavior are intrinsically valuable as ends (purposes) in themselves, as constitutive elements of a good life. In the evolutionary approach, they are valuable means to the ultimate end (purpose) of long-term fitness. They are evidence that so far, so good, one is still on track for continuing to become and need not scramble just to stay in the game.

In the capability approach, it is ethical to allocate resources preferentially to reduce the risk and uncertainty that constitute fitness cliffs simply because of the fact that people are *capable* of better health, longer lives, and (the whole point of ToM) empathy: the ability "to imagine the situation of another and to have compassion for that situation" (Nussbaum 1995:83). The fact of these capabilities exerts a moral claim on those who have achieved more of them to develop them in those who have not, for doing so is part of a *good* life. From an evolutionary perspective, it is ethical (valuable) to allocate resources preferentially to reduce the worst security shortfalls, because when too many people have to live on the edge of fitness cliffs there will be too many people with appalling shortfalls and thus nothing left to lose. When this happens freedom is in danger. Those with little to lose already suffer a capability shortfall and may feel free to use whatever means are available just to have a life at all, just to stay in the existential game of life. Directly or indirectly, this will tend to reduce everyone's well-being. At some point, this will impinge on the capabilities and freedom of those with more to lose (a good life), thereby raising their costs of continuing. There may arise some sort of equilibrium between those with little to lose and those with much to lose, but, without equality (of shortfall), insecurity will always hound freedom.

The evolutionary theory of value that I am proposing offers reason to believe that value exists as a fact of nature and that sometimes what we feel is right, is right. It offers reason to believe that the subjective moral command to increase human flourishing is rationally, objectively right – at least to the extent that it helps to maximize the number of people whose optimal reproductive strategy is to maximize future reproduction. To accomplish this intensely moral task of political planning (practical reason), evolutionary theory suggests that we must minimize risk and uncertainty. Because inequality is a major source of risk and uncertainty, we must reduce inequality. Perhaps the most direct way to reduce inequality is to allocate resources preferentially to minimize the most glaring capability shortfalls. Perhaps the most common and glaring capability shortfall in the modern world is security. Insecurity (danger; bad) is the antithesis of social exchange. Earl Shorris (1997) describes the insecurity enveloping the poor as the "surround of force." In his words, "life within the surround leaves the poor without the possibility of politics, hurrying, helpless to do anything but react, with no time to reflect, no time to do anything but react" (p. 94). Living at the edge of a cliff, incapable of anything but reaction,[10] makes it difficult to set the stage for the future, which is what social exchange and politics are all about. Again Shorris: "Political loneliness has two sources: hatred of others, who are not good enough to be friends or allies, and hatred of oneself, who is not good enough to have friends or allies" (p. 271).

---

[10] Remember, if we cannot be creative we can only be reactive.

Peter Marris (1991) is equally explicit about the relationship between security and politics:

> The qualities of good social relationships and good experiences of attachment are essentially the same: predictability, responsiveness, intelligibility, supportiveness, reciprocity of commitment. To achieve this, we have to struggle constantly against the tendency of the powerful to subordinate and marginalize others in the interest of their own greater security. The worse we fail, the more widespread insecurity becomes, and the greater the temptation to rescue our own command of circumstances at the expense of others. To save ourselves from this declining spiral, those at most risk of subordination and marginalization need to organize themselves to apply all the sanctions at hand to demand reciprocity. But this in itself is not enough, because success often only displaces marginalization elsewhere. We need also to institute a style of governing our relationships with each other which takes as its first principles reciprocity of commitment, predictability, and respect for the unique structure of meaning and attachment which makes life worthwhile for each of us. It is a radically more collaborative and democratic style of government than any we have experienced. (p. 88)

Insecurity is no basis for social exchange or politics. Nurturance (which is the essence of parental investment: "predictability, responsiveness, intelligibility, supportiveness, reciprocity of commitment") contributes to human flourishing because it increases security (good). Security maximizes the impulse to play, explore, and create, which, in turn, increases the capability to generate accurate models of one's own and other people's beliefs, desires, and intentions. This ToM capability, in its turn, increases the capability to generate realistic representations of alternative futures, to adapt to changing circumstances, and to enter into long-term exchange relations with others. Freedom, too, maximizes security. The capability to achieve a good human life includes the freedom to do so. Whatever constrains people from freely choosing and pursuing valuable futures increases their risk and uncertainty. If it is true that the optimal reproductive strategy under conditions of security is to maximize future reproduction, then to increase human flourishing it is rational to value nurturance, equality, and freedom.

References

Adler, N.E., Boyce, W.T., Chesney, M.A. et al. 1993. Socioeconomic inequalities in health: No easy solution. *Journal of the American Medical Association*, 269(24):3141–5.

Aggleton, J.P. 1992. *The Amygdala*. New York: John Wiley.

Ainslie, G. 1975. Specious reward: A behavioral theory of impulsiveness and impulse control. *Psychological Bulletin*, 82:463–509.

Ainslie, G. 1992. *Picoeconomics: The Strategic Interaction of Successive Motivational States Within the Person*. Cambridge University Press.

Ainsworth, M.D.S. 1965. Conclusions from recent research. In J. Bowlby (ed.) *Child Care and the Growth of Love*. Baltimore: Penguin Books.

Ainsworth, M.D.S. 1969. *Infancy in Uganda: Infant Care and the Growth of Love*. Baltimore: Johns Hopkins University Press.

Ainsworth, M.D.S. 1979a. Infant–mother attachment. *American Psychologist*, 34:932–7.

Ainsworth, M.D.S. 1979b. Attachment as related to mother–infant interaction. In J. Rosenblatt, R. Hinde, C. Beer, and M. Busnel (eds.), *Advances in the Study of Behavior*, Vol. 9. New York: Academic Press.

Ainsworth, M.D.S., Bell, S., and Stayton, D. 1971. Individual differences in strange situation behavior of one-year-olds. In H.R. Schaffer (ed.), *The Origins of Human Social Relations*. London: Academic Press.

Ainsworth, M.D.S., Blehar, M., Waters, E., and Wall, S. 1978. *Patterns of Attachment*. Hillsdale, N.J: Lawrence Erlbaum Associates.

Alan Guttmacher Institute (AGI). 1998. *Into a New World: Young Women's Sexual and Reproductive Lives*. New York: AGI.

Alexander, P., and Lupfer, S. 1987. Family characteristics and long-term consequences associated with sexual abuse. *Archives of Sexual Behavior*, 16(3):235–45.

Alexander, R.D. 1987. *The Biology of Moral Systems*. Hawthorne, NY: Aldine de Gruyter.

Alexander, R.D., and Borgia, G. 1979. On the origin and basis of the male–female phenomenon. In M. Blum and N. Blum (eds.), *Sexual Selection and Reproductive Competition in Insects*. New York: Academic Press.

Anderson, E. 1994. The code of the streets. *Atlantic Monthly*, 273(5):80–94.

Andrews, M., and Rosenblum, L. 1991. Attachment in monkey infants raised in variable- and low-demand environments. *Child Development*, 62:686–93.

Apter, D., and Vikho, R. 1983 Early menarche, a risk factor for breast cancer, indicates early onset of ovulatory cycles. *Journal of Clinical Endocrinology and Metabolism*, 57:82–6.

Apter, D., Reinila, M., and Vikho, R. 1989. Some endocrine characteristics of early menarche, a risk factor for breast cancer, are preserved into adulthood. *Journal of Clinical Endocrinology and Metabolism*, 57:82–6.

Archer, J. (ed.), 1994. *Male Violence*. London: Routledge.

Arnold, M. 1960. *Emotion and Personality*. New York: Columbia University Press.

Atkinson, L., and Zucker, K.J. (eds.), 1997. *Attachment and Psychopathology*. New York: Guilford Press.

Baldwin, J.M. 1896. A new factor in evolution. *American Naturalist*, 30:441–51.

Baldwin, M.W., Fehr, B., Keedian, E., Seidel, M. et al. 1993. An exploration of the relational schemata underlying attachment styles: Self-report and lexical decision approaches. *Personality and Social Psychology Bulletin*, 19(6):746–54.

Banfield, E. 1974. *The Unheavenly City Revisited*. Boston: Little, Brown.

Barker, D.J.P. (ed.), 1992. *Fetal and Infant Origins of Adult Disease*. London: British Medical Journal.

Barker, D.J.P. 1997. The fetal origins of coronary heart disease. *Acta Paediatrica*, 422:78–82.

Barkow, J. 1984. The distance between genes and culture. *Journal of Anthropological Research*, 40:367–79.

Baron-Cohen, S. 1995. *Mindblindness: An Essay on Autism and Theory of Mind*. Cambridge, MA: MIT Press.

Baron-Cohen, S., Ring, H., Moriarty, J., Schmitz, B., Costa, D., and Ell, P. 1994. Recognition of mental state terms: Clinical findings in children with autism and a functional neuroimaging study of normal adults. *British Journal of Psychiatry*, 165(5):640–9.

Baron-Cohen, S., Tager-Flusberg, H., and Cohen, D. (eds.), 1993. *Understanding Other Minds: Perspectives From Autism*. Oxford: Oxford University Press.

Barth, F. 1966. *Models of Social Organization*. Royal Anthropological Institute, Occasional Paper No. 23.

Bateson, G. 1972. *Steps to an Ecology of Mind*. New York: Ballantine.

Bateson, P.P.G. (ed.), 1983. *Mate Choice*. Cambridge University Press.

Bateson, P.P.G. 1976. Rules and reciprocity in behavioural development. In P.P.G. Bateson and R.A. Hinde (eds.), *Growing Points in Ethology*. Cambridge University Press.

Bateson, P.P.G. 1982. Behavioural development and evolutionary processes. In *Current Problems in Sociobiology*. King's College Sociobiology Study Group (eds.), Cambridge University Press.

Bateson, P.P.G. 1994. The dynamics of parent-offspring conflict in mammals. *Trends in Ecology and Evolution*, 9(10):339–403.

Bateson, P.P.G., Mendl, M., and Feaver, J. 1990. Play in the domestic cat is enhanced by rationing of the mother during lactation. *Animal Behaviour*, 40:514–25.

Beeghly, M., and Cicchetti, D. 1994. Child maltreatment, attachment, and the self system: Emergence of an internal state lexicon in toddlers at high social risk. *Development and Psychopathology*, 6:5–30.

Bell, N., and Bell, R. (eds.), 1993. *Adolescent Risk Taking*. Newbury Park, CA: Sage Publications.

Belsky, J., and Cassidy, J. 1994. Attachment: Theory and evidence. In M. Rutter and D. Hay (eds.), *Development Through Life: A Handbook for Clinicians*. Oxford: Basil Blackwell.

Belsky, J., Rovine, M., and Fish, M. 1989. The developing family system. In M. Gunnar and E. Thelen (eds.), *The Minnesota Symposium on Child Psychology: Vol. 22. Systems and Development*. Hillsdale, NJ: Lawrence Erlbaum.

Belsky, J. Steinberg, L., and Draper, P. 1991. Childhood experience, interpersonal development, and reproductive strategy: An evolutionary theory og socialization. *Child Development*, 62:647–70.

Belyaev, D.K., Plyusnina, I., and Trut, L. 1985. Domestication in the silver fox (*Vulpes fulvus* DESM): Changes in physiological boundaries of the sensitive period of primary socialization. *Applied Animal Behaviour Science*, 13:359–70.

Bennett, J. 1991. How to read minds in behavior: A suggestion from a philosopher. In A. Whiten (ed.), *Natural Theories of Mind: Evolution, Development, and Simulation of Everyday Mindreadings*. Oxford: Basil Blackwell.

Bereczkei, T., and Csanaky, A. 1996. Evolutionary pathway of child development: Lifestyles of adolescents and adults from father-absent families. *Human Nature*, 7(3): 257–80.

Bernard, J. 1975. Adolescence and socialization for motherhood. In S. Dragastin and G. Elder (eds.), *Adolesence in the Life Cycle*. New York: John Wiley.

Bernardo, J. 1993. Determinants of maturation in animals. *Trends in Ecology and Evolution*, 8(5):166–73.

Betzig, L. 1986. *Despotism and Differential Reproduction: A Darwinian View of History*. Hawthorne, NY: Lawrence Erlbaum Associates.

Biller, H. 1981. Father absence, divorce, and personality development. In M. Lamb (ed.), *The Role of the Father in Child Development*. New York: John Wiley.

Blum, R. 1987. Contemporary threats to adolescent health in the United States. *Journal of the American Medical Association*, 257:3390–5.

Blurton Jones, N.G. 1993. The lives of hunter–gatherer children: Effects of parental behavior and parental reproductive strategy. In M. Pereira and L. Fairbanks (eds.), *Juvenile Primates: Life History, Development, and Behavior*. New York: Oxford University Press.

Boehm, C. 1993. Egalitarian behavior and reverse dominance hierarchy. *Current Anthropology*, 34(3):227–54.

Boehm, C. 1997. Impact of the human egalitarian syndrome on Darwinian selection mechanics. *The American Naturalist*, 150:S100–S121.

Bogin, B. 1994. Adolescence in evolutionary perspective. *Acta Pediatrica*, Supplement, 406:29–35.

Bogin, B. 1995. Growth and development: Recent evolutionary and biocultural research. In N. Boaz and L. Wolfe (eds.), *Biological Anthropology: The State of the Science*. New York: Wiley-Liss.

Bogin, B., and Smith, B.H. 1996. Evolution of the human life cycle. *American Journal of Human Biology*, 8:703–16.

Bonner, J.T. 1965. *Size and Cycle*. Princeton University Press.

Bonner, J.T. 1993. *Life Cycles*. Princeton University Press.

Booth, A., and Dabbs, J.M. 1993. Testosterone and men's marriages. *Social Forces*, 72(2):463–77.

Borgerhoff Mulder, M. 1992. Reproductive decisions. In E.A. Smith and B. Winterhalder (eds.), *Evolutionary Ecology and Human Behavior*. Hawthorne, NY: Aldine de Gruyter.

Bornstein, R.F., and Pittman, T.S. (eds.), 1992. *Perception Without Awareness: Cognitive, Clinical, and Social Perspectives*. New York: Guilford Press.

Boswell, J. 1988. *The Kindness of Strangers: The Abandonment of Children in Western Europe from Late Antiquity to the Renaissance*. New York: Pantheon.

Bourgois, P. 1995. *In Search of Respect: Selling Crack in El Barrio*. Cambridge University Press.

Bowlby, J. 1951. Maternal care and mental health. *Bulletin of the World Health Organization*, 3:355–534.

Bowlby, J. 1969. Attachment. *Attachment and Loss*, vol. 1. New York: Basic Books. (2nd edn published 1982).

Bowlby, J. 1973. Separation: Anxiety and Anger. *Attachment and Loss*, vol. 2. New York: Basic Books.

Bowlby, J. 1980. Loss: Sadness and Depression. *Attachment and Loss*, vol. 3. New York: Basic Books.

Boyce, M.S. (ed.), 1988. *Evolution of Life Histories of Mammals*. New Haven: Yale University Press.

Boyd, R., and Richerson, P. 1985. *Culture and the Evolutionary Process*. University of Chicago Press.

Bradshaw, A.D. 1965. Evolutionary significance of phenotypic plasticity in plants. *Advances in Genetics*, 13:115–55.

Brazelton, T.B., Kozlowski, B., and Main, M. 1974. The origins of reciprocity: The early mother–infant interaction. In M. Lewis and L. Rosenblum (eds.), *The Effect of the Infant on its Caregiver*. New York: John Wiley.

Brennan, K.A., and Shaver, P. 1995. Dimensions of adult attachment, affect regulation, and romantic relationship functioning. *Personality and Social Psychology Bulletin*, 21(3):267–83.

Bretherton, I. 1985. Attachment theory: Retrospect and prospect. In I. Bretherton and E. Waters (eds.), *Growing Points in Attachment Theory and Research*. Monographs of the Society for Research in Child Development (Serial No. 309), 50(1–2):3–35.

Bretherton, I., and Ainsworth, M.D.S. 1974. Responses of one-year-olds to a stranger in a strange situation. In M. Lewis and L. Rosenblum (eds.), *The Origins of Fear.* New York: John Wiley.

Bretherton, I., and Waters, E. (eds.), 1985. *Growing Points in Attachment Theory and Research.* Monographs of the Society for Research in Child Development (Serial No. 309), 50(1–2).

Bretherton, I., McNew, S., and Beeghly, M. 1981. Early person knowledge in gestural and verbal communication: When do infants acquire a "theory of mind"? In M. Lamb and L. Sherrod (eds.), *Infant Social Cognition.* Hillsdale, NJ: Lawrence Erlbaum.

Bretherton, I., Ridgeway, D., and Cassidy, J. 1990. Assessing internal working models of the attachment relationship. In M.T. Greenberg, D. Cicchetti and E.M. Cummings (eds.), *Attachment in the Preschool Years: Theory, Research, and Intervention.* University of Chicago Press.

Brindley, D., and Rolland, Y. 1989. Possible connections between stress, diabetes, obesity, hypertension and altered lipoprotein metabolism that may result in atherosclerosis. *Clinical Science,* 77:453–61.

Bronson, G.W. 1972. *Infants' reactions to unfamiliar persons and novel objects.* Monographs of the Society for Research in Child Development, 37(3):46.

Brothers, L. 1989. A biological perspective on empathy. *American Journal of Psychiatry,* 146:10–19.

Broude, G. 1990. Protest masculinity: A further look at the causes and the concept. *Ethos,* 18:103–22.

Brown, D. 1991. *Human Universals.* New York: McGraw-Hill.

Brown, S.E. 1973. Coping and poverty in the Dominican Republic: Women and their mates. *Current Anthropology,* 14:555.

Burbank, V. 1988. *Aboriginal Adolescence: Maidenhood in an Australian Community.* New Brunswick: Rutgers University Press.

Burbank, V. 1995. Gender hierarchy and adolescent sexuality: The control of female reproduction in an Australian Aboriginal community. *Ethos,* 23:33–46.

Burbank, V.K., and Chisholm, J.S. 1989. Old and new inequalities in a Southeast Arnhem Land community. Polygyny, marriage age, and birth spacing. In J.C. Altman (ed.), *Emergent Inequalities in Aboriginal Australia.* Oceania Monograph no. 38. Sydney: University of Sydney Press.

Burbank, V.K., and Chisholm, J.S. 1998. Adolescent pregnancy and parenthood in an Australian Aboriginal community. In G. Herdt and S. Leavitt (eds.), *Adolescence in Pacific Island Societies.* University of Pittsburgh Press.

Burkhardt, F. (ed.), 1996. *Charles Darwin's Letters: A Selection 1825–1859.* Cambridge University Press.

Burton, L.M. 1990. Teenage childbearing as an alternative life-course strategy in multigenerational black families. *Human Nature,* 1(2):124–43.

Burton, L.M. 1997. Ethnography and the meaning of adolescence in high-risk neighborhoods. *Ethos*, 25(2):208–17.

Buss, L. 1987. *The Evolution of Individuality*. Princeton University Press.

Byrne, R.W. 1995. *The Thinking Ape: Evolutionary Origins of Intelligence*. New York: Oxford University Press.

Byrne, R.W., and Whiten, A. (eds.), 1988. *Machiavellian Intelligence: Social Expertise and the Evolution of Intellect in Monkeys, Apes, and Humans*. Oxford: Clarendon Press.

Campbell, B., and Udry, J.R. 1995. Stress and age at menarche of mothers and daughters. *Journal of Biosocial Science*, 27:127–34.

Campbell, D.T. 1974. Evolutionary epistemology. In P.A. Schilpp (ed.), *The Philosophy of Karl Popper*. La Salle, IL: Open Court.

Campos, J., Barrett, K., Lamb, M., Goldsmith, H., and Stenberg, C. 1983. Socioemotional development. In M. Haith and J. Campos (eds.), *Handbook of Child Psychology*, Vol. 2. *Infancy and Developmental Psychobiology*. (4h edn, Paul Mussen, series ed.). New York: John Wiley.

Caro, T., and Bateson, P.P.G. 1986. Organization and ontogeny of alternative tactics. *Animal Behaviour*, 4:1482–99.

Cassidy, J., and Berlin, J. 1994. The insecure-ambivalent pattern of attachment: Theory and research. *Child Development*, 65:971–91.

Chalmers, A. 1978. *What is this Thing Called Science: An Assessment of the Nature and Status of Science and Its Methods*. Milton Keynes: The Open University Press.

Changeux, J-P. 1985. *Neuronal Man*. New York: Pantheon.

Charlton, B.G. 1994. Is inequality bad for the national health? *Lancet*, 34:221–2.

Charlton, B.G., and White, M. 1995. Living on the margin: A salutogenic model for socio-economic differentials in health. *Public Health*, 109:235–43.

Charman, T., Swettenham, J. Baron-Cohen, S., Cox, A., Baird, G., and Drew, A. 1997. Infants with autism: An investigation of empathy, pretend play, joint attention, and imitation. *Developmental Psychology*, 33(5):781–9.

Charnov, E.L. 1982. *The Theory of Sex Allocation*. Princeton University Press.

Charnov, E.L. 1990. On evolution of age at maturity and the adult lifespan. *Journal of Evolutionary Biology*, 3:139–44.

Charnov, E.L. 1991. Evolution of life history among female mammals. *Proceedings of the National Academy of Science, USA*, 88:1134–7.

Charnov, E.L. 1993. *Life History Invariants*. Oxford University Press.

Charnov, E.L., and Berrigan, D. 1990. Dimensionless numbers and life history evolution: Age at maturity versus the adult lifespan. *Evolutionary Ecology*, 4:273–5.

Charnov, E.L., and Berrigan, D. 1993. Why do female primates have such long lifespans and so few babies? *or* Life in the slow lane. *Evolutionary Anthropology*, 1:191–4.

Chasiotis, A., Scheffer, D. Restemeier, R., and Keller, H. 1998. Intergenerational context discontinuity affects the onset of puberty: A comparison of parent–child dyads in West and East Germany. *Human Nature*, 9(3): 321–339.

Cheney, D., and Seyfarth, R. 1990. *How Monkeys See the World: Inside the Mind of Another Species.* University of Chicago Press.

Cherlin, A., Furstenberg, F., Chase-Lonsdale, P. et al. 1991. Longitudinal studies of effects of divorce on children in Great Britain and the United States. *Science*, 252:1386–9.

Chisholm, J.S. 1993. Death, hope, and sex: Life history theory and the development of reproductive strategies. *Current Anthropology*, 34(1):1–24.

Chisholm, J.S. 1995a. Love's contingencies: The developmental socioecology of romantic passion. In W. Jankowiak (ed.), *Romantic Passion: A Universal Experience.* New York: Columbia University Press.

Chisholm, J.S. 1995b. Life history theory and life style choice: Implications for Darwinian medicine. In L. Schmitt and L. Freedman (eds.), *Perspectives in Human Biology*, vol. 1. Nedlands, WA: Centre for Human Biology, University of Western Australia and River Edge, NJ: World Scientific Publishing.

Chisholm, J.S. 1996a. The evolutionary ecology of attachment organization. *Human Nature*, 7(1):1–37.

Chisholm, J.S. 1996b. Learning "respect for everything": Navajo images of development. In C.P. Hwang, M.E. Lamb, and I.E. Sigel (eds.), *Images of Childhood.* Hillsdale, NJ: Lawrence Erlbaum.

Chisholm, J.S. 1999. Attachment and time preference: Relations between early stress and sexual behavior in a sample of American university women. *Human Nature*, 10(1): 51–83.

Chisholm, J.S., and Burbank, V. 1991. Monogamy and polygyny in Southeast Arnhem Land: Male coercion and female choice. *Ethology and Sociobiology*, 12:291–313.

Chomsky, N. 1975. *Reflections on Language.* New York: Pantheon Books.

Cicchetti, D., and Carlson, V. (eds.), 1989. *Child Maltreatment: Theory and Research on the Causes and Consequences of Child Abuse and Neglect.* New York: Cambridge University Press.

Cicchetti, D., Ganiban, J., and Barnett, D. 1991. Contributions from the study of high risk populations to understanding the development of emotion. In J. Garber, K.A. Dodge et al. (eds.), *The Development of Emotion Regulation and Dysregulation.* New York: Cambridge University Press.

Cincotta, R.P., and Engelman, R. 1997. Economics and rapid change: The influence of population growth. *Population Action International*, Occasional Paper no. 3, October, 1997.

Clark, P.M., Atton, C., Law, C.M. et al. 1998. Weight gain in pregnancy, triceps skinfold thickness, and blood pressure in offspring. *Obstetrics and Gynecology*, 91(1):103–7.

Clutton-Brock, T.H. 1991. *The Evolution of Parental Care.* Princeton University Press.

Clutton-Brock, T.H., Guiness, F.E., and Albon, S.D. 1982. *Red Deer: Behavior and Ecology of Two Sexes*. University of Chicago Press.

Cohen, S., Tyrrell, D., and Smith, A. 1991. Psychological stress and susceptibility to the common cold. *New England Journal of Medicine*, 325:606–12.

Cohn, D.A. 1990. Child–mother attachment of six-year-olds and social competence at school. *Child Development*, 61:152–62.

Cohn, J., and Tronick, E.Z. 1983. Three-month-old infants' reactions to simulated depression. *Child Development*, 54:185–93.

Cole, L. 1954. The population consequences of life history phenomena. *Quarterly Review of Biology*, 29:103–37.

Conger, R.D., Ge, X., Elder, G.H. et al. 1994. Economic stress, coercive family process, and developmental problems of adolescents. *Child Development*, 65:541–61.

Conger, R.D., McCarty, J., Yang, R. et al. 1984. Perception of child, child-rearing values, and emotional distress as mediating links between environmental stressors and observed maternal behavior. *Child Development*, 54:2234–47.

Constantino, J.N. 1996. Intergenerational aspects of the development of aggression: A preliminary report. *Journal of Developmental and Behavioral Pediatrics*, 17(3):176–82.

Cooper, W.S. 1987. Decision theory as a branch of evolutionary theory: A biological derivation of the Savage axioms. *Psychological Review*, 94(4):395–411.

Coplan, J.D., Andrews, M.W., Rosenblum, L.A. et al. 1996. Persistent elevations of cerebrospinal fluid concentrations of corticotropin-releasing factor in adult nonhuman primates exposed to early-life stressors: Implications for the psychopathology of mood and anxiety disorders. *Proceedings of the National Academy of Science of the USA*, 93(4):1619–23.

Corteen, R.S., and Wood, B. 1972. Autonomic responses to shock-associated words in an unattended channel. *Journal of Experimental Psychology*, 94:308–13.

Cosmides, L. 1989. The logic of social exchange: Has natural selection shaped how humans think? Studies with the Wason selection task. *Cognition*, 31:187–276.

Craik, K.J.W. 1943. *The Nature of Explanation*. Cambridge University Press.

Crittenden, P.M. 1987. Non-organic failure-to-thrive: Deprivation or distortion? *Infant Mental Health Journal*, 8(1):51–64.

Crittenden, P.M. 1997a. Patterns of attachment and sexual behavor: Risk of dysfunction versus opportunity for creative integration. In L. Atkinson and K.J. Zucker (eds.), *Attachment and Psychopathology*. New York: Guilford Press.

Crittenden, P.M. 1997b. Toward an integrative theory of trauma: A dynamic-maturation approach. In D. Cicchetti and S. Toth (eds.), *The Rochester*

Symposium on Developmental Psychopathology: Trauma. Rochester: University of Rochester Press.

Crockenberg, S. 1981. Infant irritability, mother responsiveness, and social support influences on the security of infant–mother attachment. *Child Development,* 52:857–69.

Crook, J.H. 1980. *The Evolution of Human Consciousness.* Oxford: Clarendon Press.

Crook, J.H. 1988. The experiential context of intellect. In R. Byrne and A. Whiten (eds.), *Machiavellian Intelligence: Social Expertise and the Evolution of Intellect in Monkeys, Apes, and Humans.* Oxford: Clarendon Press.

Crook, J.H. 1991. Consciousness and the ecology of meaning. In M. Robinson and L. Tiger (eds.), *Man and Beast Revisited.* Washington, DC: Smithsonian Institution Press.

Cutright, P. 1972. The teenage sexual revolution and the myth of the abstinent past. *Family Planning Perspectives,* 4:24–31.

Cvetkovich, G., Grote, B., Lieberman, E., and Miller, W. 1978. Sex role development and teenage fertility-related behavior. *Adolesence,* 13:231–6.

Dabbs, J.M., and Morris, R. 1990. Testosterone, social class and antisocial behavior in a sample of 4,462 men. *Psychological Science,* 1(3):209–211.

Dabbs, J.M., Carr, T.S., Frady, R.L., and Riad, J.K. 1995. Testosterone, crime, and misbehavior among 692 male prison inmates. *Personality and Individual Differences,* 18(5):627–33.

Daly, M., and Wilson, M. 1983. *Sex, Evolution and Behavior.* 2nd edn. Belmont, CA: Wadsworth Publishing Co.

Daly, M., and Wilson, M. 1988. *Homicide.* Hawthorne, NY: Aldine de Gruyter.

Damasio, A. 1994. *Descartes' Error: Emotion, Reason, and the Human Brain.* New York: G.P. Putman.

Danailov, A. and Tögel, C. 1991. Evolutionary epistemology: Science philosophy. In G. Greenberg and E. Tobach (eds.), *Theories of the Evolution of Knowing.* The T.C. Schneirla Conference Series, vol. 4. Hillsdale, NJ: Lawrence Erlbaum.

Darwin, C. 1839/1936. *The Voyage of the Beagle.* London: J.M. Dent and Sons, Ltd.

Darwin, C. 1871. *The Descent of Man and Selection in Relation to Sex.* London: John Murray.

Dasser, V., Ulbaek, I., and Premack, D. 1989. The perception of intention. *Science,* 293:186–8.

Davey Smith, G., Neaton, J.D., Stamler, R. et al. 1996a. Socioeconomic differentials in mortality risk among men screened for the Multiple Risk Factor Intervention Trial: I. White men. *American Journal of Public Health,* 86 (4):486–96.

Davey Smith, G., Wentworth, D., Neaton, J.D. et al. 1996b. Socioeconomic differentials in mortality risk among men screened for the Multiple Risk Factor Intervention Trial: II. Black men. *American Journal of Public Health,* 86(4):497–504.

Davies, P.T., and Cummings, E.M. 1994. Marital conflict and child adjustment: An emotional security hypothesis. *Psychological Bulletin*, 116(3):387–411.

Dawkins, R. 1976. *The Selfish Gene*. Oxford University Press.

Dawkins, R. 1982. *The Extended Phenotype: The Gene as the Unit of Selection*. Oxford and San Francisco: Freeman.

Dawkins, R. 1986. *The Blind Watchmaker*. London: Longmans.

Dawkins, R. 1996. *Climbing Mount Improbable*. London: Viking Penguin.

de Kloet, E. 1991. Brain corticosteroid receptor balance and homeostatic control. *Frontiers in Neuroendocrinology*, 12(2):95–164.

DeBellis, M., Lefter, L., Trickett, P., and Putnam, F. 1994. Urinary catecholamine excretion in sexualy abused girls. *Journal of the American Academy of Child and Adolescent Psychiatry*, 33(3):320–7.

Degler, C. 1991. *In Search of Human Nature: The Decline and Revival of Darwinism in American Social Thought*. New York: Oxford University Press.

Denham, S.A. 1994. Mother–child emotional communication and preschoolers' security of attachment and dependency. *Journal of Genetic Psychology*, 155(1):119–21.

Dennett, D.C. 1978. Beliefs about beliefs. *Behavioral and Brain Sciences*, 4:515–26.

Dennett, D.C. 1987. *The Intentional Stance*. Cambridge, MA: MIT Press/A Bradford Book.

Dennett, D.C. 1995, *Darwin's Dangerous Idea: Evolution and the Meanings of Life*. New York: Simon and Schuster.

DeRousseau, C.J. (ed.), 1990. *Primate Life History and Evolution*. New York: Wiley-Liss.

Divale, W., and Harris, M. 1976. Population, warfare, and the male supremacist complex. *American Anthropologist*, 78:521–38.

Dobzhansky, T. 1973. Nothing in biology makes sense except in the light of evolution. *American Biology Teacher*, 35:125–129.

Doran, T.E., De Angelis, C., Baumgardner, R.A., and Mellits, E.D. 1989. Acetominophen: More harm than good for chicken pox? *Journal of Pediatrics*, 114:1045–48.

Draper, P., and Belsky, J. 1990. Personality development in evolutionary perspective. *Journal of Personality*, 58(1):141–61.

Draper, P., and Harpending, H. 1982. Father absence and reproductive strategy: An evolutionary perspective. *Journal of Anthropological Research*, 38:255–73.

Dressler, W.W. 1982. *Hypertension and Culture Change*. New York: Redgrave Publishing Company.

Drotar, D. 1991. The family context of nonorganic failure to thrive. *American Journal of Orthopsychiatry*, 61:23–34.

Dunbar, R.I.M. 1984. The ecology of monogamy. *New Scientist*, 30 August 1984.

Dunbar, R.I.M. 1995. *The Trouble with Science*. Cambridge, MA: Harvard University Press.

Duncan, G.J., Brooks-Gunn, J., and Klebanov, P.K. 1994. Economic deprivation and early childhood development. *Child Development*, 65:296–318.

Dunn, J. 1976. How far do early differences in mother–child relations affect later development? In P. Bateson and R. Hinde (eds.), *Growing Points in Ethology*. Cambridge University Press.

DuRant, R.H., Cadenhead, C., Pendergrast, R.A., Slavens, G., and Linder, C.W. 1994. Factors associated with the use of violence among urban Black adolescents. *American Journal of Public Health*, 84(4):612–17.

Durkheim, E. 1951. *Suicide: A Study in Sociology*. Translated by J. Spaulding and G. Simpson. New York: Free Press.

Durrett, M.E., Otaki, M., and Richards, P. 1984. Attachment and the mother's perception of support from the father. *International Journal of Behavioral Development*, 7(2):167–76.

Edelman, G. 1987. *Neural Darwinism*. New York: Basic Books.

Edelman, G. 1992. *Bright Air, Brilliant Fire: On the Matter of Mind*. New York: Basic Books.

Edgerton, R. 1992. *Sick Societies: Challenging the Myth of Primitive Harmony*. New York: Free Press.

Edwards, W. 1954. The theory of decision making. *Psychological Bulletin*. 51:380–417.

Egeland, B., and Farber, E. 1984. Infant–mother attachment: Factors related to its development and changes over time. *Child Development*, 55:753–71.

Egeland, B., Carlson, E., and Sroufe, L.A. 1993. Resilience as process. *Development and Psychopathology*, 5(4):517–28.

Egeland, B., Jacobvitz, D., and Papatola, K. 1987. Intergenerational continuity of abuse. In R. Gelles and J. Lancaster (eds.), *Child Abuse and Neglect: Biosocial Dimensions*. New York: Aldine de Gruyter.

Elicker, J., England, M., and Sroufe, L.A. 1992. Predicting peer competence and peer relationships in childhood from early parent–child relationships. In R.D. Parke and G.W. Ladd (eds.), *Family–Peer Relationsips: Modes of Linkage*. Hillsdale, NJ: Lawrence Erlbaum.

Ellison, P.T. 1990. Human ovarian function and reproductive ecology: New hypotheses. *American Anthropologist*, 92:933–52.

Ellison, P.T. 1994. Extinction and descent. *Human Nature*, 5(2):155–65.

Elzanowski, A. 1993. The moral career of vertebrate values. In M. Nitecki and D. Nitecki (eds.), *Evolutionary Ethics*. Albany: State University of New York Press.

Emlen, J.M. 1985. Evolutionary ecology and the optimality assumption. In J. Dupré (ed.), *The Latest on the Best: Essays on Evolution and Optimality*. Cambridge University Press.

Emlen, S.T. 1995. An evolutionary theory of the family. *Proceedings of the National Academy of Science USA*. 92:8092–9.

Emlen, S.T., and Oring, L. 1977. Ecology, sexual selection, and the evolution of mating systems. *Science*, 197:215–23.

Erdal, D., and Whiten, A, 1994. On human egalitarianism: An evolutionary product of Machiavellian status escalation? *Current Anthropology*, 35(2): 175–83.

Erdal, D., and Whiten, A. 1996. Egalitariansm and Machiavellian intelligence in human evolution. In P. Mellars and K. Gibson (eds.), *Modelling the Early Human Mind*. McDonald Institute Monographs. McDonald Institute for Archaeological Research, Cambridge.

Erickson, M., Sroufe, L.A., and Egeland, B. 1985. The relationship between quality of attachment and behavior problems in preschool in a high-risk sample. In I. Bretherton and E. Waters (eds.), *Growing Points of Attachment Theory and Research*. Monographs of the Society for Research in Child Development. (Serial no. 309), 50(1–2):147–66.

Eveleth, P., and Tanner, J. 1990. *Worldwide Variation in Human Growth*. New York: Cambridge University Press.

Fagen, R. 1977. Selection for optimal age-dependent schedules of play behavior. *American Naturalist*, 111:395–414.

Fagen, R. 1982. Evolutionary issues in the development of behavioral flexibility. In P.P.G. Bateson and P. Klopfer (eds.), *Perspectives in Ethology*, vol. 5. New York: Academic Press.

Fagen, R. 1993. Primate juveniles and primate play. In M.E. Pereira and L.A. Fairbanks (eds.), *Juvenile Primates: Life History, Development, and Behavior*. New York: Oxford University Press.

Featherman, D.L., and Lerner, R.M. 1985. Ontogenesis and sociogenesis: Problematics for theory and research about development and socialization across the lifespan. *American Sociological Review*, 50:659–76.

Feldman, S., and Downey, G. 1994. Rejection sensitivity as a mediator of childhood exposure to family violence on adult attachment behavior. *Development and Psychopathology*, 6:231–47.

Fenichel, O. 1945. *The Psychoanalytic Theory of Neurosis*. New York: Norton.

Field, T.M. 1985. Attachment as psychobiological attunement: Being on the same wavelength. In M. Reite and T. Field (eds.), *The Psychobiology of Attachment and Separation*. Orlando, FL: Academic Press.

Field, T.M. 1994. The effects of mother's physical and emotional unavailability on emotion regulation. In N. Fox (ed.), *The Development of Emotion Regulation: Biological and Behavioral Considerations*. Monographs of the Society for Reseach in Child Development (Serial no. 240), 59(2–3):208–27.

Fisher, R.A. 1930. *The Genetical Theory of Natural Selection*. New York: Dover.

Flinn, M. and England, B. 1995a. Childhood stress and family environment. *Current Anthropology*, 36(5):854–66.

Flinn, M., Quinlan, R., Decker, S., Turner, M., and England, B. 1995b. Male–female differences in effects of parental absence on glucocorticoid stress response. *Human Nature*, 7(2):125–62

Fodor, J. 1975. *The Language of Thought.* New York: Thomas Crowell.

Fodor, J. 1983. *The Modularity of Mind.* Cambridge, MA: Bradford/MIT Press.

Fodor, J. 1994. *The Elm and the Expert: Mentalese and Its Semantics.* Cambridge, MA: MIT Press.

Foley, R. 1992. Evolutionary ecology of fossil hominids. In E.A. Smith and B. Winterhalder (eds.), *Evolutionary Ecology and Human Behavior.* Hawthorne, NY: Aldine de Gruyter.

Fonagy, P. 1991. Thinking about thinking: Some clinical and theoretical considerations in the treatment of a borderline patient. *International Journal of Psychoanalysis*, 72:639–56.

Fonagy, P. 1996. The significance of the development of metacognitive control over mental representations in parenting and infant development. *Journal of Clinical Psychoanalysis*, 5(1):67–86.

Fonagy, P., Redfern, S., and Charman, T. 1997a. The relationship between belief–desire reasoning and a projective measure of attachment security. *British Journal of Developmental Psychology*, 15(1):51–61.

Fonagy, P., Steele, M., Steele, H., Moran, G., and Higgitt, A. 1991. The capacity for understanding mental states: The reflexive self in parent and child and its significance for security of attachment. *Infant Mental Health Journal*, 13:200–17.

Fonagy, P., Target, M., Steele, M., et al. 1997b. Morality, disruptive behavior, borderline personality disorder, crime, and their relationship to security of attachment. In L. Atkinson and K.J. Zucker (eds.), *Attachment and Psychopathology.* New York: Guilford Press.

Fox, N.A. 1991. If it's not left, it's right: Electroencephalography asymmetry and the development of emotion. *American Psychologist*, 46:863–72.

Fox, N.A., Kimmerly, N., and Schafer, W. 1991. Attachment to mother/ attachment to father: A meta-analysis. *Child Development*, 62(1):210–25.

Fox, R. 1975. *Encounter With Anthropology.* New York: Harcourt Brace Jovanovich.

Fox, R. 1989. *The Search for Society: Quest For a Biosocial Science and Morality.* New Brunswick: Rutgers University Press.

Frank, R.H. 1988. *Passions Within Reason: The Strategic Role of the Emotions.* New York: Norton.

Frank, R.H. 1992. The role of moral sentiments in the theory of intertemporal choice. In G. Loewenstein and J. Elster (eds.), *Choice Over Time.* New York: Russell Sage Foundation.

Frank, S.A. 1996. The design of natural and artificial adaptive systems. In M.R. Rose and G.V. Lauder (eds.), *Adaptation.* New York: Academic Press.

Freedman, D.G., and Gorman, J. 1993. Attachment and the transmission of culture: An evolutionary perspective. *Journal of Social and Biological Systems*, 16(3):297–329.

Freud, S. 1911/1956. Formulations of the two principles of mental functioning.

In J. Strachey and A. Freud (eds.), *The Standard Edition of the Complete Psychological Works of Sigmund Freud*, vol. 12. London: Hogarth Press.

Freud, S. 1921/1955. Group psychology and the analysis of the ego. In J. Strachey and A. Freud (eds.), *The Standard Edition of the Complete Psychological Works of Sigmund Freud*, vol. 18. London: Hogarth Press.

Freud, S. 1940. *An Outline of Psychoanalysis.* New York: Norton.

Friedman, H.S., Tucker, J.S., Schwartz, J.E. et al. 1995. Psychosocial and behavioral predictors of longevity. *American Psychologist*, 50(2):69–78.

Frijda, N. 1993. The place of appraisal in emotion. *Cognition and Emotion*, 7:357–88.

Furstenberg, F.F. 1991. As the pendulum swings: Teenage childbearing and social concern. *Family Relations*, 40:127–38.

Gadgil, M., and Bossert, W. 1970. Life history consequences of natural selection. *American Naturalist*, 104:1–24.

Gardner, W. 1993. A life-span rational-choice theory of risk taking. In N. Bell and R. Bell (eds.), *Adolescent Risk Taking.* Newbury Park, CA: Sage Publications.

Gardner, W., and Herman, J. 1990. Adolescents' AIDS risk taking: A rational choice perspective. *New Directions for Child Development*, 50:17–34.

Garn, S.M. 1985. Relationship between birthweight and subsequent weight gain. *American Journal of Clinical Nutrition*, 42(1):57–60.

Garn, S.M., Pesick, S., and Petzold, A. 1986a. The biology of teenage pregnancy: The mother and the child. In J. Lancaster and B. Hamburg (eds.), *School-Age Pregnancy and Parenthood: Biosocial Dimensions.* New York: Aldine de Gruyter.

Garn, S.M., LaVelle, M., Rosenberg, K.R., and Hawthorne, V.M. 1986b. Maturational timing as a factor in female fatness and obesity. *American Journal of Clinical Nutrition*, 43(6):879–83.

Geertz, C. 1973. *The Interpretation of Cultures.* New York: Basic Books.

Geertz, C. 1984. Anti anti-relativism. *American Anthropologist*, 86:263–78.

Geronimus, A. 1987. On teenage childbearing and neonatal mortality in the United States. *Population and Development Review*, 13(2):245–79.

Geronimus, A. 1994. The health of African American women and infants: Implications for reproductive strategies and policy analysis. In G. Sen and R. Snow (eds.), *Power and Decision: The Social Control of Reproduction.* Cambridge, MA: Harvard University Press.

Geronimus, A. 1996. What teen mothers know. *Human Nature*, 7(4):323–52.

Gibson, E.J., and Walk, R.D. 1960. The "visual cliff." *Scientific American*, 202:64–71.

Gillespie, J. 1977. Natural selection for variances in offspring numbers: A new evolutionary principle. *American Naturalist*, 111:1010–14.

Gillett, G. 1993. 'Ought' and well-being. *Inquiry*, 36:287–306.

Goel, V., Grafman, J., Sadato, N., and Hallett, M. 1995. Modeling other minds. *Neuroreport*, 6(13):1741–6.

Goldsmith, H., and Harmon, C. 1994. Temperament and attachment: Individuals and relationships. *Current Directions in Psychological Science*, 3:53–7.

Gomendio, M. 1991. Parent–offspring conflict and maternal investment in rhesus macaques. *Animal Behavior*, 42:993–1005.

Goodwin, B. 1994. *How the Leopard Changed its Spots*. London: Weidenfeld and Nicholson.

Gottfredson M., and Hirschi, T. 1990. *A General Theory of Crime*. Palo Alto, CA: Stanford University Press.

Gottlieb, G. 1992. *Individual Development and Evolution: The Genesis of Novel Behavior*. New York: Oxford University Press.

Gould, S.J. 1977. *Ontogeny and Phylogeny*. Cambridge, MA: Harvard University Press.

Gould, S.J. 1989. *Wonderful Life: The Burgess Shale and the Nature of History*. New York: Norton.

Gould, S.J. 1991. Exaption: A crucial tool for an evolutionary psychology. *Journal of Social Issues*, 47(3):43–65.

Gould, S.J., and Lewontin, R. 1979. The spandrels of San Marcos and the panglossian paradigm: A critique of the adaptationist program. *Proceedings of the Royal Society of London* B, 205:581–98.

Gould, S.J., and Vrba, E.S. 1982. Exaptation – a missing term in the science of form. *Paleobiology*, 8:4–15.

Graber, J.A., Brooks-Gunn, J., and Warren, M.P. 1995. The antecedents of menarcheal age: Heredity, family environment, and stressful life events. *Child Development*, 66:346–59.

Grafen, A. 1984. Natural selection, kin selection, and group selection. In J. Krebs and N. Davies (eds.), *Behavioral Ecology: An Evolutionary Approach*. 2nd edn. Sunderland, MA: Sinauer Associates.

Green, L., Fry, A., and Myerson, J. 1994. Discounting of delayed rewards: A life-span comparison. *Psychological Science*, 5(1):33–6.

Greenberg, M.T., and Speltz, M. 1988. Attachment and the ontogeny of conduct problems. In J. Belsky and T. Nezworski (eds.), *Clinical Implications of Attachment*. Hillsdale, NJ: Lawrence Erlbaum

Gregory, R.L. 1981. *Mind in Science: A History of Explanations in Psychology and Physics*. Cambridge University Press.

Gregory, R.L. (ed.), 1987. *The Oxford Companion to the Mind*. Oxford University Press.

Gross, P., and Levitt, N. 1994. *Higher Superstition: The Academic Left and its Quarrels with Science*. Baltimore: Johns Hopkins University Press.

Gunnar, M.R. 1994. Psychoendocrine studies of temperament and stress in early childhood: Expanding current models. In J.E. Bates and T.D. Wachs (eds.), *Temperament: Individual Differences at the Interface of Biology and Behavior*. Washington, DC. American Psychological Association.

Gunnar, M., Brodersen, L., Nachmias, M., Buss, K., and Rigatuso, J. 1996. Stress reactivity and attachment security. *Developmental Psychobiology*, 29(3):191–204.

Gunnar, M., Malone, S., Vance, G., and Fisch, R. 1985. Coping with aversive stimulation in the neonatal periods: Quiet sleep and plasma cortisol levels during recovery from circumcision in newborns. *Child Development*, 56:290–303.

Gunnar, M., Mangelsdorf, S., Larson, M., and Hertsgaard, L. 1989. Attachment, temperament, and adrenocortical activity in infancy: A study of neuroendocrine regulation. *Developmental Psychology*, 25:355–63.

Hahlweg, K., and Hooker, C. 1989. Evolutionary epistemology and philosophy of science. In K. Hahlweg and C. Hooker (eds.), *Issues in Evolutionary Epistemology*. Albany: State University of New York Press.

Hall, B. 1992. *Evolutionary Developmental Biology*. London: Chapman and Hall.

Hall, F. Pawlby, S., and Wolkind, S. 1979. Early life experiences and later mothering behaviors: A study of mothers and their 20-week-old babies. In D. Schaffer and j. Dunn (eds.), *The First Year of Life*. London: John Wiley.

Hamburg, D.A. 1993. The American family transformed. *Society*, 30(2):60–9.

Hamilton, W. 1964. The genetical evolution of social behaviour, I, II. *Journal of Theoretical Biology*, 7:1–52.

Hansen, C.H., and Hansen, R.D. 1988. Finding the face in the crowd: An anger superiority effect. *Journal of Personality and Social Psychology*, 54:917–24.

Harden, P., and Pihl, R. 1995. Cognitive function, cardiovascular reactivity, and behavior in boys at high risk for alcoholism. *Journal of Abnormal Psychology*, 104(1):94–103.

Hardy, J.B., Shapiro, S., Astone, N.M. et al. 1997. Adolescent childbearing revisited: The age of inner-city mothers at delivery is a determinant of their children's self- sufficiency at age 27 to 33. *Pediatrics*, 100(5):802–9.

Harlow, H.F. 1958. The nature of love. *American Psychologist*, 13:673–85.

Harpending, H., Draper, P., and Pennington, R. 1990. Culture, evolution, parental care, and mortality. In A. Swedland and G. Armelagos (eds.), *Disease in Populations in Transition*. South Hadley, MA: Bergin and Garvey.

Harris, P.L. 1991. The work of imagination. In A. Whiten (ed.), *Natural Theories of Mind: Evolution, Development, and Simulation of Everyday Mindreading*. Oxford: Basil Blackwell.

Harris, P.L. 1994. Thinking by children and scientists: False analogies and neglected similarities. In L.A. Hirschfield and S.A. Gelman (eds.), *Mapping the Mind: Domain Specificity in Cognition and Culture*. Cambridge University Press.

Harvey, P.H., and Nee, S. 1991. How to live like a mammal. *Nature*, 350:23–4.

Haukioja, E., Lemmetyinen, R., and Pikkola, M. 1989. Why are twins so rare in *Homo sapiens*? *American Naturalist*, 133:572–7.

Hausfater, G., and Hrdy, S.B. (eds.), 1984. *Infanticide: Comparative and Evolutionary Perspectives*. Hawthorne, NY: Aldine de Gruyter.

Hayden, B. 1986. Resources, rivalry, and reproduction: The influence of basic resource characteristics on reproductive behavior. In W.P. Handwerker (eds.), *Culture and Reproduction: An Anthropological Critique of Demographic Transition Theory.* Boulder, CO: Westview Press.

Hazan, C., and Shaver, P. 1987. Romantic love concetualized as an attachment process. *Journal of Personality and Social Psychology*, 52:511–24.

Hebb, D.O. 1953. Heredity and environment in mammalian behavior. *British Journal of Animal Behaviour*, 1:43–7.

Hendrick, C., and Hendrick, S. 1986. A theory and method of love. *Journal of Personality and Social Psychology*, 50(2):392–402.

Herman-Giddens, M.E., Sandler, A.D., and Friedman, N.E. 1988. Sexual precocity in girls: An association with sexual abuse? *American Journal of Diseases of Children*, 142:431–3.

Hetherington, E.M. 1972. Effects of paternal absence on personality development in adolescent daughters. *Developmental Psychology*, 7:313–26.

Hetherington, E.M., and Clingempeel, W.G. 1992. *Coping with Marital Transitions: A Family Systems Perspective.* Monographs of the Society for Research in Child Development, 57(2–3):1–242.

Hill, E.M., Ross, L.T., and Low, B.S. 1997. The role of future unpredictability in human risk-taking. *Human Nature*, 8(4):287–325.

Hill, E.M., Young, J.P., and Nord, J.L. 1994. Childhood adversity, attachment security, and adult relationships: A preliminary study. *Ethology and Sociobiology*, 15:323–38.

Hill, K. 1993. Life history theory and evolutionary anthropology. *Evolutionary Anthropology*, 2(3):78–88.

Hill, K., and Hurtado, A.M. 1991. The evolution of premature reproductive senescence and menopause in human females: An evaluation of the "grandmother" hypothesis. *Human Nature*, 2(4):313–50.

Hinde, R.A. 1961. The establishment of the parent–offspring relation in birds, with some mammalian analogies. In W.H. Thorpe and O.L. Zangwill (eds.), *Current Problems in Animal Behaviour.* London: Cambridge University Press.

Hinde, R.A. 1982. Attachment: Some conceptual and biological issues. In C.M. Parkes and J. Stevenson-Hinde (eds.), *The Place of Attachment in Human Behavior.* New York: Basic Books.

Hinde, R.A. 1983. Ethology and child development. In M. Haith and J. Campos (eds.), *Handbook of Child Psychology, Vol. 2. Infancy and Developmental Psychobiology.* (4th edn, Paul Mussen, series ed.). New York: John Wiley.

Hinde, R.A. 1987. *Individuals, Relationships, and Culture: Links Between Ethology and the Social Sciences.* Cambridge University Press.

Hirschfield, M., and Tinkle, D. 1975. Natural selection and the evolution of reproductive effort. *Proceedings of the National Academy of Science*, 72:2227–31.

Hirshleifer, J. 1985. On the emotions as guarrantors of threats and promises. In J. Dupré (ed.), *The Latest on the Best: Essays on Evolution and Optimality.* Cambridge University Press.

Hofer, M.A. 1990. Early symbiotic processes: Hard evidence from a soft place. In R. Glick and S. Bone (eds.), *Pleasure Beyond the Pleasure Principle*. New Haven: Yale University Press.

Hofer, M.A. 1994. Hidden regulators in attachment, separation, and loss. In N. Fox (ed.), *The Development of Emotion Regulation: Biological and Behavioral Considerations*. Monographs of the Society for Research in Child Development (Serial no. 240), 59(2–3):192–207.

Hofer, M.A. 1995. Hidden regulators: Implications for a new understanding of attachment, separation, and loss. In S. Goldberg, R. Muir. And J. Kerr (eds.)., *Attachment Theory: Social, Developmental, and Clinical Perspectives*. Hillsdale, NJ: Analytic Press.

Holland, J. H. 1992. Complex adaptive systems. *Daedalus*, 121(1):17–30.

Holloway, M. 1994. Trends in women's health: A global view. *Scientific American*, August 1994 (pp. 76–83).

Holton, G. 1993. *Science and Anti-Science*. Cambridge, MA: Harvard University Press.

Horn, H.S., and Rubenstein, D.J. 1984. Behavioural adaptations and life history. In J.R. Krebs and N.B. Davies (eds.), *Behavioural Ecology: An Evolutionary Approach*. Oxford: Blackwell Scientific Publishing.

Howes, P., and Markman, H.J. 1989. Marital quality and child functioning: A longitudinal investigation. *Child Development*, 60:1044–51.

Hrdy, S.B. 1977. Infanticide as a primate reproductive strategy. *American Scientist*, 65:40–9.

Hrdy, S.B. 1979. Infanticide among animals: A review, classification, and examination of the implication for the reproductive strategies of females. *Ethology and Sociobiology*, 1:13–40.

Hrdy, S.B. 1981. *The Woman That Never Evolved*. Cambridge, MA: Harvard University Press.

Hrdy, S.B. 1992. Fitness tradeoffs in the history and evolution of delegated mothering with special reference to wet-nursing, abandonment, and infanticide. *Ethology and Sociobiology*, 13:409–42.

Hrdy, S.B. 1997. Raising Darwin's consciousness: Female sexuality and the prehominid origins of patriarchy. *Human Nature,* 8(1):1–49.

Hull, D. 1988. A mechanism and its metaphysics: An evolutionary account of the social and conceptual development of science. *Biology and Philosophy*, 3:123–55.

Hume, D. [1740] 1978. *A Treatise on Human Nature*. L. Selby-Bigge. 2nd edn, revised by P. Nidditch. Oxford: Clarendon Press.

Humphrey, N. 1976. The social function of intellect. In P. Bateson and R. Hinde (eds.), *Growing Points in Ethology*. Cambridge University Press.

Humphrey, N. 1984. *Consciousness Regained*. New York: Oxford University Press.

Hunter, E. 1993. *Aboriginal Health and History: Power and Prejudice in Remote Australia*. Cambridge University Press.

Huxley, J. 1964. *Essays of a Humanist.* Harmondsworth: Penguin Books.

Irons, W.T. 1983. Human female reproductive strategies. In S. Wasser (ed.), *Social Behavior of Female Vertebrates.* New York: Academic Press.

Isabella, R.A., and Belsky, J. 1985. Marital change during the transition to parenthood and security of infant–parent attachment. *Journal of Family Issues*, 6:505–22.

Isabella, R.A., and Belsky, J. 1991. Interactional synchrony and the origins of mother-infant attachment: A replication study. *Child Development*, 62:373–84.

Jackendoff, R. 1993. *Patterns in the Mind: Language and Human Nature.* Cambridge, MA: MIT Press/A Bradford Book.

Janson, J., and Van Schaik, C. 1993. Ecological risk aversion in juvenile primates: Slow and steady wins the race. In M. Pereira and L. Fairbanks (ed.), *Juvenile Primates: Life History, Development, and Behavior.* New York: Oxford University Press.

Johnson, D.B. 1982 Altruistic behavior and the development of the self in infants. *Merrill-Palmer Quarterly*, 28(3):379–88.

Johnson, M. 1987. *The Body in the Mind: The Bodily Basis of Meaning, Imagination, and Reason.* University of Chicago Press.

Johnson, M. 1993. *Moral Imagination: Implications of Cognitive Science for Ethics.* University of Chicago Press.

Johnson-Laird, P.N. 1983. *Mental Models: Towards a Cognitive Science of Language, Inference, and Consciousness.* Cambridge, MA: Harvard University Press.

Johnston, T. D. 1982. Selective costs and benefits in the evolution of learning. In J.S. Rosenblatt, R.A. Hinde, C. Beer, and M-C. Busnel (eds.), *Advances in the Study of Behavior*, vol. 12. New York: Academic Press.

Jones, B., Leeton, J., McLeod, I., and Wood, C. 1972. Factors influencing the age of menarche in a lower socio-economic group in Melbourne. *The Medical Journal of Australia*, 2:533–5.

Kacelnik, A., and Bateson, M. 1996. Risky theories – The effects of variance on foraging decisions. *American Zoologist*, 36:402–34.

Kagan, J. 1994. *Galen's Prophecy: Temperament in Human Nature.* New York: Basic Books.

Kagan, J., Kearsley, P., and Zalazo, P. 1978. *Infancy: Its Place in Human Development.* Cambridge, MA: Harvard University Press.

Kagan, J., Reznick, J.S., and Snidman, N. 1988. Biological basis of childhood shyness. *Science*, 240(4849):167–71.

Kahneman, D., and Tversky, A. 1979. Prospect theory: An analysis of decision under risk. *Econometrica*, 47:262–91.

Kahneman, D., and Tversky, A. 1984. Choices, values, and frames. *The American Psychologist*, 39:341–50.

Kahneman, D., Slovic, P., and Tversky, A. 1982. *Judgment Under Uncertainty: Heuristics and Biases.* Cambridge University Press.

Kaplan, H. 1994. Evolutionary and wealth flows theories of fertility: Empirical tests and new models. *Population and Development Review*, 20(4):753–91.

Karp, R.J., Scholl, T.O., Decker, E., and Ebert, E. 1989. Growth of abused children: Contrasted with the non-abused in an urban poor community. *Clinical Pediatrics*, 28(7):317–20.

Keil, F. 1992. The origins of an autonomous biology. In M. Gunnar and M. Maratsos (eds.), *Modularity and Constraints in Language and Cognition*. The Minnesota Symposia on Child Psychology, vol. 25. Hillsdale, NJ: Lawrence Erlbaum.

Kelley, A.C., and Schmidt, R.M. 1996. Toward a cure for the myopia and tunnel vision of the population debate: A dose of the historical perspective. In D.A. Ahlburg, A.C. Kelley, and K.O. Mason (eds.), *The Impact of Population Growth on Well- being in Developing Countries*. Berlin: Springer Verlag.

Kelsey, J.L., Gammon, M.D., and John, E.M. 1993. Reproductive factors and breast cancer. *Epidemiologic Reviews*, 15(1):36–47.

Kestenbaum, R., Farber, E., and Sroufe, L.A. 1989. Individual differences in empathy among preschoolers: Relation to attachment history. *New Directions for Child Development*, 44:51–64.

Keyfitz, N. 1977. *Introduction to the Mathematics of Population, with Revisions*. Reading, MA: Addison Wesley.

Khan, A., Schroeder, D., Martorell, R., Haas, J., and Rivera, J. 1996. Early childhood determinants of age at menarche in rural Guatemala. *American Journal of Human Biology*, 8:717–23.

Kim, K., Smith, P.K., and Palermiti, A-L. 1997. Conflict in childhood and reproductive development. *Evolution and Human Behavior*, 18:109–42.

Kingma, J. 1994. The young male peak in different categories of trauma victims. *Perceptual and Motor Skills*, 79:920–2.

Kinsey, A.C., Pomeroy, W.B., and Martin, C.E. 1948. *Sexual Behavior in the Human Male*. Philadelphia: W.B. Saunders.

Kinsey, A.C., Pomeroy, W.B., Martin, C.E., and Gebhard, P.H. 1953. *Sexual Behavior in the Human Female*. Philadelphia: W.B. Saunders.

Kitcher, P. 1985. *Vaulting Ambition: Sociobiology and the Quest for Human Nature*. Cambridge, MA: MIT Press.

Kitcher, P. 1993. *The Advancement of Science*. Oxford University Press.

Klama, J. 1988. *Aggression: The Myth of the Beast Within*. New York: John Wiley.

Kleiman, D., and Malcolm, J. 1981. The evolution of male parental investment in mammals. In D. Gubernick and P. Klopfer (eds.), *Parental Care in Mammals*. New York: Plenum Press.

Knauft, B.B. 1991. Violence and sociality in human evolution. *Current Anthropology*, 32:391–428.

Kobak, R. and Hazan, C. 1991. Attachment in marriage: Effects of security and accuracy of working models. *Journal of Personality and Social Psychology*, 60(6):861–9.

Konner, M.J. 1991. Universals of behavioral development in relation to brain myelination. In K.R. Gibson and A.C. Petersen (eds.), *Brain Maturation and Cognitive Development: Comparative and Cross-Cultural Perspectives*. Hawthorne, NY: Aldine de Gruyter.

Krebs, J., and Kacelnik, A. 1991. Decision-making. In J. Krebs and N. Davies (eds.), *Behavioural Ecology: An Evolutionary Approach*, (3rd edn). Oxford: Basil Blackwell.

Kushner, M.G., Sher, J., and Beitman, B.D. 1990. The relation between alcohol problems and the anxiety disorders. *American Journal of Psychiatry*, 147:685–95.

Lack, D. 1947. The significance of clutch size. *Ibis*, 89:302–52.

Lack, D. 1966. *Population Studies of Birds*. Oxford: Clarendon Press.

Lakoff, G. 1987. *Women, Fire, and Dangerous Things: What Categories Reveal About the Mind*. University of Chicago Press.

Lalonde, C.E., and Chandler, M.J. 1995. False belief understanding goes to school: On the social-emotional consequences of coming early or late to a first theory of mind. *Cognition and Emotion*, 9(2):167–85.

Lamb, M. 1981. Fathers and child development: An integrative overview. In M. Lamb (ed.), *The Role of the Father in Child Development*. New York: John Wiley.

Lamb, M. 1987. Introduction: The emergent American father. In M.E. Lamb (ed.), *The Father's Role: Cross-Cultural Perspectives*. Hillsdale, NJ: Lawrence Erlbaum.

Lamb, M., Thompson, R., Gardner, W., and Charnov, E. 1985. *Infant–Mother Attachment: The Origins and Developmental Significance of Individual Differences in Strange Situation Behavior*. Hillsdale, NJ: Lawrence Erlbaum.

Lancaster, J.B. 1989. Evolutionary and cross-cultural perspectives on single-parenthood. In R. Bell and N. Bell (eds.), *Sociobiology and the Social Sciences*. Lubbock, TX: Texas Tech University Press.

Lancaster, J.B. 1997. The evolutionary history of human parental investment in relation to population growth and social stratification. In P.A. Gowaty (ed.), *Feminism and Evolutionary Biology*, New York: Chapman and Hall.

Lancaster, J.B., and Lancaster, C.S. 1983. Parental investment: The hominid adaptation. In D.J. Ortner (ed.), *How Humans Adapt: A Biocultural Odyssey*. Washington, DC: Smithsonian Institution Press.

Lancaster, J.B., and Lancaster, C.S. 1987. The watershed: Change in parental-investment and family-formation strategies in the course of human evolution. In J.B. Lancaster, J. Altmann, A.S. Rossiand, and L.R. Sherrod (eds.), *Parenting Across the Life Span: Biosocial Dimensions*. Hawthorne, NY: Aldine de Gruyter.

Lawrence, E. 1991. Poverty and the rate of time preference: Evidence from panel data. *Journal of Political Economy*, 99(1):54–75.

Lazarus, R.S. 1991. Cognition and motivation in emotion. *American Psychologist*, 46(4):352–67.

Leacock, E.B. 1971. Introduction. In E.B. Leacock (ed.), *The Culture of Poverty: A Critique*. New York: Simon and Schuster.

LeDoux, J. 1989. Cognitive–emotional interactions in the brain. *Cognition and Emotion,* 3:267–289.

LeDoux, J. 1995. Emotion: Clues from the brain. *Annual Review of Psychology,* 46:209–35.

LeDoux, J. 1996. *The Emotional Brain.* New York: Simon and Schuster.

Lee, P.C. 1987. Nutrition, fertility and maternal investment in primates. *Journal of the Zoological Society of London,* 213:409–22.

Leslie, A.M. 1987. Pretense and representation: The origins of "theory of mind." *Psychological Review,* 94:412–26.

Leslie, A.M. 1994. ToMM, ToBy, and agency: Core architecture and domain-specificity. In L. Hirschfield and S. Gelman (eds.), *Mapping the Mind: Domain Specificity in Cognition and Culture.* Cambridge University Press.

Leslie, A.M. 1995. Pretending and believing: Issues in the theory of ToMM. In J. Mehler and S. Franck (eds.), *Cognition on Cognition.* Cambridge, MA: MIT Press.

Leutnegger, W. 1974. Functional aspects of pelvic morphology in simian primates. *Journal of Human Evolution,* 3:207–22.

Levine, N. 1987. Differential child care in three Tibetan communities: Beyond son preference. *Population and Development Review,* 13(2):281–304.

Levins, R. 1968. *Evolution in Changing Environments.* Princeton University Press.

Lewis, O. 1959. *Five Families: Mexican Case Studies in the Culture of Poverty.* New York: Basic Books.

Lewis, O. 1967. *La Vida: A Puerto Rican Family in the Culture of Poverty – San Juan and New York.* London: Secker and Warburg.

Lickliter, R.F., and Berry, T.D. 1990. The phylogeny fallacy: Developmental psychology's misapplication of evolutionary theory. *Developmental Review,* 10:348–64.

Loewenstein, G. and Elster, J. 1992. *Choice over Time.* New York: Russell Sage Foundation.

Logue, A. 1988. Research on self-control: An integrating framework. *Behavioral and Brain Sciences,* 11:665–709.

Lorenz, K. 1935. Der Kumpan in der Umwelt des Vogels [Companionship in bird life]. *Journal of Ornithology,* 83:137–213.

Lorenz, K. 1941/1982. Kant's doctrine of the a priori in the light of contemporary biology. In H.C. Plotkin (ed.), *Learning, Development, and Culture: Essays in Evolutionary Epistemology.* New York: John Wiley.

Lovejoy, C.O. 1981. The origin of man. *Science,* 211:341–50.

Low, B. 1978. Environmental uncertainty and the parental strategies of marsupials and placentals. *American Naturalist,* 112:197–213.

Luker, K. 1996. *Dubious Conceptions: The Politics of Teenage Pregnancy.* Cambridge, MA: Harvard University Press.

Lundberg, O. 1993. The impact of living conditions on illness and mortality in adulthood. *Social Science and Medicine*, 36:1047–52.

Main, M. 1981. Avoidance in the service of attachment: A working paper. In K. Immelmann, G. Barlow, L. Petrinovich, and M. Main (eds.), *Behavioral Development: The Bielefeld Interdisciplinary Project.* New York: Cambridge University Press.

Main, M. 1983. Exploration, play, and cognitive functioning as related to infant–mother attachment. *Infant Behavior and Development*, 6:167–74.

Main, M. 1990. Cross-cultural studies of attachment organization: Recent studies, changing methodologies, and the concept of conditional strategies. *Human Development*, 33:48–61.

Main, M. 1991. Metacognitive knowledge, metacognitive monitoring, and singular (coherent) vs. multiple (incoherent) models of attachment. In C.M. Parkes, J. Stevenson-Hinde, and P. Marris (eds.), *Attachment Across the Life Cycle.* New York: Tavistock/Routledge.

Main, M., and Goldwyn, R. 1984. Predicting rejection of her infant from mother's representation of her own experiences: A preliminary report. *International Journal of Child Abuse and Neglect*, 8(2):203–17.

Main, M., Kaplan, N., and Cassidy, J. 1985. Security in infancy, childhood, and adulthood: A move to the level of representation. In I. Bretherton and E. Waters (eds.), *Growing Points in Attachment Theory and Research*. Monographs of the Society for Research in Child Development (Serial no. 309), 50(1–2):66–104.

Maital, S., and Maital, S. 1977. Time preference, delay of gratification, and the intergenerational transmission of economic instability: A behavioral theory of income distribution. In O. Ashenfelter and W. Oates (eds.), *Essays in Labor Market Analysis.* New York: John Wiley.

Mangel, M., and Clark, C. 1988. *Dynamic Modeling in Behavioral Ecology.* Princeton University Press.

Marks, I. 1987. *Fears, Phobias, and Rituals: Panic, Anxiety, and Their Disorders.* New York: Oxford University Press.

Marris, P. 1991. The social construction of uncertainty. In C. Parkes, J. Stevenson-Hinde and P. Marris (eds.), *Attachment Across the Life Cycle.* London: Routledge.

Marshall, W., and Tanner, J. 1986. Puberty. In F. Falkner and J. Tanner (eds.), *Human Growth: A Comprehensive Treatise. Vol. 2, Postnatal Growth: Neurobiology*, 2nd edn. New York: Plenum Press.

Martin, R.D. 1983. *Human Brain Evolution in an Ecological Context.* New York: American Museum of Natural History.

Mascie-Taylor, C.G. 1991. Biosocial influences on stature: A review. *Journal of Biosocial Science*, 23:113–28.

Mathews, A., and MacLeod, C. 1994. Cognitive approaches to emotion and emotional disorders. *Annual Review of Psychology*, 45:25–50.

Mauss, M. 1924/1969. *The Gift: Forms and Functions of Exchange in Archaic Societies.* Translated by Ian Cunnison. London: Routledge & Kegan Paul.

Maxwell, N. 1984. *From Knowledge to Wisdom: A Revolution in the Aims and Methods of Science.* Oxford: Basil Blackwell.

Maynard Smith, J. 1978. Optimization theory in evolution. *Annual Review of Ecology and Systematics*, 9:31–56.

Maynard Smith, J. 1982. *Evolution and the Theory of Games.* Cambridge University Press.

Maynard Smith, J. 1989. Weismann and modern biology. In P. Harvey and L. Partridge (eds.), *Oxford Surveys in Evolutionary Biology*, vol. 6. Oxford University Press.

Mayr, E. 1974. Behavior programs and evolutionary strategies. *American Scientist* 62:650–9.

Mayr, E. 1982. *The Growth of Biological Thought.* Cambridge, MA: Harvard University Press.

Mayr, E. 1983. How to carry out the adaptationist program. *American Naturalist*, 121:324–34.

Mayr, E. 1988. *Toward a New Philosophy of Biology.* Cambridge, MA: Harvard University Press.

Mayr, E. 1997. *This is Biology: The Science of the Living World.* Cambridge, MA: Harvard University Press.

McCord, C., and Freeman, H.P. 1990. Excess mortality in Harlem. *New England Journal of Medicine*, 322:173–7.

McCormick, M.C. 1985. The contribution of low birthweight to infant mortality and childhood morbidity. *New England Journal of Medicine*, 312(2):82–90.

McEwen, B.S. 1995. Stressful experience, brain, and emotions: Development, genetic, and hormonal influences. In M.S. Gazzaniga (ed.), *The Cognitive Neurosciences*. Cambridge, MA: MIT Press.

McLanahan, S., and Booth, K. 1989. Mother-only families: Problems, prospects, and politics. *Journal of Marriage and the Family*, 51: 557–80.

McLoyd, V. 1990. The declining fortune of black children: Psychological distress, parenting, and socioemotional development in the context of economic hardship. *Child Development*, 61:311–46.

McLoyd, V. 1997. The impact of poverty and low socioeconomic status on the socioemotional functioning of Afro-American children and adolescents: Mediating effects. In R.D. Taylor and M.C. Wang (eds.), *Social and Emotional Adjustment and Family Relations in Ethnic Minority Families*. Hillsdale, NJ: Lawrence Erlbaum.

McNamara, J.M., and Houston, A.L. 1996. State-dependent life histories. *Nature*, 380:215–21.

Medawar, P.B. 1952. *An Unsolved Problem of Biology.* London: H.K. Lewis.

Mencher, J.P., and Okongwu, A. (eds.), 1993. *Where Did All the Men Go? Female-*

Headed/Female-Supported Households in Cross-Cultural Perspective. Boulder, CO: Westview Press.

Miller, G., Galanter, E., and Pribram, K. 1960. *Plans and the Structure of Behavior.* New York: Holt, Rinehart and Winston.

Mischel, W. 1958. Preference for delayed reinforcement: An experimental study of a cultural observation. *Journal of Abnormal and Social Psychology*, 56:57–61.

Mischel, W. 1961a. Delay of gratification, need for achievement, and acquiescence in another culture. *Journal of Abnormal and Social Psychology*, 62:543–52.

Mischel, W. 1961b. Father absence and delay of gratification. *Journal of Abnormal and Social Psychology*, 63:116–24.

Mischel, W., Shoda, Y., and Rodriguez, M.L. 1989. Delay of gratification in children. *Science*, 244:933–8.

Moffitt, T.E., Caspi, A., and Belsky, J. 1992. Childhood experience and the onset of menarche: A test of a sociobiological model. *Child Development*, 63:47–58.

Moncher, F.J. 1996. The relationship of maternal adult attachment style and risk of child abuse. *Journal of Interpersonal Violence*, 11(3):335–50.

Monckberg, F. 1992. Nutrition, emotional factors, and growth. In M. Hernandez and J. Argente (eds.), *Human Growth: Basic and Clinical Aspects*. New York: Elsevier.

Montgomery, S.M., Bartley, M.J., and Wilkinson, R.G. 1997. Family conflict and slow growth. *Archives of Disease in Childhood*, 77(4):326–30.

Moore, G. 1903. *Principia Ethica*. Cambridge University Press.

Munroe, R., Munroe, R., and Whiting, J. 1981. Male sex-role resolutions. In R. Munroe, R. Munroe, and B. Whiting (eds.), *Handbook of Cross-Cultural Human Development*. New York: Garland STPM Press.

Nesse, R. 1991. What good is feeling bad? *The Sciences*, Nov./Dec., 30–37.

Nesse, R., and Williams, G.C. 1995. *Why We Get Sick: The New Science of Darwinian Medicine*. New York: Times Books/Random House.

Newman, L.F. 1987. Fitness and survival. In N. Scheper-Hughes (ed.), *Child Survival*. Boston: D. Reidel Publishing Company.

Niedenthal, P.M. and Kitayama, E. (eds.), 1994. *The Heart's Eye: Emotional Influences in Perception and Attention*. San Diego, CA: Academic Press.

Nussbaum, M.C. 1993. Charles Taylor: Explanation and practical reason. In M. Nussbaum and A. Sen (eds.), *The Quality of Life*. Oxford: Clarendon Press.

Nussbaum, M.C. 1994. *The Therapy of Desire: Theory and Practice in Hellenistic Ethics*. Princeton University Press.

Nussbaum, M.C. 1995. Human capabilities, female human beings. In M.C. Nussbaum and J. Glover (eds.), *Women, Culture, and Development: A Study of Human Capabilities*. Oxford: Clarendon Press.

Nussbaum, M.C., and Sen, A. 1993. Introduction. In M.C. Nussbaum and A. Sen (eds.), *The Quality of Life*. Oxford: Clarendon Press.

Nyström Peck, M., and Lundberg, O. 1995. Short stature as an effect of economic and social conditions in childhood. *Social Science and Medicine*, 41:733–8.

O'Rand, A., and Ellis, R. 1974. Social class and social time perspective. *Social Forces*, 53(1):53–62.

Ortiz, S. 1979. Expectations and forecasts in the face of uncertainty. *Man*, 14:64–80.

Orzack, S., and Sober, E. 1994. Optimality models and the test of adaptationism. *American Naturalist*, 143:361–80.

Oyama, S. 1985. *The Ontogeny of Information: Developmental Systems and Evolution.* New York: Cambridge University Press.

Oyama, S. 1994. Rethinking development. In P.K. Bock (ed.), *Psychological Anthropology*. Westport, CT: Praeger.

Pagel, M.D., and Harvey, P.H. 1993. Evolution of the juvenile period in mammals. In M.E. Pereira and L. Fairbanks (eds.), *Juvenile Primates: Life History, Evolution, and Behavior*. New York: Oxford University Press.

Parker, G. 1989. Hamilton's rule and conditionality. *Ethology, Ecology, and Evolution*, 1:195–211.

Parker, G., and Maynard Smith, J. 1990. Optimality theory in evolutionary biology. *Nature*, 348:27–33.

Pascal, B. 1670/1976. *Pensées*. Paris: Mercure de France.

Pavelka, M.S.M., and Fedigan, L.M. 1991. Menopause: A comparative life history perspective. *Yearbook of Physical Anthropology*, 34:13–38.

Peacock, N. 1990. Comparative and cross-cultural approaches to the study of human reproductive failure. In C. DeRousseau (ed.), *Primate Life History and Evolution*. New York: Wiley-Liss.

Peacock, N. 1991. An evolutionary perspective on the patterning of maternal investment in pregnancy. *Human Nature*, 2(4):351–85.

Peccei. J.S. 1995. The origin and evolution of menopause: The altriciality-lifespan hypothesis. *Ethology and Sociobiology*, 16(5):425–49.

Pennington, R. and Harpending, H. 1988. Fitness and fertility among Kalahari !Kung. *American Journal of Physical Anthropology*, 7:303–13.

Pereira, M., and Fairbanks, L. (eds.), 1993. *Juvenile Primates: Life History, Development, and Behavior*. New York: Oxford University Press.

Petrinovich, L. 1995. *Human Evolution, Reproduction, and Morality*. New York: Plenum.

Philmore, P., Beattie, A., and Townsend, P. 1994. The widening gap: Inequality of health in Northern England, 1981–1991. *British Medical Journal*, 308:1125–8.

Phoenix, A. 1993. The social construction of teenage motherhood: A black and white issue? In A. Lawson and D. Rhode (eds.), *The Politics of Pregnancy: Adolescent Sexuality and Public Policy*. New Haven: Yale University Press.

Piaget, J. 1970. *Genetic Epistemology*. New York: Columbia University Press.

Piaget, J. 1971. *Biology and Knowledge*. University of Chicago Press.

Pihl, R.O., and Peterson, J. 1996. Characteristics and putative mechanisms in boys at risk for drug abuse and aggression. *Annals of the New York Academy of Sciences,* 794:238–52.

Pinker, S. 1994. *The Language Instinct.* New York: Morrow.

Pipp, S., and Harmon, R.J. 1987. Attachment as regulation: A commentary. *Child Development,* 58:648–52.

Plomin, R. 1986. *Development, Genetics, and Psychology.* Hillsdale, NJ: Lawrence Erlbaum.

Plomin, R., and Bergeman, C.S. 1991. The nature of nurture: Genetic influences on "environmental" measures. *Behavioral and Brain Sciences,* 14:373–427,

Plotkin, H.C. (ed.), 1982. *Learning, Development, and Culture: Essays in Evolutionary Epistemology.* New York: John Wiley.

Plotkin, H.C. 1994. *Darwin Machines and the Nature of Knowledge.* Cambridge, MA: Harvard University Press.

Plotkin, H.C., and Odling-Smee, F.J. 1981. A multiple-level model of evolution and its implications for sociobiology. *The Behavioral and Brain Sciences,* 4:225–68.

Popper, K. 1959. *The Logic of Scientific Discovery.* London: Hutchinson.

Popper, K. 1978. Natural selection and the emergence of mind. *Dialectica,* 32:339–55.

Popper, K. 1994. *Knowledge and the Body–Mind Problem: In Defence of Interactionism.* London: Routledge.

Povenelli, D.J., and Preuss, T.M. 1995. Theory of mind: Evolutionary history of a cognitive specialization. *Trends in Neuroscience,* 18(9):418–24.

Pratto, F. 1994. Consciousness and automatic evaluation. In P. Niedenthal and S. Kitayama (eds.), *The Heart's Eye: Emotional Influences in Perception and Attention.* New York: Academic Press.

Pratto, F., and John, O.P. 1991. Automatic vigilance: The attention-grabbing power of negative social information. *Journal of Personality and Social Psychology,* 61:380–91.

Preece, M.A. 1985. Prepubertal and pubertal endocrinology. In F. Falkner and J.M. Tanner (eds.), *Human Growth,* 2nd edn. London: Plenum Press.

Premack, D. 1990. The infant's theory of self-propelled objects. *Cognition,* 36:1–16.

Premack, D., and Premack, A.J. 1995. Intention as psychological cause. In D. Sperber, D. Premack, and A.J. Premack (eds.), *Causal Cognition: A Multidisciplinary Debate.* Oxford: Clarendon Press.

Premack, D., and Woodruff, G. 1978. Does the chimpanzee have a theory of mind? *Behavioral and Brain Sciences,* 4:515–26.

Presser, H. 1978. Age at menarche, socio-sexual behavior, and fertility. *Social Biology,* 25:94–101.

Preuss, T.M. 1995. Do rats have prefrontal cortex? The Rose–Woolsey–Akert program reconsidered. *Journal of Cognitive Neuroscience,* 7(1):1–24.

Promislow, D., and Harvey, P.H. 1990. Living fast and dying young: A comparative analysis of life-history variation in mammals. *Journal of the Zoological Society of London*, 220:417–37.

Promislow, D., and Harvey, P.H. 1991. Mortality rates and the evolution of mammal life histories. *Acta Oecologica*, 12:94–101.

Proos, L.A., Hofvander, Y., and Tuvemo, T. 1991. Menarcheal age and growth of Indian girls adopted in Sweden. *Acta Pediatrica*, 80:852–8.

Purvis, A., and Harvey, P.H. 1995. Mammal life-history evolution: A comparative test of Charnov's model. *Journal of the Zoological Society of London*, 237:259–83.

Putnam, F., and Trickett, P. 1993. Child sexual abuse: A model of chronic trauma. *Psychiatry*, 56:82–95.

Radke-Yarrow, M. 1991. Attachment patterns in children of depressed mothers. In C. Parkes, J. Stevenson-Hinde, and P. Marris (eds.), *Attachment Across the Lifespan*. New York: Tavistock/Routledge.

Rakic, P. 1995. Corticogenesis in human and nonhuman primates. In M. Gazzaniga (ed.), *The Cognitive Neurosciences*. Boston: MIT Press.

Renken, B., Egeland, B., Marvinney, D., Mangelsdorf, S., and Sroufe, L.A. 1989. Early childhood antecedents of aggression and passive-withdrawal in early elementary school. *Journal of Personality*, 57(2):60–7.

Rholes, W.S., Simpson, J.A., Blakely, B.S. et al. 1997. Adult attachment styles, the desire to have children, and working models of parenthood. *Journal of Personality*, 65(2):357–85.

Richards, R. 1987. *Darwin and the Emergence of Evolutionary Theories of Mind and Behavior*. University of Chicago Press.

Richards, R. 1993. Birth, death, and ressurection of evolutionary ethics. In M. Nitecki and D. Nitecki (eds.), *Evolutionary Ethics*. Albany: State University of New York Press.

Ricks, M.H. 1985. The social transmission of parental behavior: Attachment across generations. In I. Bretherton and E. Waters (eds.), *Growing Points in Attachment Theory and Research*. Monographs of the Society for Research in Child Development (Serial no. 309), 50(1–2):211–27.

Robertson, A.F. 1991. *Beyond the Family: The Social Organization of Human Reproduction*. Berkeley: University of California Press.

Rodseth, L., Wrangham, R.W., Harrigan, A.M., and Smuts, B.B. 1991. The human community as a primate society. *Current Anthropology*, 32:221–54.

Roff, D. 1992. *The Evolution of Life Histories: Theory and Analysis*. New York: Chapman and Hall.

Rogers, A. 1990. The evolutionary economics of reproduction. *Ethology and Sociobiology*, 11:479–95.

Rogers, A. 1994. Evolution of time preference by natural selection. *American Economic Review*, 84(3):460–81.

Rona, R., and Pereira, G. 1974. Factors that influence age of menarche in girls in Santiago, Chile. *Human Biology*, 46(1):33–42.

Roscoe, P. 1995. The perils of 'positivism' in cultural anthropology. *American Anthropologist*, 97(3):492–504.

Rose, M.R. 1991. *The Evolutionary Biology of Ageing*. Oxford University Press.

Rosenblum, L., and Andrews, M. 1994. Influences of environmental demand on maternal and infant development. *Acta Pediatrica*, Supplement, 397:57–63.

Rosenblum, L., Caplan, J., Freedman, S., Bassoff, T. et al. 1994. Adverse early experiences affect noradrenergic and serotonergic functioning in adult primates. *Biological Psychiatry*, 35(4):91–111.

Rosenzweig, M.R., Bennet, E., and Diamond, M.C. 1972. Brain changes in response to experience. *Scientific American*, 226:22–9.

Rubenstein, D. 1982. Risk, uncertainty, and evolutionary strategies. In King's College Sociobiology Study Group (eds.), *Current Problems in Sociobiology*. Cambridge University Press.

Rubenstein, D. 1993. On the evolution of juvenile lifestyles in mammals. In M. Pereira and L. Fairbanks (eds.), *Juvenile Primates: Life History, Development, and Behavior*. New York: Oxford University Press.

Ruddick, S. 1989. *Maternal Thinking: Toward a Politics of Peace*. New York: Ballantine Books.

Ruse, M. 1989 *Philosophy of Biology*. London: Macmillan.

Ruse, M., and Wilson, E.O. 1985. The evolution of ethics. *New Scientist*, 17:50–2. (Reprinted in Ruse 1989).

Ryckmans, P. 1996. The signature of humanity. *The Australian*, Tuesday, 12 November, 1996 (p. 13).

Sahlins, M. 1972. *Stone Age Economics*. Chicago: Aldine.

Sameroff, A.J. 1975. Early influences on development: Fact or fancy? *Merrill-Palmer Quarterly*, 21(4):267–94.

Sampson, R., and Laub, J. 1994. Urban poverty and the family context of delinquency: A new look at structure and process in a classic study. *Child Development*, 65:523–40.

Sapolsky, R.M., Krey, L.C., and McEwen, B.S. 1985. Prolonged glucocorticoid exposure reduces hippocampal neuron number. *Journal of Neuroscience*, 5:1221–6.

Sartre, J-P. 1943/1958. *Being and Nothingness*. London: Methuen.

Scarr, S., and McCartney, K. 1983. How people make their own environments: A theory of genotype → environment effects. *Child Development*, 54:424–35.

Schaffer, W. 1983. The application of optimal control theory to the general life history problem. *American Naturalist*, 121:418–31.

Scheper-Hughes, N. 1987. The cultural politics of child survival. In N. Scheper-Hughes (ed.), *Child Survival*. Boston: D. Reidel.

Scheper-Hughes, N. 1992. *Death Without Weeping: The Violence of Everyday Life in Brazil*. Berkeley: University of California Press.

Scheper-Hughes, N. 1995. The primacy of the ethical: Propositions for a militant anthropology. *Current Anthropology*, 36(3):409–40.

Scherer, K.R. 1993. Neuroscience projections to current debates in emotion psychology. *Cognition and Emotion*, 7:1–41.

Schneider-Rosen, K., and Cicchetti, D. 1984. The relationship between affect and cognition in maltreated infants: Quality of attachment and the development of visual self-recognition. *Child Development*, 55:648–58.

Scholl, T.O., Hediger, M.L., Vasilenko, P., Ances, I.G., Smith, W., and Salmon, R.W. 1989. Effects of early maturation on fetal growth. *Annals of Human Biology*, 16(4):335–45.

Schore, A.N. 1994. *Affect Regulation and the Origin of Self: The Neurobiology of Emotional Development*. Hillsdale, NJ: Lawrence Erlbaum.

Schulkin, J., McEwen, B., and Gold, P. 1994. Allostasis, amygdala, and anticipatory angst. *Neuroscience and Biobehavioral Review*, 18:385–96.

Schulman, S., Elicker, J., and Sroufe, L.A. 1994. Stages of friendship growth in preadolescence as related to attachment history. *Journal of Social and Personal Relationships*, 11(3):341–61.

Scott, F.J., and Baron-Cohen, S. 1996. Logical, analogical, and psychological reasoning in autism: A test of the Cosmides theory. *Development and Psychopathology*, 8(1):235–45.

Seger, J., and Brockmann, J. 1987. What is bet-hedging? In P. Harvey and L. Partridge (eds.), *Oxford Surveys in Evolutionary Biology*, vol. 4. Oxford University Press.

Seger, J., and Stubblefield, J.W. 1996. Optimization and adaptation. In M.R. Rose and G.V. Lauder (eds.), *Adaptation*. New York: Academic Press.

Segerstråle, U. 1992. Reductionism, "bad science," and politics: A critique of anti-reductionist reasoning. *Politics and the Life Sciences*, 11(2):199–214.

Sen, A. 1980. Equality of what? In S. McMurrin (ed.), *Tanner Lectures in Human Values, I*. Salt Lake City: University of Utah Press, and Cambridge University Press.

Sen, A. 1990. More than a million women are missing. *New York Review of Books*, 37:61–6.

Sen, A. 1992. *Inequality Reexamined*. New York: Russell Sage Foundation.

Sen, A. 1993a. The economics of life and death. *Scientific American*, May, 1993 (pp. 40–7).

Sen, A. 1993b. Capability and well-being. In M. Nussbaum and A. Sen (eds.), *The Quality of Life*. Oxford: Clarendon Press.

Sennett, R., and Cobb, J. 1972/1993. *The Hidden Injuries of Class*. New York: Norton.

Shangold, M.M., Kelley, M., Berkeley, A.S., Freedman, K.S., and Groshen, S. 1989. Relationship between menarcheal age and adult height. *Southern Medical Journal*, 82(4):443–5.

Shaver, P., and Hazan, C. 1994. Adult romantic attachment. In D. Perlman and W. Jones (eds.), *Advances in Personal relationships*, vol. 4. Greenwich, CT: JAI Press.

Shaver, P.R., and Clark, C.L. 1996. Forms of adult romantic attachment and their cognitive and emotional underpinnings. In G. Noam and K. Fischer (eds.), *Development and Vulnerability in Close Relationships*. Hillsdale, NJ: Lawrence Erlbaum.

Sheline, Y., Wang, P., Gado, M., Csernansky, J., and Vannier, M. 1996. Hippocampal atrophy in recurrent major depression. *Proceedings of the National Academy of Science of the USA*. 93(9):3908–13.

Shoda, Y., Mischel, W., and Peake, P. 1990. Predicting adolescent cognitive and self- regulatory competencies from preschool delay of gratification: Identifying diagnostic conditions. *Developmental Psychology*, 26(6):978–86.

Shore, B. 1996. *Culture in Mind: Cognition, Culture, and the Problem of Meaning*. New York: Oxford University Press.

Shorris, E. 1997. *New American Blues: A Journey Through Poverty to Democracy*. New York: Norton.

Shweder, R.A. 1990. Cultural psychology – what is it? In J. Stigler, R. Shweder, and G. Herdt (eds.), *Cultural Psychology: Essays on Comparative Human Development*. Cambridge University Press.

Shweder, R.A. 1996. The view from manywheres. *Anthropology Newsletter*, 37(9):1–5.

Simpson, J., and Gangestad, S. 1991. Individual differences in sociosexuality: Evidence for divergent and discriminative validity. *Journal of Personality and Social Psychology*, 60:870–83.

Skolnick, A. 1986. Early attachment and personal relationships across the life course. In R. Lerner and D Featherman (eds.), *Life Span Development and Behavior*, vol.7. Hillsdale, NJ: Lawrence Erlbaum.

Slobodkin, L., and Rapoport, A. 1974. An optimal strategy of evolution. *Quarterly Review of Biology*, 49:181–200.

Smith, E.A., and Winterhalder, B. 1992. Natural selection and decision-making: Some fundamental principles. In E.A. Smith and B. Winterhalder (eds.), *Evolutionary Ecology and Human Behavior*. Hawthorne, NY: Aldine de Gruyter.

Smith, E.F.S. 1991. The influence of nutrition and postpartum mating on weaning and subsequent play behaviour of hooded rats. *Animal Behaviour*, 41:513–24.

Smuts, B.B. 1985. *Sex and Friendship in Baboons*. Hawthorne, NY: Aldine de Gruyter.

Smuts, B.B. 1992. Male aggression against women: An evolutionary perspective. *Human Nature*, 3(1):1–44.

Smuts, B.B. 1995. The evolutionary origins of patriarchy. *Human Nature*, 6(1):1–32.

Smuts, B.B., and Gubernick, D.J. 1992. Male-infant relationships in nonhuman primates: Paternal investment or mating effort? In B.S. Hewlett (ed.),

Father–Child Relations: Cultural and Biosocial Contexts. New York: Aldine de Gruyter.

Soefer, E., Scholl, T., Sobel, E. et al. 1985. Menarche: Target age for reinforcing sex education for adolescents. *Journal of Adolescent Health Care*, 6:383–6.

Solomon, C.G., and Manson, J.E. 1997. Obesity and mortality: A review of the epidemiologic data. *American Journal of Clinical Nutrition*, 66(4):1044S- 1050S.

Spitz, R. 1945. Hospitalism: An inquiry into the genesis of psychiatric conditions in early childhood. *Psychoanalytic Study of the Child*, 1:53–74.

Sroufe, L.A. 1983. Infant–caregiver attachment and patterns of adaptation in preschool: The roots of maladaptation and competence. In M. Perlmutter (ed.), *Minnesota Symposia on Child Psychology*, vol. 16. Hillsdale, NJ: Lawrence Erlbaum.

Sroufe, L.A. 1988. The role of infant–caregiver attachment in development. In J. Belsky and T. Nezworski (eds.), *Clinical Implications of Attachment*. Hillsdale, NJ: Lawrence Erlbaum.

Sroufe, L.A., and Fleeson, J. 1986. Attachment and the construction of relationships. In W.W. Hartup and Z. Rubin (eds.), *The Nature and Development of Relationships*. Hillsdale, NJ: Lawrence Erlbaum.

Sroufe, L.A., and Waters, E. 1977. Attachment as an organizational construct. *Child Development*, 48:1184–99.

Stack, C. 1974. *All Our Kin: Strategies for Survival in a Black Community*. New York Harper and Row.

Stamps, J. 1991. Why evolutionary issues are reviving interest in proximate behavioral mechanisms. *American Zoologist*, 31:339–48.

Stansbury, K., and Gunnar, M. 1994. Adrenocortical activity and emotion regulation. In N. Fox (ed.), *The Development of Emotion Regulation: Biological and Behavioral Considerations*. Monographs of the Society for Reseach in Child Development (Serial no. 240), 59(2–3):108–34.

Stearns, S. 1982. The role of development in the evolution of life histories. In J.T. Bonner (ed.), *Evolution and Development*. Dahlem Konferenzen. New York: Springer-Verlag.

Stearns, S. 1989. Trade-offs in life-history evolution. *Functional Ecology*, 3:259–68.

Stearns, S. 1992. *The Evolution of Life Histories*. New York: Oxford University Press.

Sterelny, K. 1990. *The Representational Theory of Mind*. Oxford: Basil Blackwell.

Stern, D. 1977. *The First Relationship*. Cambridge, MA: Harvard University Press.

Strassmann, B. 1997. Polygyny as a risk factor for child mortaility among the Dogon. *Current Anthropology*, 38(4):681–95.

Suess, G.J., Grossman, K.E., and Sroufe, L.A. 1992. Effects of infant attachment to mother and father on quality of adaptation in preschool: From dyadic to individual organization of self. *International Journal of Behavioral Development*, 15(1):43–65.

Suomi, S. 1991. Primate models of affective disorders. In J. Madden (ed.), *Neurobiology of Learning, Emotion, and Affect.* New York: Raven Press.

Surbey, M.K. 1990. Family composition, stress, and the timing of human menarche. In T.E. Zeigler and F.B. Bercovitch (eds.), *Socioendocrinology of Primate Reproduction.* New York: Wiley-Liss.

Tanner, J. 1962. *Growth at Adolescence.* Oxford: Blackwell Scientific Publications.

Tauber, A. 1994. Darwinian aftershocks: Repercussions in late twentieth-century medicine. *Journal of the Royal Society of Medicine,* 87:27–31.

Taylor, C. 1993. Explanation and practical reason. In M. Nussbuam and A. Sen (eds.), *The Quality of Life.* Oxford University Press.

Thompson, D'A. 1942. *Growth and Form,* 2nd edn. New York: Macmillan.

Thompson, R.A. 1997. Early sociopersonality development. In W. Damon (ed.), *Handbook of Child Psychology,* 5th edn., vol. 3, *Social, Emotional, and Personality Development* (N. Eisenberg, vol. ed.) (pp. 25–104). New York: John Wiley.

Thornhill, R., and Gangestad, S. 1993. Human facial beauty: Averageness, symmetry, and parasite resistance. *Human Nature,* 4(3):237–69.

Thornton, A., and Camburn, D. 1987. The influence of the family on premarital sexual attitudes and behavior. *Demography,* 24:323–40.

Tinbergen, N. 1963. On the aims and methods of ethology. *Zeitschrift für Tierpsychologie,* 20:410–33.

Tomasello, M., Kruger, A.C., and Ratner, H.H. 1993. Cultural learning. *Behavioral and Brain Sciences,* 16:495–552.

Tooby, J., and Cosmides, L. 1989. Evolutionary psychology and the generation of culture, Part I. Theoretical considerations. *Ethology and Sociobiology,* 10:29–49.

Tooby, J., and Cosmides, L. 1990. The past explains the present: Emotional adaptations and the structure of ancestral environments. *Ethology and Sociobiology,* 11(4/5): 375–424.

Tooby, J., and DeVore, I. 1987. The reconstruction of hominid behavioral evolution through strategic modeling. In W.G. Kinzey (ed.), *The Evolution of Human Behavior: Primate Models.* Albany: State University of New York Press.

Treloar, S.A., and Martin, N.G. 1990. Age at menarche as a fitness trait: Nonadditive genetic variance detected in a large twin sample. *American Journal of Human Genetics,* 47:137–48.

Trevathan, W. 1987. *Human Birth: An Evolutionary Perspective.* Hawthorne, NY: Aldine de Gruyter.

Trickett, P., and Putnam, F. 1993. Impact of child sexual abuse on females: Toward a developmental, psychobiological integration. *Psychological Science,* 4(2):81–7.

Trivers, R. 1971. The evolution of reciprocal altruism. *Quarterly Review of Biology,* 46:35–57.

Trivers, R. 1972. Parental investment and sexual selection. In B. Campbell (ed.), *Sexual Selection and the Descent of Man, 1871–1971.* Chicago: Aldine.

Trivers, R. 1974. Parent–offspring conflict. *American Zoologist*, 14:249–62.

Tronick, E.Z. 1989. Emotions and emotion communication in infants. *American Psychologist*, 44:112–19.

Tronick, E.Z., Morelli, G., and Winn, S. 1987. Multiple caretaking of Efe (Pygmy) infants. *American Anthropologist*, 89:96–106.

Troy, M., and Sroufe, L.A. 1987. Victimization among preschoolers: Role of attachment relationship history. *Journal of the American Academy of Child and Adolescent Psychiatry*, 26(2):166–72.

Turner, F. 1995. *The Culture of Hope: A New Birth of the Classic Spirit*. New York: Free Press.

Turner, P. 1991. Relations between attachment, gender, and behavior with peers in preschool. *Child Development*, 62:1475–88.

Tversky, A. and Kahneman, D. 1981. The framing of decisions and the psychology of choice. *Science*, 211:453–8.

Udry, J.R. 1988. Biological predispositions and social control in adolescent sexual behavior. *American Sociological Review*, 53:709–22.

Udry, J., and Cliquet, R. 1982. A cross-cultural examination of the relationship between ages at menarche, marriage, and first birth. *Demography*, 19:53–63.

Udry, J.R., and van den Berg, B. 1995. Childhood precursors of age at first intercourse for females. *Archives of Sexual Behavior*, 24(3):329–37.

Valenzuela, M. 1990. Attachment in chronically underweight young children. *Child Development*, 61:1984–96.

van IJzendoorn, M.H. 1995. Adult attachment representations, parental responsiveness, and infant attachment: A meta-analysis on the predictive validity of the Adult Attachment Interview. *Psychological Bulletin*, 117(3):387–403.

van Schaik, C., and Dunbar, R. 1990. The evolution of monogamy in large primates: A new hypothesis and some crucial tests. *Behaviour*, 115:31–62.

Vaughn, B., and Waters, E. 1990. Attachment behavior at home and in the laboratory: Q- sort observations and strange situation classifications of one-year-olds. *Child Development*, 61:1965–73.

Vila, B. 1994. A general paradigm for understanding criminal behavior: Extending evolutionary ecological theory. *Criminology*, 32(3):311–59.

Vila, B. 1997. Human nature and crime control: Improving the feasibility of nurturant strategies. *Politics and the Life Sciences*, 16(1):3–55.

Vogel, V.G. 1996. Assessing women's potential risk of developing breast cancer. *Oncology*, 10(10):1451–61.

Waddington, C.H. 1957. *The Strategy of the Genes: A Discussion of Some Aspects of Theoretical Biology*. London: George Allen and Unwin.

Waddington, C.H. 1968. The theory of evolution today. In A. Koestler and R. Smythies (eds.), *Beyond Reductionism*. New York: Macmillan.

Waddington, C.H. 1969. Paradigm for an evolutionary process. In C.H. Waddington (ed.), *Towards a Theoretical Biology*, vol. 2, *Sketches*. Edinburgh University Press.

Waddington, C.H. 1975. *The Evolution of an Evolutionist*. Ithaca, NY: Cornell University Press.

Wadsworth, M., MacLean, M., Kuh, D., and Rodgers, B. 1990. Children of divorced and separated parents: Summary and review of findings from a long-term follow-up study in the UK. *Family Practice*, 7(1):104–9.

Waldron, I. 1983. The role of genetic and biological factors in sex differences in mortality. In A.D. Lopez and L.T. Ruzicka (eds.), *Sex Differences in Mortality*. Canberra: Australian National University Press.

Waller, N., and Shaver, P. 1994. The importance of nongenetic influences on romantic love styles: A twin-family study. *Psychological Science*, 5:268–74.

Wallerstein, J.S. 1991. The long-term effects of divorce on children: A review. *Journal of the American Academy of Child & Adolescent Psychiatry*, 30(3):349–60.

Wark, M. 1996. Postmodern jokers. *The Australian*, Wednesday 5 June, 1996 (p. 28).

Washburn, S.L. 1960. Tools and human evolution. *Scientific American*, 203:63–75.

Waters, E., and Deane, K. 1985. Defining and assessing individual differences in attachment relationships: Q-methodology and the organization of behavior in infancy and early childhood. In I. Bretherton and E. Waters (eds.), *Growing Points in Attachment Theory and Research*. Monographs of the Society for Research in Child Development (Serial no. 309), 50(1–2):41–65.

Watson, J.S. 1972. Smiling, cooing, and "the game." *Merrill-Palmer Quarterly*, 18:323–9.

Watson, J.S. 1985. Contingency perception in early social development. In T. Field and N. Fox (eds.), *Social Perception in Infants*. Norwood, NJ: Ablex.

Weinberg, E.D. 1984. Iron withholding: A defence against infection and neoplasia. *Physiological Review*, 64:65–102.

Weinrich, J.D. 1977. Human sociobiology: Pair-bonding and resource predictability (effects of social class and race). *Behavioral Ecology and Sociobiology*, 2:91–118.

Wellens, R., Malina, R., Roche, A., Chumlea, W., Guo, S., and Siervogel, R. 1992. Body size and fatness in young adults in relation to age at menarche. *American Journal of Human Biology*, 4:783–7.

Wellman, H. 1990. *Children's Theories of Mind*. Cambridge, MA: MIT Press.

Werner, E.E., and Smith, R.S. 1992. *Overcoming the Odds: High Risk Children From Birth to Adulthood*. Ithaca: Cornell University Press.

West, M., and Konner, M. 1976. The role of the father in anthropological perspective. In M. Lamb (ed.), *The Role of the Father in Child Development*. New York: John Wiley.

West-Eberhard, M.J. 1989. Phenotypic plasticity and the origins of diversity. *Annual Review of Ecology and Systematics*, 20:249–78.

West-Eberhard, M.J. 1992. Behavior and evolution. In P.R. Grant and H.S. Horn (eds.), *Molds, Molecules, and Metazoa: Growing Points in Evolutionary Biology.* Princeton University Press.

Whiten, A. (ed.), 1991. *Natural Theories of Mind: Evolution, Development, and Simulation of Everyday Mindreading.* Oxford: Basil Blackwell.

Whiten, A., and Byrne, R. 1988. The Machiavellian intelligence hypothesis: Editorial. In R. Byrne and A. Whiten (eds.), *Machiavellian Intelligence: Social Expertise and the Evolution of Intellect.* Oxford University Press.

Whiting, B. 1965. Sex identity conflict and physical violence: A cross-cultural study. *American Anthropologist,* 67:123–40.

Whiting, J., and Whiting, B. 1975. Aloofness and intimacy of husbands and wives: A cross-cultural study. *Ethos,* 3:183–207.

Widdowson, E.M. 1951. Mental contentment and physical growth. *Lancet,* June 16: 1316–18.

Wierson, M., Long, P.J., and Forehand, R.L. 1993. Toward a new understanding of early menarche: The role of environmental stress in pubertal timing. *Adolescence,* 28(112):913–24.

Wiley, A. 1992. Adaptation and the biocultural paradigm in medical anthropology: A critical review. *Medical Anthropology Quarterly,* 6:216–36.

Wilkinson, R.G. 1996. *Unhealthy Societies: The Afflictions of Inequality.* London: Routledge.

Williams, G.C. 1957. Pleiotropy, natural selection, and the evolution of senescence. *Evolution,* 11:398–411.

Williams, G.C. 1966. *Adaptation and Natural Selection: A Critique of Some Current Evolutionary Thought.* Princeton University Press.

Williams, G.C. 1996. *Plan and Purpose in Nature.* London: Weidenfeld and Nicolson.

Williams, G.C., and Nesse, R.M. 1991. The dawn of Darwinian medicine. *The Quarterly Review of Biology,* 66 (1):1–22.

Wilson, E.O. 1975. *Sociobiology: The New Synthesis.* Cambridge, MA: Harvard University Press.

Wilson, E.O. 1978. *On Human Nature.* Cambridge, MA: Harvard University Press.

Wilson, J.Q. 1993. *The Moral Sense.* New York: Free Press.

Wilson, J.Q., and Herrnstein, R. 1985. *Crime and Human Nature.* New York: Simon and Schuster.

Wilson, M., and Daly, M. 1985. Competitiveness, risk-taking, and violence: The young male syndrome. *Ethology and Sociobiology,* 6:59–73.

Wilson, M., and Daly, M. 1997. Life expectancy, economic inequality, homicide, and reproductive timing in Chicago neighborhoods. *British Medical Journal,* 314:1271–4.

Wilson, W.J. 1987. *The Truly Disadvantaged: The Inner City, the Underclass, and Public Policy.* University of Chicago Press.

Wilson, W.J. 1996. *When Work Disappears: The World of the New Urban Poor*. New York: Alfred A. Knopf.

Wimmer, H. and Perner, J. 1983. Beliefs about beliefs: Representation and constraining function of wrong beliefs in young children's understanding of deception. *Cognition*, 13:103–28.

Wittenberger, J.F., and Tilson, R.L. 1980. The evolution of monogamy: Hypotheses and evidence. *Annual Review of Ecology and Systematics*, 11:197–232.

Wolkind, S., and Rutter, M. 1985. Separation, loss, and family relationships. In M. Rutter and L. Hersov (eds.), *Child and Adolescent Psychiatry: Modern Approaches*. Palo Alto: Blackwell Scientific Publications.

Woodburn, J. 1982 Egalitarian societies. *Man*, 17:431–51.

Worthman, C.M. 1993. Biocultural interactions in human development. In M.E. Pereira and L.A. Fairbanks (eds.), *Juvenile Primates: Life History, Development, and Behavior*. New York: Oxford University Press.

Worthman, C.M. 1994. Developmental microniche: A concept for modelling relationships of biology, behavior and culture in development. Paper presented at the session on "Human Growth and development: Modelling relationships of biology and context." Annual Meeting of the American Association of Physical Anthropologists, Denver, CO, March 31 – April 2, 1994.

Worthman, C.M. 1996. Dual embodiment: "Hidden" developmental pathways of socialization. Paper presented at the Symposium "The Evolution of the Ontogeny of Enculturation," Keith McNeal and John Bing, Organizers. Annual Meeting of the American Anthropological Association. San Francisco, CA.

Wrangham, R.W. 1980. An ecologcal model of female-bonded groups. *Behaviour*, 75:262–300.

Wright, S. 1931. Evolution in Mendelian populations. *Genetics*, 16:97–159.

Wyatt, G.E. 1988. The relationship between child sexual abuse and adolescent sexual functioning in Afro-American and White American women. *Annals of the New York Academy of Science*, 258:111–22.

Wyatt, G.E. 1990. Changing influences on adolescent sexuality over the past forty years. In J. Bancroft and J. Reinisch (eds.), *Adolescence and Puberty*. Kinsey Institute Series 3. New York: Oxford University Press.

Yarrow, L. 1967. The development of focused relationships during infancy. In J. Hellmuth (ed.), *Exceptional Infant*, vol. 1. Seattle: Special Child.

Zabin, L., Smith, M., Hirsch, M. et al. 1986. Age of physical maturation and first intercourse in black teenage males and females. *Demography*, 23:595–605.

Zahn-Waxler, C., Radke-Yarrow, M., and King, R.A. 1979. Childrearing and children's prosocial initiations towards victims of distress. *Child Development*, 50:319–30.

Index

CHESTER COLLEGE LIBRARY